CASE STUDY METHOD

D0067751

CASE STUDY METHOD

Key Issues, Key Texts

Edited by
Roger Gomm, Martyn Hammersley and Peter Foster

SAGE Publications
London • Thousand Oaks • New Delhi

ISBN 0-7619-6413-4 (hbk)   ISBN-13 978-0-7619-6413-1 (hbk)
ISBN 0-7619-6414-2 (pbk)   ISBN-13 978-0-7619-6414-8 (pbk)

© Roger Gomm, Martyn Hammersley and Peter Foster 2000
    Editorial arrangement, Introduction and Chapter 5 and 12
For © information on individual chapters, see Acknowledgements
First published 2000
Reprinted 2002, 2004, 2006

Apart from any fair dealing for the purposes of research or private study,
or criticism or review, as permitted under the Copyright, Designs and
Patents Act, 1988, this publication may be reproduced, stored or
transmitted in any form or by any means, only with the prior permission
in writing of the publishers, or in the case of reprographic reproduction,
in accordance with the terms of licences issued by the Copyright
Licensing Agency. Inquiries concerning reproduction outside those
terms should be sent to the publishers.

SAGE Publications Ltd
1 Oliver's Yard, 55 City Road
London EC1Y 1SP

SAGE Publications Inc
2455 Teller Road
Thousand Oaks, California 91320

SAGE Publications India Pvt Ltd
B–42 Panchsheel Enclave
PO Box 4109
New Delhi 110 017

British Library Cataloguing in Publication data

A catalogue record for this book is available
from the British Library

Typeset by SIVA Math Setters, Chennai, India
Printed digitally and bound in Great Britain by
Biddles Ltd., King's Lynn, Norfolk

CONTENTS

PREFACE

We had the idea for this book when the three of us were writing a set of conference papers on case study research in late 1997 and early 1998. In the course of this, we gained a reasonably comprehensive sense of the literature in the field, of what could be learned from it, and of what were the key issues that needed to be addressed. And we were surprised to find that, while there were several collections of articles dealing with case study, none of them brought together the most influential and important articles. Indeed, we noted that the literature was fragmented across different disciplines and topic areas, with little sign of any cumulative understanding of the problems this kind of research raises. As a result, we decided to continue our collaboration to produce a book that would bring a little more coherence to the field.

Most books take longer to produce than anticipated, and it is usually a relief to reach the point of writing the preface: by that time most of the work has been done. In this case, however, pleasure is mixed with deep sorrow because one of us, Peter Foster, died at the beginning of 1999, when we were still in the throes of editing the collection and finalizing our contributions to it. There is a great deal of him in the book; it was the fruit of a collaboration spreading over many years. We are very sad that he did not see it completed. We still miss his voice in our discussions, and are only too painfully aware of how much his family also miss him.

Roger Gomm and Martyn Hammersley

ACKNOWLEDGEMENTS

We would like to thank the following people and organizations for permission to reprint the articles included in this volume:

American Educational Research Association and *Educational Researcher* for permission to reprint Robert E. Stake 'The case study method in social inquiry', *Educational Researcher*, 7, February 1978: 5–8.

Sage for permission to reprint Yvonna S. Lincoln and Egon G. Guba 'The only generalization is: there is no generalization', from Yvonna S. Lincoln and Egon G. Guba, *Naturalistic Inquiry*, Newbury Park, CA: Sage, 1985.

Teachers College Press, Columbia University, for permission to reprint Robert Donmoyer, 'Generalizability and the single-case study', from Elliot W. Eisner and Alan Peshkin (eds), *Qualitative Inquiry in Education: The Continuing Debate*, New York: Teachers College Press. © 1990 by Teachers College, Colombia University. All rights reserved.

Teachers College Press for permission to reprint Janet Ward Schofield, 'Increasing the generalizability of qualitative research', from Elliot W. Eisner and Alan Peshkin (eds), *Qualitative Inquiry in Education: The Continuing Debate*, New York: Teachers College Press. © 1990 by Teachers College, Colombia University. All rights reserved.

University of California Press for permission to reprint Harry Eckstein, 'Case study and theory in political science', from Harry Eckstein, *Regarding Politics: Essays on Political Theory, Stability and Change*, Berkeley: University of California Press, 1992.

Blackwell Press and the editors of *Sociological Review* for permission to reprint J. Clyde Mitchell, 'Case and situation analysis', *Sociological Review*, 31 (2) 1983: 187–211.

American Sociological Review for confirmation of the public domain status of W.S. Robinson 'The logical structure of analytic induction', *American Sociological Review*, 16 (6) 1951: 812–18.

American Sociological Review for confirmation of the public domain status of Ralph H. Turner, 'The quest for universals', *American Sociological Review*, 18 (6) 604–11.

Cambridge University Press and Stanley Lieberson for permission to reprint Stanley Lieberson 'Small N's and big conclusions: an examination of the reasoning in comparative studies based on a small number of cases', from Charles C. Ragin and Howard S. Becker (eds), *What is a Case? Exploring the Foundations of Social Inquiry*, Cambridge: Cambridge University Press, 1992.

Cambridge University Press and Howard S. Becker for permission to reprint Howard S. Becker, 'Cases, causes, conjunctures, stories and imagery', from Charles C. Ragin and Howard S. Becker (eds), *What is a Case? Exploring the Foundations of Social Inquiry*, Cambridge: Cambridge University Press, 1992.

INTRODUCTION

Martyn Hammersley and Roger Gomm

In the early 1980s, Jennifer Platt and J. Clyde Mitchell both commented, in separate articles, on what Mitchell referred to as 'the eclipse of interest in case studies as a method of sociological research' (see Mitchell, Chapter 7, this volume; Platt, 1981). The situation is very different today. Case study research has become extremely popular in sociology and also in many other areas of social inquiry. However, this story of demise and resurrection is misleading. To a large extent, it traces the fortunes of the *term* 'case study', rather than the history of the research approach or approaches to which it refers. Indeed, one of the problems with the phrase 'case study' is that it is not used in a standard way. This stems from the fact that what it has been contrasted with has varied considerably. Furthermore, in some of its uses the meaning of the term has overlapped substantially with that of others – notably with 'ethnography', 'participant observation', 'fieldwork', 'qualitative research' and 'life history'.

To complicate matters further, the notion of case study is not restricted to the research context. Lawyers deal with cases, so do detectives, medical practitioners, social workers and others; and, for this reason, the case method has been an influential component of several fields of professional education, and has also figured significantly in the training of managers, most famously at the Harvard Business School. Indeed, it seems likely that case study *research* arose out of, or at least was strongly influenced by, case study approaches in other fields. Thus, Becker (1968) traces it back to the medical model, while Platt (1981) notes that 'historically, the origin of the idea of case study [in American sociology] seems to have had a lot to do with the social worker's "case history" or "case work"' (p. 19). She notes that data from social work case records were used in some early studies that have come to be treated as classics of case study inquiry, notably Thomas and Znaniecki's *The Polish Peasant in Europe and America* (1918–20). Furthermore, while – in general – case study research has become increasingly distant from the practical treatment of cases, this is not always true. Thus, Bromley (1986) discusses case study in psychology as a form of clinical science (he also refers to it as a 'quasi-judicial' method), in which the aim is not just to develop knowledge but also to search for a remedy to some problem present in the case. A slightly different link to professional practice is provided by Stenhouse's argument for case study in education. He sees this as concerned with the development and testing of curricular and pedagogical strategies (Stenhouse, 1975, 1978, 1980); and locates it within a conception of the teacher as researcher, an idea which has stimulated a flourishing class-room action research tradition in Britain, Australia and elsewhere. A similarly close relationship between case study research and attempts to solve practical problems can also be found in some other areas, including management studies (see Eisenhardt, 1989).

The existence of close links between case study inquiry and various forms of occupational practice has sometimes been regarded as a weak-ness, as indicating the less-than-scientific or even unscientific character of this kind of research. However, such criticism has become less com-mon, and less widely accepted, in recent years. One reason for this has been growing public suspicion of science, and increasing doubts about the possibility or desirability of a science of social life. Equally signifi-cant has been greater emphasis on the need for research of all kinds to be practically applicable, or even for it to be integrated into practical activities (see Gibbons et al., 1994). At the same time, these trends have by no means eliminated the commitment of some case study researchers to a scientific approach, interpreted in a variety of ways.

So, 'case study' is not a term that is used in a clear and fixed sense. Given this, our first task is to sketch the central components of its meaning.

What is case study research?

In one sense all research is case study: there is always some unit, or set of units, in relation to which data are collected and/or analysed.[1] Usually, though, the term 'case study' is employed to identify a specific form of inquiry; notably, one which contrasts with two other influen-tial kinds of social research: the experiment and the social survey. And we can use these contrasts to mark the boundaries of the currently accepted meaning of the term; though a *range* of dimensions is involved, so that the meaning is fuzzy-edged.

The most important dimension relates to the *number of cases* investi-gated. Another, closely related, one is the *amount of detailed information* that the researcher collects about each case studied. Other things being equal, the fewer cases investigated, the more information can be col-lected about each of them. Many social surveys gather only a relatively small amount of data from each case (cases here are usually, though not always, individual respondents: see Platt, 1992). We can contrast this with research in which large amounts of information are collected about one case, across a wide range of dimensions; here the case may be an individual (as in life-history work), an event, an institution or even a whole national society. So, usually, 'case study' refers to research that investigates a few cases, often just one, in considerable depth.[2]

Number of cases studied and amount of information collected about each case are not the only dimensions built into the concept of case study, as it is used in social research today. A further element in the meaning of the term is highlighted by the contrast with experimental research. While the latter also usually involves the investigation of a small number of cases compared to survey work, what distinguishes it from case study is not so much the amount of data collected as the fact that it involves direct control of variables. In experiments, the researcher *creates* the case(s) studied, whereas case study researchers construct cases out of naturally occurring social situations.

The term 'case study' is also often taken to carry implications for the kind of data that are collected, and perhaps also for how these are analysed. Frequently, but not always, it implies the collection of unstructured data, and qualitative analysis of those data. Moreover, this relates to a more fundamental issue about the purpose of the research. It is sometimes argued that the aim of case study research should be to capture cases in their uniqueness, rather than to use them as a basis for wider generalization or for theoretical inference of some kind. And this is often held to require a narrative approach rather than one framed in terms of variable analysis.

Closely related is the question of objectivity. Is the aim to produce an account of each case from an external or research point of view, one that may contradict the views of the people involved? Or is it solely to portray the character of each case 'in its own terms'? This contrast is most obvious where the cases are people, so that the aim may be to 'give voice' to them rather than to use them as respondents or even as informants. (Table 1 summarizes these various dimensions of the meaning of 'case study'; and the similarities and differences between this approach, on the one hand, and experimental and survey research, on the other.)

Method or paradigm?

Some commentators treat case study as a method – to be used as and when appropriate, depending on the problem under investigation. Like other methods, it is believed to have both advantages and disadvantages. However, even from this point of view there can be variation in the specific form that case study research take:

- in the number of cases studied, and the role of comparison;
- in how detailed the case studies are;

Table 1   A schematic comparison of case study with experimental and survey approaches

Experiment	Case study	Survey
Investigation of a relatively small number of cases.	Investigation of a relatively small number of cases (sometimes just one).	Investigation of a relatively large number of cases.
Information gathered and analysed about a small number of features of each case.	Information gathered and analysed about a large number of features of each case.	Information gathered and analysed about a small number of features of each case.
Study of cases created in such a way as to control the important variables.	Study of naturally occurring cases; or, in 'action research' form, study of cases created by the actions of the researcher but where the primary concern is *not* controlling variables to measure their effects.	Study of a sample of naturally occurring cases; selected in such a way as to maximize the sample's representativeness in relation to some larger population.
Quantification of data is a priority.	Quantification of data is *not* a priority. Indeed, qualitative data may be treated as superior.	Quantification of data is a priority.
The aim is either theoretical inference – the development and testing of theory – or the practical evaluation of an intervention.	The main concern may be with understanding the case studied in itself, with no interest in theoretical inference or empirical generalization. However, there may also be attempts at one or other, or both, of these. Alternatively, the wider relevance of the findings may be conceptualized in terms of the provision of vicarious experience, as a basis for 'naturalistic generalization' or 'transferability'.	The aim is empirical generalization, from a sample to a finite population, though this is sometimes seen as a platform for theoretical inference.

- in the size of the case(s) dealt with;
- in the extent to which researchers document the *context* of the case, in terms of the wider society and/or historically;
- in the extent to which they restrict themselves to description and explanation, or engage in evaluation and prescription.

Variation in these respects depends to some extent on the purpose that the case study is intended to serve. Where it is designed to test or illustrate a theoretical point, then it will deal with the case as an instance of a type, describing it in terms of a particular theoretical framework (implicit or explicit). Where it is concerned with developing theoretical ideas, it is likely to be more detailed and open-ended in character. The same is true where the concern is with describing and/or explaining what is going on in a particular situation for its own sake. Where the interest is in some problem in the situation investigated, then the discussion will be geared to diagnosing that problem; and identifying its sources and what can be done about it. Moreover, here, the analysis will go beyond description and explanation to include evaluation and prescription.

Many commentators, however, regard case study as more than just a method: as involving quite different assumptions about how the social world can and should be studied from those other underlying approaches (see, for example, Hamilton, 1980; Simons, 1996). In other words, it is seen as a distinct research paradigm. Sometimes, this is formulated in terms of a contrast between positivism, on the one hand, and naturalism, interpretivism or constructionism, on the other. At the extreme, case study is viewed as more akin to the kind of portrayal of the social world that is characteristic of novelists, short-story writers and even poets. Those who see case study in this way may regard as fundamentally misconceived any comparison of it with other methods in terms of advantages and disadvantages.

A series of methodological issues arise from these differences in view about the purpose and nature of case study; and these have been subject to considerable debate:

1 *Generalizability.* In some case study work the aim is to draw, or to provide a basis for drawing, conclusions about some general type of phenomenon or about members of a wider population of cases. A question arises here, though, as to how this is possible. Some argue that what is involved is a kind of inference or generalization that is quite different in character from statistical analysis, being 'logical', 'theoretical' or 'analytical' in character (Mitchell, Chapter 7; Yin, 1994). Others suggest that there are ways in which case studies can be used to make what are in effect the same kind of generalizations as those which survey researchers produce.[3] Still others argue that case studies need not make any claims about the generalizability of their findings, that what is crucial is the use others make of them: that they feed into processes of 'naturalistic generalization' (Stake, Chapter 1; Donmoyer, Chapter 3), or facilitate the 'transfer' of findings from one setting to another on the basis of 'fit' (Lincoln and Guba, Chapter 2; Guba and Lincoln, 1989).

2 *Causal or narrative analysis.* Case study researchers sometimes claim that by examining one or two cases it is possible to identify causal processes in a way that is not feasible in survey research (Connolly, 1998). This is because the case(s) are studied in depth, and over time rather than at a single point. It is also often argued that, by contrast with experiments, case study research can investigate causal processes

'in the real world' rather than in artificially created settings. Other formulations of this argument emphasize that outcomes can always be reached by multiple pathways, so that narrative accounts of events in particular cases are essential if we are to understand those outcomes (see Becker, Chapter 11). Here, parallels may be drawn with the work of historians. However, whichever form this argument takes, there are questions about how to distinguish contingent from necessary relationships among events if only one or a small number of cases is being studied, and about what role theory plays in causal/narrative analysis (see Hammersley et al., Chapter 12).

Some case study researchers argue that they can identify causal relations through comparative analysis, for example by means of John Stuart Mill's methods of agreement and difference or via analytic induction. Sometimes, comparative method is seen as analogous to statistical analysis (Skocpol, 1979, pp. 35–6); but, often, a sharp distinction is drawn between the 'logics' involved in 'statistical' and 'case study' work (see, for example, Mitchell, Chapter 7; and Becker, Chapter 11). Nevertheless, questions have been raised about whether there is any such difference in logic (Robinson, Chapter 8); as well as about the adequacy of Mill's canons and of analytic induction as a means of producing theory via case study (Lieberson, Chapter 10; Goldenberg, 1993).

3   *The nature of theory.* While many case study researchers emphasize the role of theory, they differ in their views about the nature of the theoretical perspective required. For some it must be a theory which makes sense of the case as a bounded system (see, for instance, Smith, 1978). Here, the emphasis is on cases as unique configurations that can only be understood as wholes. For others, the task of theory is more to locate and explain what goes on within a case in terms of its wider societal context (see Sharp, 1982 and Burawoy, 1998). Without this, it is argued, intra-case processes will be misunderstood. Indeed, it is often argued that analysis of a case always presumes some wider context; so the issue is not whether or not a macro theory is involved but rather how explicit this is and whether it is sound.

4   *Authenticity and authority.* Sometimes, case study research is advocated on the basis that it can capture the unique character of a person, situation, group, and so on. Here there may be no concern with typicality in relation to a category, or generalizability to a population. The aim is to represent the case authentically: 'in its own terms'. In some versions, this is seen as a basis for discovering symbolic truths of the kind that literature and art provide (see Simons, 1996). There are questions here, though, about what this involves. After all, different aesthetic theories point in divergent directions.[4]

The commitment to authenticity may also be based on rejection of any claim to authority on the part of the case study researcher, and/or on the idea that case study can be used to amplify the unique voices of those whose experience in, and perspective on, the world are unknown, neglected or suppressed. However, questions have been raised about this position, not just by those committed to the natural science model or by those who emphasize the role of macro theory, but also by some constructionists and postmodernists. Their arguments undermine the notion of authenticity by denying the existence of any real situation that is independent of investigations of it; by questioning the legitimacy of researchers speaking on behalf of (or even acting as mediators for) others; and/or by challenging the idea that people have unitary perspectives which are available for case study description.

In editing this book, we have not adopted any particular line about the proper nature of case study research. Indeed, our aim has been to display the range of views to be found in the literature; especially about the first and second issues listed above, since these have been given the most attention. Our own views are presented in the two chapters we have written.

An outline of the contents

In the first half of the book we collect together articles that address the question of whether case study research can and should draw general conclusions; and, more specifically, whether it can draw conclusions of the kind that are characteristic of survey research. In the opening chapter, a widely cited paper entitled 'The case study method in social inquiry', Robert Stake argues that case studies can have general relevance even though they may not provide a sound basis for scientific generalization of a conventional kind. Moreover, he suggests that if research is to be of value to people, it needs to be framed in the same terms as the everyday experience through which they learn about the world firsthand. So, the great strength of case studies, he argues, is that they provide vicarious experience, in the form of 'full and thorough knowledge of the particular'. In doing this they facilitate what he calls 'naturalistic generalization', and thereby build up the body of tacit knowledge on the basis of which people act. Indeed, Stake suggests that, by contrast with naturalistic generalization, abstract propositional generalizations of the kind aimed at by conventional social science can be harmful in practical terms: false laws foster misunderstandings, and even true laws distract attention from direct experience and may lead people to see phenomena more simplistically than they should. The conclusion that he draws is that what is required of case study researchers is not that they provide generalizations but rather that they describe the case they have studied properly: in a way that captures its unique features. For Stake, a case is a bounded system that exists independently of inquiry; and he emphasizes the importance of respecting the boundaries of the case – in particular, of coming to understand how people operating within it view their world (see also Stake and Trumbull, 1982; Stake, 1994).

In Chapter 2, entitled 'The only generalization is: there is no generalization', Lincoln and Guba begin by criticizing the frequently held idea that generalization is the aim of science; in the sense of the discovery of laws. They attribute this belief to positivism, and identify a number of problems with it. They suggest that it depends on: the assumption of determinism; the possibility of inductive logic; the idea that we can produce knowledge that is free of time and context; the belief that law-like generalizations can provide a self-sufficient basis for understanding and action in particular cases; and a discredited reductionism. They then examine the alternative to law-like generalization put forward by Stake: naturalistic generalization. They point to some uncertainties in this, in particular about whether it is tacit or propositional in character. Furthermore, they argue that we are not faced with a choice between either searching for general laws or studying the unique; that between these extremes there is 'the broad range of the related'. In other words, there are ways of stating conclusions from studying one context that might hold in another context. More specifically, case study research produces 'working hypotheses' (Cronbach, 1975, p. 125) that can be used in attempts to understand other cases. Lincoln and Guba argue that transferability of conclusions from one case to another is a function of the similarity, or 'fit', between the two. And, for judgements about this to be possible, researchers must provide 'thick descriptions' of the cases they study. In the final section of the chapter the authors appeal to the analogy of holographic film, one of whose features is that any fragment of it can produce the whole picture. The implication is that case studies can do the same.

In Chapter 3, Donmoyer builds on the work of Stake, and Lincoln and Guba, seeking to provide a more adequate account of the concept of naturalistic generalization. He argues that adopting the approach to generalizability enshrined in quantitative research, and concerned with identifying law-like regularities, is not appropriate in applied areas like education. This is because it assumes a model of the applicability of research findings, in terms of using empirical generalizations to control action, which is unacceptable in these cases – given that practice there deals with unique situations. Donmoyer further suggests that the complexity of the social world, and the assumption-laden nature of all knowledge, also undermines adoption of the conventional model of science. However, he finds recent moves toward a qualitative understanding of generalizability insufficiently developed, and reliant on some false assumptions. For example, he criticizes Lincoln and Guba for assuming that we can only use knowledge from one case to understand another when the two cases are *similar*. Instead, he argues that *differences* can be equally illuminating. He also suggests that their notion of working hypotheses, derived from Cronbach, fails to recognize the way in which tacit knowledge is rendered communicable by being turned into narrative form. Furthermore, he underlines that what is involved here is not just a matter of cognition but also of affect. Like Stake, he bases his approach to generalizability on experiential knowledge, knowledge that is tacit rather than propositional. In order to clarify the nature of this knowledge he employs Piaget's schema theory, in which learning takes place by assimilation and accommodation, leading to integration and/or differentiation of what is known. In these terms, case studies may facilitate learning by substituting for firsthand experience; indeed, they may be more effective than real life because they are less threatening. Above all, they have important advantages over more conventional kinds of research product: in accessibility, and in portraying events from a personal perspective.

In the next chapter, Schofield takes a rather different line. While she rejects the idea that generalizability consists of the production of laws, she insists that this does not rule out case study researchers putting forward general conclusions. And she argues that two key questions must be addressed in thinking about generalizability: to *what* do we want to generalize; and how can we design qualitative studies so as to maximize the generalizability of their findings in this respect? Addressing these issues, she distinguishes between generalizing to what *is*, to what *may be*, and to what *could be*. In discussing each sort of generalization, she identifies useful strategies and illustrates them with examples. In addition, she examines strategies for generalization on the basis of already published work, through the 'aggregation or comparison of independent studies'. She discusses three of these strategies: Yin and Heald's 'case survey method' (Yin and Heald, 1975), Ragin's qualitative comparative method (Ragin, 1987), and Noblit and Hare's 'meta-ethnography' (Noblit and Hare, 1988).

In the final chapter in this section, Gomm et al. begin by addressing the question of whether naturalistic generalization or transferability – as advocated by Stake, Lincoln and Guba, and Donmoyer – offers an alternative to the drawing of general conclusions by case study researchers. They argue that it does not. Furthermore, they claim that case study research is not barred from producing general conclusions of the kind that survey researchers pursue. To assume that this is impossible, they suggest, is to forget that statistical sampling theory is not the only basis for drawing such conclusions; and that, even though a highly effective one, it is often not usable. Moreover, they point out that, in practice, case study researchers often *do* claim this kind of general conclusion. The authors draw a distinction between generalization across and within cases; pointing out that the latter is virtually unavoidable in case study work. In the central sections of the chapter, they outline the strategies case study researchers can use to make these two sorts of empirical generalization. However, at the same time, they underline the serious danger of drawing misleading conclusions about aggregates and trends from the study of a few cases; or of mistaking what is going on in one part of a case as representative of what is going on elsewhere.

The second part of the book is concerned with influential arguments to the effect that the main task of case study research is to develop and test theoretical ideas. In Chapter 6, writing in the context of political science, Eckstein argues that case study is valuable at all stages of inquiry, but particularly in testing theories. He defines a 'case' as 'a phenomenon for which we report and interpret only a single measure on any pertinent variable' (p. 124), and contrasts it with comparative analysis, by which he means large-scale quantitative studies dealing with several countries. The aim of case study, he suggests, is to contribute, with other strategies, towards theorizing which is designed to arrive at 'statements of regularity about the structure, behaviour and interaction of phenomena'. He outlines different stages of inquiry – from developing explanations for particular events, through theory application, to theory development and testing – and then identifies and elaborates the various types of case study suited to each. One of the most distinctive features of the discussion here is his argument that while the social world is multivariate in phenomenal terms, in reality it may be no more so than the physical world; so that it could be possible to identify a few powerful theories that account for much of the variation, with case study playing an important role in this task.

In 'Case and situation analysis', Mitchell puts forward a similar argument to Eckstein, but writes from the point of view of sociology and social anthropology rather than political science. He contrasts case study with the social survey, and argues that whereas the latter is concerned with representativeness – with describing social morphology – case study is designed to draw inferences about general, abstract theoretical principles which the case is taken to exemplify. He elaborates Gluckman's distinction between the apt illustration, the social situation and the case study (Gluckman, 1961), and outlines Eckstein's typology, distinguishing heuristic case studies, plausibility probes and crucial case studies. He draws a sharp distinction between statistical inference, from sample to population on the basis of random sampling, and logical inference, which involves identifying an 'essential linkage between two or more characteristics in terms of some systematic explanatory schema'. He clarifies this distinction through a discussion of the contrast between enumerative and analytic induction, drawing on the work of Znaniecki and Turner. Central to case study work – for Mitchell – is identifying the essential, theoretically conceptualized processes embodied in a case, rather than representing it in its uniqueness or using it as a basis for wider survey-type generalizations.[5]

In Chapter 8, an article that was written in the early 1950s, Robinson provides a detailed analysis of the logic of analytic induction; this often being held to underpin case study research. He examines it as 'a research procedure', 'a method of causal analysis' and 'a method of proof'. He argues that Znaniecki's sharp distinction between enumerative and analytic induction is unconvincing. He suggests that it is a product (on one side) of the failure of much statistical work to pursue the investigation of deviant cases and (on the other) of the formulation of analytic induction in such a way as only to investigate necessary, not sufficient, conditions for the occurrence of a phenomenon. Robinson insists that an adequate scientific explanation requires the specification of both necessary and sufficient conditions. From this point of view, the only remaining difference between analytic and enumerative induction is that the former is committed to deterministic rather than probabilistic generalizations. He argues that while it is proper to try to approximate deterministic laws, we must recognize that even natural science now involves probabilistic ones. And, as a result, modern views of science underline the need for strategies designed to ensure representative sampling in sociological investigations. In short, Robinson argues that, once the respective practical failings of enumerative and analytic induction are remedied, we are left with a single form of scientific inference.

In response to Robinson's critique, Ralph Turner's article 'The quest for universals in sociological research' (Chapter 9) examines the arguments in support of analytic induction. He claims that Robinson translates analytic induction into the terms of statistical method, and thereby misinterprets it. Turner explores some examples of analytic induction in use (notably those of Lindesmith, 1937 and Cressey, 1950; 1953), concurring with Robinson that, generally speaking, it does not provide the basis for empirical prediction. However, rather than seeing this as a failing, and as requiring a reformulation of analytic induction along statistical lines, he presents it as reflecting a fundamental difference in purpose between analytic and enumerative induction. The task of the former, he suggests, is to discover definitions of scientific concepts that capture the 'universal and uniform' relationships operating within closed, causal systems. Moreover, these relationships are logical ones, so that cause is not independent of effect. He argues that these systems are put into operation by external factors, but that the effects of those factors are always mediated by the system. As a result, the relationship between outside factors and the outcomes from the system is always a matter of probability, rather than being deterministic. For example, in discussing Cressey's theory of embezzlement, Turner points out that while, according to this theory, a 'non-shareable problem' *always* leads to 'financial trust-violation' (when other specified conditions are met), the occurrence of non-shareable problems itself is produced by factors outside the theoretical system (such as gambling debts and extra-marital affairs) whose relationship to the decision to embezzle can only be probabilistic. On this basis, Turner argues that analytic and enumerative induction are complementary. The identification of closed systems provides a basis for 'organizing and interpreting observed statistical associations': 'It is through conceiving the "essential" conditions in a closed system as the avenues through which correlated factors can operate as causes, that generalizations about closed systems can escape their self-containment, and probability associations may be organized into meaningful patterns' (p. 206). In other words, theories representing closed causal systems can be used to interpret empirical correlations found by enumerative induction, thereby providing for complex, multivariate explanations and predictions. Equally important, they can point to factors outside the causal system whose relationship to the phenomenon concerned might be worth investigating through statistical method.

In a much more recent article, Lieberson examines the rationale behind case study research from a position that is similar in many respects to that of Robinson. He starts from a dispute within comparative history about the possibility of drawing general conclusions from the study of a small number of cases. This dispute was focused on Skocpol's investigation of 'successful social revolutions', notably the French, Russian and Chinese revolutions (Skocpol, 1979; Nicols, 1986; Skocpol, 1986). In justifying this kind of comparative historical analysis Skocpol appeals to J.S. Mill's methods of agreement and difference (Mill, 1843). Lieberson notes that, like analytic induction, these methods assume that causal relations are deterministic – implying that X *always* produces Y rather than simply that X *tends to* produce Y. And he argues that, whether we assume deterministic or probabilistic causal theories, we usually have to rely on probabilistic results. This is because of measurement error, the multivariate nature of causation in the social world, and the fact that often we cannot measure all the factors that we believe influence what we are investigating. Lieberson then outlines some problems with using Mill's two methods in the analysis of small numbers of cases, using the example of road accidents. Looking first at the method of difference, he argues that it simply *assumes* that there are no interaction effects: that whatever is constant cannot affect the outcome. He notes that this does not seem a reasonable assumption as regards traffic accidents, or about social phenomena more generally. In relation to the method of agreement, he argues that this assumes that there is only one cause of the phenomenon concerned. Yet, in the case of road accidents, it is fairly clear that there are multiple causes; and this is true of many other types of event. Furthermore, he points out that both of Mill's methods are extremely vulnerable to the exclusion of relevant variables: different conclusions will be reached depending on which variables are included. However, there is a dilemma here: the more variables that are taken into account, the less likely is any clear result to be achieved from these methods, especially when the number of cases is small. So, Lieberson's conclusion is that using Mill's methods with a small number of cases is fraught with difficulties. It requires zero measurement error, and therefore careful attention to where the cut-off points are drawn – for example between a driver being drunk and not being drunk. It also makes assumptions about the phenomena under investigation – that there are single causes and no interaction effects; assumptions which cannot be tested through the method itself, and which are highly implausible. He concludes that this kind of comparative case analysis may be usable in some areas, but that its validity remains to be demonstrated.

In Chapter 11, Howard Becker argues that case study research is based on a different logic from that taken for granted by Lieberson's approach. He points out how the latter assumes that all the variables studied operate simultaneously and independently, and that this is false. He therefore examines Ragin's version of comparative analysis (Ragin, 1987), which recognizes that variables operate in concert. However, Becker also finds this unsatisfactory. He emphasizes that case study work is interested in processes; in other words, it recognizes that variables impact at different point in time, as events unfold. Given this, he suggests that a more appropriate method is narrative analysis, concerned with capturing the processes by which various outcomes are produced over time.[6] He takes the classic studies employing analytic induction, those of Lindesmith and Cressey, as exemplifying this narrative approach. He points out how analytic induction requires the construction of hypotheses and reconceptualization of the dependent variable in such a way as to render the latter causally homogeneous. He argues that this relies on social imagery, in order to make sense of the kinds of causal processes that could be involved. Furthermore, the narrative analyses that result are deterministic in character: they do not tell us that an outcome is likely but, rather, why it occurred; and they do this by documenting the path that led to it. Becker concludes by outlining a number of problems, relating to generalization from case studies, that need further consideration.

In the final chapter, Hammersley et al. examine the idea that general conclusions can be drawn from case studies by means of theoretical inference. They discuss two approaches to this. The first assumes that causal relationships can be uncovered through in-depth study of a single case, by relying on direct perception and/or on empathy. They suggest that this assumption is false, and that only the second approach, comparative analysis, can provide a sound basis for theoretical conclusions. Here, they outline the history of J.S. Mill's 'eliminative induction' and of Znaniecki's 'analytic induction', two versions of theoretical inference that have been widely appealed to by case study researchers. It is argued that these share much in common, but also serve as a corrective to one another: they point the way to a form of comparative analysis that could identify the necessary and sufficient conditions underlying causal relationships – at least in principle. However, the authors also highlight some problems which remain with case study researchers' reliance on comparative method. Notable here is the fact that it assumes the existence of universal laws of human behaviour. Furthermore, these have to be deterministic, rather than probabilistic, in character. Yet case study researchers today generally reject the possibility of laws. Hammersley et al. conclude that how serious an obstacle these problems are to achieving sound theoretical conclusions through comparative case analysis can only be discovered by pursuing that goal in full awareness of the difficulties involved.

Conclusion

This book brings together a range of key articles dealing with case study research, and especially with its capacity to produce general conclusions. Some of the chapters (for example, those by Stake, Lincoln and Guba, and Donmoyer) suggest that this is unnecessary or impossible, arguing in favour of thick description, naturalistic generalization and/or transferability. Others (those by Schofield and Gomm et al.) suggest that case study research can provide the basis for empirical generalization of the kind that survey researchers aim at, and they outline some of the strategies available for doing this, and some of the problems involved. The second half of the book is concerned with theoretical inference. It presents the most influential statements about the capacity of case study research to produce theoretical conclusions (the chapters by Eckstein, Mitchell, Turner and Becker), as well as articles which raise questions about various aspects of this (those by Robinson, Lieberson and Hammersley et al.). We hope that this collection will be of interest and use to all those who carry out or read case study research; and that presenting the various arguments side by side will assist in clarifying the nature and potential of this kind of work.

Notes

1 Ragin (1989, pp. 7–9) points out that the reference of 'case' need not coincide with that of 'unit of analysis'; see also Hammersley and Atkinson's (1995, pp. 40–2) distinction between 'setting' and 'case'.

2 The relationship between depth of investigation and number of cases is complicated by other factors, not least by the scale of the cases studied: the larger the case, other

things being equal, the less depth of investigation is possible. For example, if classroom lessons in schools are the cases with which a researcher is concerned, it may be possible to study a substantial number of them in considerable detail. If national education systems are the cases, however, there will be much greater tension between the number studied and the amount of detailed information that can be collected about each one; unless all the relevant information is already available via national statistics or some other readily accessible source. For more discussion of this tension, see Hammersley (1992, Chap. 11).

3 This seems to be the implication of Schofield's argument (Chapter 4). See also Gomm et al., Chapter 5.

4 Some of the scope for disagreement here is illustrated by the dispute between those who advocate realism in literature and art, and those who deny that these can or should be mimetic. See, for example, the debates about aesthetics and politics within German Marxism in the early part of this century (Adorno et al., 1977).

5 For a critical assessment of Mitchell's argument, see Hammersley (1992, Chap. 10).

6 'Narrative' here refers to the form of analysis; it does not necessarily indicate a focus on the study of narratives supplied by informants.

References

Adorno, T.W., Benjamin, W., Bloch, E., Brecht, B. and Lukács, G. (1977) *Aesthetics and Politics.* London: Verso.

Becker, H.S. (1968) 'Social observation and case studies', in D.L. Sills (ed.), *International Encyclopedia of the Social Sciences* (Vol. 14). New York: Crowell, Collier and Macmillan. Reprinted in H.S. Becker (1971) *Sociological Work.* Chicago: Aldine.

Bromley, D.B. (1986) *The Case Study Method in Psychology and Related Disciplines.* Chichester: Wiley.

Burawoy, M. (1998) 'The extended case method', *Sociological Theory,* 16 (1): 4–33.

Connolly, P. (1998) '"Dancing to the wrong tune": ethnography, generalization, and research on racism in schools', in P. Connolly and B. Troyna (eds), *Researching Racism in Education.* Buckingham: Open University Press.

Cressey, D.R. (1950) 'Criminal violation of financial trust', *American Sociological Review,* 15: 738–43.

Cressey, D.R. (1953) *Other People's Money.* Glencoe, IL: Free Press.

Cronbach, L.J. (1975) 'Beyond the two disciplines of scientific psychology', *American Psychologist,* 30: 116–27.

Eisenhardt, K. (1989) 'Building theories from case study research', *Academy of Management Review,* 14 (4): 532–50.

Gibbons, M., Limoges, C., Nowotny, H., Schwartzman, S., Scott, P. and Trow, M. (1994) *The New Production of Knowledge: The Dynamics of Science and Research in Contemporary Societies.* London: Sage.

Gluckman, M. (1961) 'Ethnographic data in British social anthropology', *Sociological Review,* 9: 5–17.

Goldenberg, S. (1993) 'Analytic induction revisited', *Canadian Journal of Sociology,* 18 (2): 161–76.

Guba, E. and Lincoln, Y.S. (1989) *Fourth Generation Evaluation.* Newbury Park, CA: Sage.

Hamilton, D. (1980) 'Some contrasting assumptions about case study research and survey analysis', in H. Simons (ed.), *Towards a Science of the Singular: Essays about Case Study in Educational Research and Evaluation.* Norwich: Centre for Applied Research in Education University of East Anglia.

Hammersley, M. (1992) *What's Wrong with Ethnography?* London: Routledge.

Hammersley, M. and Atkinson, P. (1995) *Ethnography: Principles in practice* (2nd edn). London: Routledge.

Lindesmith, A.R. (1937) *The Nature of Opiate Addiction.* Chicago: University of Chicago Libraries.

Lindesmith, A.R. (1968) *Addiction and Opiates.* Chicago: Aldine.

Mill, J.S. (1843) *A System of Logic.* London: Longman.

Nichols, E. (1986) 'Skocpol and revolution: comparative analysis vs historical conjuncture', *Comparative Social Research*, 9: 163–86.

Noblit, G.W. and Hare, R.D. (1988) *Meta-ethnography: Synthesizing Qualitative Studies.* Beverly Hills, CA: Sage.

Platt, J. (1981) '"Case study" in American methodological thought', *Current Sociology*, 40: 17–48.

Platt, J. (1992) 'Cases of cases ... of cases', in C.C. Ragin and H.S. Becker (eds), *What is a Case? Exploring the Foundations of Social Inquiry.* Cambridge: Cambridge University Press.

Ragin, C.C. (1987) *The Comparative Method: Moving beyond Qualitative and Quantitative strategies.* Berkeley: University of California Press.

Sharp, R. (1982) 'Self-contained ethnography or a science of phenomenal forms and inner relations', *Boston University Journal of Education*, 164 (1): 48–63.

Simons, H. (1996) 'The paradox of case study', *Cambridge Journal of Education*, 26 (2): 225–40.

Skocpol, T. (1979) *States and Social Revolutions: A Comparative Analysis of France, Russia, and China.* Cambridge: Cambridge University Press.

Skocpol, T. (1986) 'Analyzing causal configurations in history: a rejoinder to Nichols', *Comparative Social Research*, 9: 187–94.

Smith, L.M. (1978) 'An evolving logic of participant observation, educational ethnography and other case studies', in L. Shulman (ed.) *Review of Educational Research*, Vol. 6. Itasca, IL: F.E. Peacock. pp. 316–77.

Stake, R.E. (1994) 'Case Studies', in N.K. Denzin and Y.S. Lincoln (eds), *Handbook of Qualitative Research.* Thousand Oaks, CA: Sage.

Stake, R.E. and Trumbull, D. (1982) 'Naturalistic generalization', *Review Journal of Philosophy and Social Science*, 7: 1–12.

Stenhouse, L. (1975) *An Introduction to Curriculum Research and Development.* London: Heinemann.

Stenhouse, L. (1978) 'Case study and case records: towards a contemporary history of education', *British Educational Research Journal*, 4 (2): 21–39.

Stenhouse, L. (1980) 'The study of samples and the study of cases', *British Educational Research Journal*, 6 (1): 1–6.

Thomas, W.I. and Znaniecki, F. (1918–20) *The Polish Peasant in Europe and America* (5 Vols). Chicago: University of Chicago Press/Boston: Badger Press.

Yin, R.K. (1994) *Case Study Research: Design and Methods* (2nd edn). Thousand Oaks, CA: Sage.

Yin, R.K. and Heald, K.A. (1975) 'Using the case survey method to analyze policy studies', *Administrative Science Quarterly*, 20: 371–81.

INTRINSIC CASE STUDY AND GENERALIZABILITY

Chapter 1

THE CASE STUDY METHOD IN SOCIAL INQUIRY

Robert E. Stake

It is widely believed that case studies are useful in the study of human affairs because they are down-to-earth and attention-holding but that they are not a suitable basis for generalization. In this paper, I claim that case studies will often be the preferred method of research because they may be epistemologically in harmony with the reader's experience and thus to that person a natural basis for generalization.

Experience

We expect an inquiry to be carried out so that certain audiences will benefit – not just to swell the archives, but to help persons toward further understandings. If the readers of our reports are the persons who populate our houses, schools, governments and industries; and if we are to help them understand social problems and social programmes, we must perceive and communicate (see Bohm, 1974; Schön, 1977) in a way that accommodates their present understandings.[1] Those people have arrived at their understandings mostly through direct and vicarious experience.

And those readers who are most learned and specialized in their disciplines are little different. Though they write and talk with special languages, their own understandings of human affairs are for the most part attained and amended through personal experience. I believe that it is reasonable to conclude that one of the more effective means of adding to understanding for all readers will be by approximating, through the words and illustrations of our reports, the natural experiences acquired in ordinary personal involvement.

At the turn of the century, German philosopher Wilhelm Dilthey (1910) claimed that more objective and 'scientific' studies did not do the best job of acquainting man with himself:

> Only from his actions, his fixed utterances, his effects upon others, can man learn about himself; thus he learns to know himself only by the round-about

Originally published in (1978) *Educational Researcher*, 7 February: 5–8.

way of understanding. What we once were, how we developed and became what we are, we learn from the way in which we acted, the plans which we once adopted, the way in which we made ourselves felt in our vocation, from old dead letters, from judgements on which were spoken long ago. ...we understand ourselves and others only when we transfer our own lived experience into every kind of expression of our own and other people's lives.

He distinguished between the human studies and other kinds of studies:

The human studies are thus founded on this relation between lived experience, expression and understanding. Here for the first time we reach a quite clear criterion by which the delimitation of the human studies can be definitively carried out. A study belongs to the human studies only if its object becomes accessible to us through the attitude which is founded on the relation between life, expression and understanding.

Dilthey was not urging us merely to pay more attention to humanistic values or to put more affective variables into our equations. He was saying that our methods of studying human affairs need to capitalize upon the natural powers of people to experience and understand.

Knowledge

In statements fundamental to the epistemology of social inquiry, Polanyi[2] distinguished between propositional and tacit knowledge. Propositional knowledge – the knowledge of both reason and gossip – was seen to be composed of all interpersonally sharable statements, most of which for most people are observations of objects and events. Tacit knowledge may also dwell on objects and events, but it is knowledge gained from experience with them, experience with propositions about them, and rumination:

Through reason man observes himself; but he knows himself only through consciousness. (Tolstoy, 1869).

Tacit knowledge is all that is remembered somehow, minus that which is remembered in the form of words, symbols or other rhetorical forms. It is that which permits us to recognize faces, to comprehend metaphors and to 'know ourselves'. Tacit knowledge includes a multitude of unexpressible associations which give rise to new meanings, new ideas and new applications of the old. Polanyi recognized that each person, expert or novice, has great stores of tacit knowledge with which to build new understandings.

It is a common belief that these ordinary understandings, both new and old, are merely the pieces from which mighty explanations are made. And that explanation is the grandest of understandings.

But explanation and understanding are perhaps not so intimately interwoven:

> Practically every explanation, be it causal or teleological or of some other kind, can be said to further our understanding of things. But 'understanding' also has a psychological ring which 'explanation' has not. This psychological feature was emphasized by several of the nineteenth-century antipositivist methodologists, perhaps most forcefully by Simmel who thought that understanding as a method characteristic of the humanities is a form of *empathy* or re-creation in the mind of the scholar of the mental atmosphere, the thoughts and feelings and motivations, of the objects of his study.
>
> ... Understanding is also connected with *intentionality* in a way that explanation is not. One understands the aims and purposes of an agent, the meaning of a sign or symbol, and the significance of a social institution or religious rite. This intentionalistic ... dimension of understanding has come to play a prominent role in more recent methodological discussion. (Von Wright, 1971)

Explanation belongs more to propositional knowledge, understanding more to tacit.

Philosophers of the positivist school, Carl Hempel and Karl Popper particularly, have posited that propositional statements of lawful relationship are the closest approximations of Truth – whether we are talking about physical matter or human. They would have us speak of attributes and constructs, such as energy and mass or work ethic and masculinity, and the relationships among them. Anti-positivists such as Dilthey, Von Wright and William Dray have claimed that Truth in the fields of human affairs is better approximated by statements that are rich with the sense of human encounter: to speak not of underlying attributes, objective observables and universal forces, but of perceptions and understanding that come from immersion in and holistic regard for the phenomena.

In American research circles most methodologists have been of positivistic persuasion. The more episodic, subjective procedures, common to the case study, have been considered weaker than the experimental or correlational studies for explaining things.

When explanation, propositional knowledge and law are the aims of an inquiry, the case study will often be at a disadvantage. When the aims are understanding, extension of experience and increase in conviction in that which is known, the disadvantage disappears.

Generalizations

The scientist and the humanist scholar alike search for laws that tell of order in their disciplines. But so do all other persons look for regularity and system in their experience. Predictable covariation is to be found in all phenomena. In 1620 Francis Bacon said:

> There are and can be only two ways of searching and discovering truth. The one flies from the senses and particulars to the most general axioms ... this is now the fashion. The other derives axioms from the senses and particulars, rising by a gradual and unbroken ascent, so that it arrives at the most general axioms last of all. This is the true way, but as yet untried.

He claimed that Truth lies in the most general of axioms, a far and laboured trek from experience.[3]

Another point of view holds that Truth lies in particulars. William Blake (1808) offered these intemperate words:

> To generalize is to be an idiot. To particularize is the lone distinction of merit. General knowledges are those that idiots possess.

Generalizations may not be all that despicable, but particularization does deserve praise. To know particulars fleetingly of course is to know next to nothing. What becomes useful understanding is a full and thorough knowledge of the particular, recognizing it also in new and foreign contexts.

That knowledge is a form of generalization too, not scientific induction but *naturalistic generalization*, arrived at by recognizing the similarities of objects and issues in and out of context and by sensing the natural covariations of happenings. To generalize this way is to be both intuitive and empirical, and not idiotic.

Naturalistic generalizations develop within a person as a product of experience. They derive from the tacit knowledge of how things are, why they are, how people feel about them, and how these things are likely to be later or in other places with which this person is familiar. They seldom take the form of predictions but lead regularly to expectation. They guide action, in fact they are inseparable from action (Kemmis, 1974). These generalizations may become verbalized, passing of course from tacit knowledge to propositional; but they have not yet passed the empirical and logical tests that characterize formal (scholarly, scientific) generalizations.

Sociologist Howard Becker (1964)[4] spoke of an irreducible conflict between sociological perspective and the perspective of everyday life. Which is superior? It depends on the circumstance, of course. For publishing in the sociological journals, the scientific perspective is better; but for reporting to lay audiences and for studying lay problems, the lay perspective will often be superior. And frequently that everyday-life perspective will be superior for discourse among scholars for they, too, often share among themselves more of ordinary experience than of special conceptualization. The special is often too special. It is foolish to presume that a more scholarly report will be the more effective.

The other generalizations, that is, rationalistic, propositional, law-like generalizations, can be useful for understanding a particular situation. And they can be hurtful. Obviously, bad laws foster misunderstandings. And abstract statements of law distract attention from direct experience. Good generalizations aid the understanding of general conditions, but good generalizations can lead one to see phenomena more simplistically than one should.

It is the legitimate aim of many scholarly studies to discover or validate laws. But the aim of the practical arts is to get things done. The better generalizations often are those more parochial, those more personal. In fields such as education and social work, where few laws have been validated and where inquiry can be directed toward gathering information that has use other than for the cultivation of laws, a persistent attention to laws is pedantic.

Cases

The object (target) of a social inquiry is seldom an individual person or enterprise. Unfortunately, it is such single objects that are usually thought of as 'cases'. A case is often thought of as a constituent member of a target population. And since single members poorly represent whole populations, one case study is seen to be a poor basis for generalization.

Often, however, the situation is one in which there is need for generalization about that particular case or generalization to a similar case rather than generalization to a population of cases. Then the demands for typicality and representativeness yield to needs for assurance that the target case is properly described. As readers recognize essential similarities to cases of interest to them, they establish the basis for naturalistic generalization.

The case need not be a person or enterprise. It can be whatever 'bounded system' (to use Louis Smith's term) is of interest. An institution, a programme, a responsibility, a collection or a population can be the case. This is not to trivialize the notion of 'case' but to note the generality of the case study method in preparation for noting its distinctiveness.

It is distinctive in the first place by giving great prominence to what is and what is not 'the case' – the boundaries are kept in focus. What is happening and deemed important within those boundaries (the emic) is considered vital and usually determines what the study is about, as contrasted with other kinds of studies where hypotheses or issues previously targeted by the investigators (the etic) usually determine the content of the study.

Case studies can be used to test hypotheses, particularly to examine a single exception that shows the hypothesis to be false. Case studies can be highly statistical; institutional research and vocational counselling case studies often are. But in the social science literature, most case studies feature: descriptions that are complex, holistic and involving a myriad of not highly isolated variables; data that are likely to be gathered at least partly by personalistic observation; and a writing style that is informal, perhaps narrative, possibly with verbatim quotation, illustration and even allusion and metaphor. Comparisons are implicit rather than explicit. Themes and hypotheses may be important, but they remain subordinate to the understanding of the case.[5]

Although case studies have been used by anthropologists, psychoanalysts and many others as a method of exploration preliminary to theory development,[6] the characteristics of the method are usually more suited to expansionist than reductionist pursuits. Theory building is the search for essences, pervasive and determining ingredients, and the makings of laws. The case study, however, proliferates rather than narrows. One is left with more to pay attention to rather than less. The case study attends to the idiosyncratic more than to the pervasive.[7] The fact that it has been useful in theory building does not mean that that is its best use.

Its best use appears to me to be for adding to existing experience and humanistic understanding. Its characteristics match the 'readiness' people have for added experience. As Von Wright and others stressed, intentionality and empathy are central to the comprehension of social problems, but so also is information that is holistic and episodic. The discourse of persons struggling to increase their understanding of social matters features and solicits these qualities. And these qualities match nicely the characteristics of the case study.[8]

The study of human problems is the work of scientists, novelists, journalists, everybody of course – but especially historians. The historian Herbert Butterfield (1951) recognized the centrality of experiential data and said:

> ...the only understanding we ever reach in history is but a refinement, more or less subtle and sensitive, of the difficult – and sometimes deceptive – process of imagining oneself in another person's place.

Case studies are likely to continue to be popular because of their style and to be useful for exploration for those who search for explanatory laws. And, moreover, because of the universality and importance of experiential understanding, and because of their compatability with such understanding, case studies can be expected to continue to have an epistemological advantage over other inquiry methods as a basis for naturalistic generalization. Unlike Bacon's 'true way' of discovering

Truth, this method *has been* tried and found to be a direct and satisfying way of adding to experience and improving understanding.

Notes

Written at the Centre for Applied Research in Education, University of East Anglia, as part of an assignment for the Organization for Economic Cooperation and Development, Paris.

1 In this paper I am writing about the formal inquiry to be done by people, on or off the campus, who are subject to greater rewards for scholarly work and knowledge production and to lesser rewards for professional support and problem solving. In the USA there are few civil service or applied research agencies which validate their inquiries according to its service value more than to its 'internal and external validities', as defined by Campbell and Stanley (1966). I see it as unfortunately necessary to overstate the distinction between academic research and practical inquiry as a step toward improving and legitimizing inquiries that are needed for understanding and problem solving but which are unlikely to produce vouchsafed generalizations.

2 I am indebted to statements by Harry Broudy (1972) and Andrew Ortony (1975) for helping me understand the educational relevance of the writing of Polanyi.

3 But he noted that at least before 1620 *that* was not the way humans reached understanding.

4 Important ideas about the special use of case study as precursor to theoretical study are found in his 'Problems of inference and proof in participant observation,' (1958).

5 This is not to say that all case studies are as described here. Medical 'write-ups', for example, are very different. But these characteristics are commonly expected and little different than those specified by Louis Smith (1974), for example, to be: credible, holistic, particularistic, individualizable, process-oriented, ego-involving, and blending of behavioural and phenomenological methodologies.

6 In Julian Simon (1969), for example.

7 Barry MacDonald and Rob Walker have made the strongest case I know for using idiosyncratic instances to create understanding of more general matters, as in 'Case study and the social philosophy of educational research' (1975).

8 It would be of interest to get empirical data on the perceived utility of case studies. It can be presumed, I fear, that some respondents, having heard objections to the case study method from such authorities as Julian Stanley and Donald Campbell and thinking more of political value than informational value, would underrate their utility for understanding and generalization.

References

Bacon, F. (1620) *Novum Organum.*

Becker, H.S. (1958) 'Problems of inference and proof in participant observation', *American Sociological Review,* 23: 652–9.

Becker, H.S. (1964) 'Problems in the publication of field studies', in A.J. Vidich, J. Bensman and M.R. Stein (eds), *Reflections on Community Studies.* New York: John Wiley.

Blake, W. (1808) *Annotations to Sir Joshua Reynolds' 'Disclosures'.*

Bohm, D. (1974) 'Science as perception–communication', in F. Suppe (ed.), *The Structure of Scientific Theories.* Urbana, IL: University of Illinois Press.

Broudy, H.S. (1972) 'The life uses of schooling as a field for research', in L.G. Thomas (ed.), *Philosophical Redirection of Educational Research*. 71st Yearbook of NSEE.

Butterfield, H. (1951) *History and Human Relations*. London: Collins.

Campbell, D.T. and Stanley, J.C. (1966) *Experimental and Quasi-experimental Designs for Research*. Chicago: Rand McNally.

Dilthey, W. (1910) 'Der Aufbauder Welt in den Geisteswissenschaften' ('The construction of the historical world of the human studies'), in *Gesammelte Schriften*, I–VII Leipzig, B.G. Teubner, 1914–27 [Translated in Rickman (1976)].

Dray, W.H. (1957) *Laws and Explanation in History*. Oxford: Oxford University Press.

Hempel, C.G. (1942) 'The function of general laws in history', *Journal of Philosophy*, 39: 35–48.

Kemmis, S. (1974) 'An ecological perspective on innovation' (mimeo). Urbana, IL: University of Illinois College of Education.

MacDonald, B. and Walker, R. (1975) 'Case study and the philosophy of educational research', *Cambridge Journal of Education*, 5 (1): 2–11.

Ortony, A. (1975) 'Knowledge, language, and thinking' (mimeo). Urbana, IL: University of Illinois College of Education.

Polanyi, M. (1958) *Personal Knowledge*. New York: Harper & Row.

Popper, K. (1957) *The Poverty of Historicism*. London: Routledge and Kegan Paul.

Rickman, H.P. (ed.) (1976) *Wilhelm Dilthey: Selected Writings*. Cambridge: Cambridge University Press.

Schön, D.A. (1977) 'Metaphor and the social conscience'. Paper delivered at the Conference on Metaphor and Thought, University of Illinois, September.

Simon, J. (1969) *Basic Research Methods in Social Science: The Art of Empirical Investigation*. New York: Random House.

Smith, L. (1974) 'An aesthetic education workshop for administrators: some implications for a theory of case studies'. Paper presented at the annual meeting of the American Educational Research Association, Chicago. [See also Smith, L. (1978) 'An evolving logic of participant observation, educational ethnography and other case studies, in Shulman, L. (ed.) *Review of Research in Education*, Vol. 6, pp. 316–77. Itasca, IL: Peacock.]

Tolstoy, L. (1869) *War and Peace*.

Von Wright, G.H. (1971) *Explanation and Understanding*. London: Routledge & Kegan Paul.

CHAPTER 2

THE ONLY GENERALIZATION IS: THERE IS NO GENERALIZATION

Yvonna S. Lincoln and Egon G. Guba

The trouble with generalizations is that they don't apply to particulars.

Generalization as the aim of science

A frequently mentioned aim of science is prediction and control. But prediction and control cannot be accomplished without something on which to base predictions or formulate controlling actions. It is the role of laws, those statements that Kaplan (1964) calls 'nomic' or 'nomological' generalizations, to provide such a base. While such nomic generalizations have a number of defining characteristics, possibly the most important is that

> the generalization must be truly universal, *unrestricted as to time and space*. It must formulate what is always and everywhere the case, provided only that the appropriate conditions are satisfied. (Kaplan, 1964, p. 91; emphasis added)

That is to say, generalizations are assertions of *enduring* value that are *context-free*. Their value lies in their ability to modulate efforts at prediction and control.

Indeed, so convinced are many scientists that generalizations are the be-all and end-all of inquiry that they seriously question whether scientific activity aimed at something other than the establishment of generalizations is worth the effort. They assert that if one rejects the goal of achieving generalizations, all that can be left is knowledge of the particular – and they ask, 'What value could there be in knowing only the unique?' But this posture ignores the fact that we are not dealing with an either/or proposition; the alternatives include more than deciding between nomic generalizations, on the one hand, and unique, particularized knowledge, on the other. We shall spend much of this chapter exploring an intermediate position.

From Y.S. Lincoln and E.G. Guba (1979) *Naturalistic Inquiry*. Newbury Park, CA: Sage.

Generalization, it must be admitted, is an appealing concept. The dictionary defines the general as 'pertaining to, affecting, or applicable to each and all of a class, kind, or order'. Each and all! When a generalization has been devised, no member of that class, kind or order can escape its pervasive influence. What could be more appropriate if the aim is prediction and control? The concept oozes determinism, and seems to place the entire world at the feet of those persons who can unlock its deepest and most pervasive generalities. How grandly these concepts fit in with political processes too; social science can discover generalizations that make it unnecessary for lawgivers to think through the particulars of each case. Rather, generalizations will serve their purposes, and what is good for one is good for all – at least all in that class.

It should not be doubted that the concept of generalization has the influence that we have ascribed to it here. Beginning with John Stuart Mill and continuing to today's post-positivists, many have subscribed to the proposition that generalization is among the most basic of scientists' goals. Hamilton (1976) has observed that among Mill's assumptions [...] is that the social and natural sciences have identical aims, namely the discovery of general laws that serve for explanation and prediction, and that Mill's 'ultimate major premise' was that there exists a uniformity of nature in time and space. Indeed, Mill felt that the latter premise was essential to overcome certain objections that had been raised about the inductive nature of generalization. For if the postulated uniformity did indeed characterize nature, then inductive logic was as procedurally certain as was deductive logic – a mistaken notion, but one nevertheless persuasive to Mill and many of his adherents [(Mill, 1906)].

Schwartz and Ogilvy (1979) comment that among the positivists' major assumptions was that

> the laws that govern matter and energy on the small scale must be similar, and hopefully identical, to those that apply on the very large scale. The governing laws thus would be universal, so that we ought to be able to build a picture of planets moving about the sun out of an understanding of the particles of which matter is composed. (p. 32)

Unfortunately, that belief has turned out to have been mistaken also.

Hesse (1980) suggests that the aim of prediction and control is primary even in post-positivist thought through the adoption of what she terms the 'pragmatic criterion' for science. This criterion states, simply enough, that science will be judged successful to the degree that it is able to produce 'increasingly successful prediction and control of the environment' (p. 188), a statement that certainly supports the continuation of dependence on generalizability. There are of course some post-positivists, particularly naturalists, who disagree with this position.

Despite the interest in generalizability, and the almost universal appeal that the idea has for all of us, serious questions can be raised about the feasibility of this concept in its classic form. We shall first examine several of the more important of these issues, stopping thereafter to comment on a form recently proposed by Stake and others that is termed 'naturalistic generalization', and finally make a counterproposal: the working hypothesis.

Some problems with the classic concept of generalizability

The classic concept of generalizability, as defined by Kaplan, suffers from a number of deficiencies, which are briefly outlined below:

(1) Dependence on the assumption of determinism

In the final analysis, there can be no generalization unless there is also determinism; if there are no fixed and reliable linkages among elements, then one cannot derive statements about those linkages (laws) that will be found to hold in 'truly universal' ways.

[...] The Newtonian and, more broadly, the positivist metaphor for the world was the machine. Indeed, scientists did not take the machine to be simply a metaphor but believed that, in fact, the world *was* one Great Machine. Dickson (1982) suggests the term 'mechanomorphism' to denote 'the belief that god is a mechanical force and that the universe is governed by natural law' (p. 137). Wolf (1981) quotes the eminent French scientist, the Marquis de Laplace, as pontificating, at the turn of the nineteenth century:

> We ought, then, to regard the present state of the universe as the effect of its previous state and as the cause of the one which is to follow. Given for one instant a mind which could comprehend all the forces by which nature is animated and the respective situation of the beings who compose it – a mind sufficiently vast to submit these data to analysis – it would embrace *in the same formula* the movements of the greatest bodies of the universe and those of the lightest atom; for it, nothing would be uncertain and the future, as the past, would be present to its eyes. (p. 43; emphasis added)

Wolf goes on to comment, 'Perfect determinism, from a heartbreak to an empire's rise and fall, was no more than the inevitable workings of the Great Machine' (p. 43).

The existence of a 'grand' formula as envisioned by Laplace was not an uncommon assumption; again, it should be stressed that this expression was taken literally and not metaphorically by its adherents. The ultimate generalization, in effect, *was* this grand formula, which has a very large number of terms, sufficiently large to embrace every particle in the universe. Any particular phenomenon was a special case; many of the 'coefficients' of terms in the formula would go to zero, but what remained would describe the phenomenon perfectly. It was only the natural limits on the human mind that prevented the discovery and utilization of the formula; had Laplace known about the power that would eventually be built into computers, he probably would have nourished the hope that this formula would, sooner or later, be known.

But of course the very idea of determinism rests, as we now understand, on shifting sand. Indeed, as Schwartz and Ogilvy (1979) remind us, determinism is rapidly being replaced by indeterminism in the 'new' paradigm; indeterminism is now the basic belief that determinism once was. And without the base of determinism on which to rest, the possibility of generalizability comes seriously into question. Generalizability becomes, at best, probabilistic.

(2) Dependence on inductive logic

Generalizations are not found in nature; they are active creations of the mind. Empirically, they rest upon the generalizer's experience with a limited number of particulars not with 'each and all' of the members of a 'class, kind, or order'. From that experience springs, as Ford (1975) suggests, an *imaginative* generalization, one that goes beyond the bounds of the particulars, making assertions that presumably apply not only to its generating particulars but to all other similar particulars.

Now the rules of *deduction* are *closed*; given certain premises, it is possible to derive conclusions that are *absolutely* true [...], conclusions that are compelling and binding upon the receiver. But induction is essentially an *open* process, as Reese (1980) suggests:

> The widespread distinction between induction as an inference moving from specific facts to general conclusions, and deduction as moving from general premises to specific conclusions is no longer respectable philosophically. This distinction distinguished one kind of induction from one kind of deduction. It is much more satisfactory to think of induction as *probable* inference and deduction as *necessary* inference. (p. 251; emphasis added)

Epistemologists such as Hesse (1980) have stressed the fact that theories are underdetermined; the same arguments might well hold for the generalizations (laws) that are sometimes said to be the component elements of theories. Thus Hesse on theory:

> Theories are logically constrained by facts, but are underdetermined by them: that is while, to be acceptable, theories should be more or less plausibly

coherent with facts, they can be neither conclusively refuted nor uniquely derived from statements of fact alone, and hence no theory in a given domain is uniquely acceptable. (p. 187)

That is to say, while generalizations are constrained by facts (especially if the facts are the particulars from which the generalization is induced), there is no single necessary generalization that *must* emerge to account for them. There are always (logically) multiple possible generalizations to account for any set of particulars, however extensive and inclusive they may be.

If the logical consequence of indeterminism is that generalizations can be, at best, probabilistic, the logical consequence of reliance on induction is that generalizations can be at best relativistic expressions (Hesse, 1980, p. xiv). There are no absolutes; all 'truth' is relative; there are no final metacriteria. And there are certainly no absolute laws. The issue, as we shall, see, is *what it is to which the 'generalization' is relative.*

(3) Dependence on the assumption of freedom from time and context

Kaplan has reminded us that nomic generalizations, at least, must be of a form that is 'always and everywhere the case, provided only that the appropriate conditions are satisfied'. But all of our experience tells us that there are always many 'conditions, contingencies, and disjunctions' (Wiles, 1981) that must be taken into account.

It is difficult to imagine a human activity that is context-free. Your response, reader, to what is on these pages may take a variety of forms. For example, you might turn to a colleague and remark, 'What nonsense this is!' If you were using these materials to instruct a class in research methods, you might wish to pose certain counter-arguments, in order to appear constructive and scholarly in your critique. If you were to question the authors about their beliefs while they were on the podium of a national meeting, you might be a bit more snide and acerbic in your statements. If you were to discuss this chapter with the authors over a bottle of beer at a convenient pub, your demeanour might be very different yet. And so on. [...]

But the problem is much more intractable than this small example suggests. Listen to Lee J. Cronbach, as he ruminates 'Beyond the two disciplines of scientific psychology' (1975):

> Generalizations decay. At one time a conclusion describes the existing situation well, at a later time it accounts for rather little variance, and ultimately it is valid *only as history*. The half-life of an empirical proposition may be great or small. The more open the system, the shorter the half-life of relations within it are likely to be.

Propositions describing atoms and electrons have a long half-life, and the physical theorist can regard the processes in his world as steady. Rarely is a social or behavioral phenomenon isolated enough to have this steady-state property. Hence the explanation we live by will perhaps always remain partial, and distant from real events ... and rather short-lived. The atheoretical regularities of the actuary are even more time-bound. An actuarial table describing human affairs *changes from science into history* before it can be set in type. (pp. 122–3; emphasis added)

Cronbach's analysis is a powerful one because it takes into account not only changes in sociobehavioural generalizations, which have short half-lives and might be explained on the basis that our knowledge is so rudimentary in these areas that frequent updates are necessary, but also changes in physical/chemical/biological generalizations, for example the failure of DDT to control mosquitoes as genetic transformations make them resistant to that pesticide, and the shifting of the value of the gravitational constant, so that while s will continue to equal gt^2, the actual distances covered by falling bodies will differ.

Cronbach's metaphor of the radioactive substance, constantly decaying and displaying a characteristic half-life, seems a particularly apt one. Further, his notion that all science eventually becomes history demolishes the proposition that generalizations are time-free; generalizations inevitably alter, usually radically, over time, so that, eventually, they have only historical interest.

Some critics, unwilling to give up easily on the Kaplan definition, point out that we have so far overlooked the phrase therein contained: 'provided only that the appropriate conditions are satisfied'. If the difficulty is that generalizations do not take adequate account of time factors and contextual conditions, they assert, there is an easy solution: enlarge the generalization to include as many of these temporal/contextual variables as may be necessary so that the generalization *will* hold. But this proposal poses two difficulties of its own: first, it tends to move us back to the Laplacian grand equation (for surely if, in their view, we included *all* variables there could be no doubt that the generalization would hold – and there need be only one generalization!); and, second, it defeats the purpose of seeking generalizations in the first place: to facilitate prediction and control. For if the equation becomes too complex, has built into it so many spatiotemporal factors as may be necessary, then of course the mind boggles (even when computer-aided) at the task, and the resources needed to set up the controls are stretched beyond all bounds. It is far easier, and more epistemologically sound, simply to give up on the idea of generalization, at least as prescribed by Kaplan. Accepting generalizations (to whatever extent they may be possible) as indeterminate, relative and time- and context-bound, while not a wholly satisfying solution, is at least a feasible one.

(4) Entrapment in the nomothetic–idiographic dilemma

The terms 'nomothetic' and 'idiographic' were coined by German philosopher Wilhelm Windelband to describe, on the one hand, the natural sciences (the term 'nomothetic' implies 'based on law'), and, on the other, the 'cultural' or human sciences (the term 'idiographic' implies 'based on the particular individual'). The essential dilemma is simply this: generalizations are nomothetic in nature, that is, law-like, but in order to use them – for purposes of prediction or control, say – the generalizations must be applied to particulars. And it is precisely at that point that their probabilistic, relative nature comes into sharpest focus.

Consider the example of the woman who comes in to see her gynaecologist for her routine annual examination. In response to the physician's questions, she reports that she has suffered certain symptoms for some months. The physician's reaction is one of immediate alarm: 'Madam,' he says, 'fully 80 per cent of the women who report those symptoms have cervical cancer. I will call the hospital at once and arrange to have you admitted. Tomorrow morning at the latest we will do a complete hysterectomy on you.' Aside from the fact that the woman in question might be well advised [...] to seek a second opinion, she has other intelligent grounds for questioning the proposed course of action. She might well ask, 'But suppose I am one of that group of 20 per cent who do *not* have cancer of the cervix, despite displaying these symptoms? Aren't you going to examine me to find out? Wouldn't you like to determine the particulars of this case before making a judgement that condemns me to expense, pain and loss of productive time, when it might not be necessary at all to have this operation?' The woman would be quite right in insisting that idiographic elements be considered rather than basing a judgement entirely on a nomothetic generalization.

If in fact there were a one-to-one relationship between particulars and generalizations – that is, that generalizations did not suffer from inductive loss in their formulation but could be counted on to be determinately and absolutely true – then this problem would not arise. But generalizations unfortunately cannot meet these stringent criteria; they are always inductively underdetermined, and they are always temporally and contextually relative.

The nomothetic–idiographic problem continues to haunt particularly the social/behavioural sciences and the helping professions. Consider the dilemma of the therapist trying to deal with an individual's problem within the context of psychiatric generalizations. Or the teacher attempting to get children to learn in a particular class by using only general pedagogical principles. Or the warden seeking to control the prisoners in a particular penitentiary on the basis of general correctional theories. That the dilemma continues to be of pervasive interest is evident from the literature; the reader may wish to consult Marceil (1977) for [an] analysis. Perhaps the professional group that has dealt best with this problem is the law, built largely on precedent cases (case law) that are powerful precisely because they take particulars into account.

(5) Entrapment in a reductionist fallacy

Generalizations represent a special case of reductionism: attempting to reduce all phenomena of a given class to the purview of a single (or single set of) generalization(s). There are several difficulties with this posture. First, generalizations are of necessity parts of formal systems: sets of laws, theories, and the like, that are directed at some phenomenological arena. Such formal systems, sometimes called formal languages, are by definition *closed* systems, that is, they are not open to the influence of any elements or factors that are not accounted for in the system. Hamilton (1979) observes:

> As closed systems, formal languages are logically isolated from extraneous elements (e.g., undefined 'variables') in the same way that laboratory experiments are empirically isolated from 'field' settings. In general, ... formal languages cannot fully comprehend natural (i.e., open) systems. (p. 2)

But there are more powerful grounds for reaching the conclusion that generalizations will always fall short of 'full comprehension'. Perhaps the most pervasive argument that can be brought to bear is Gödel's theorem, which, while developed in relation to number theory in mathematics, has wider applicability, that is, can lead one to better understanding in fields other than mathematics as well. The theorem itself, as quoted in Hofstadter (1979, p. 18), is simply this:

> All consistent axiomatic formulations of number theory include undecidable propositions.

Restated, the assertion of the theorem is that there exists no *consistent* set of statements (reduced to their most basic undergirding axioms) that can *ever hope* to deal with all propositions; some propositions will inevitably fall outside its purview (unless, of course, one wishes to take the option implied by Gödel: to start with an *inconsistent* axiomatic formulation!). That is, there can be no set of generalizations, consistent with one another, that can effectively account for all known phenomena (the Laplacian 'grand equation' is at best an idle dream!).

This concept is an extremely difficult one to comprehend; it flies in the face of traditional positivist (and some post-positivist) postures so violently as to demand rejection. But perhaps a metaphoric explanation developed by Hofstadter will contribute to our appreciation of the full

Figure 2.1   Metaphoric representation of Gödel's theorem:
No consistent formulation can include all propositions

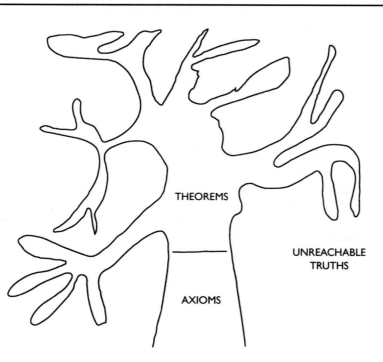

significance of this important theorem. Consider Figure 2.1, which is based on Figure 18 in Hofstadter's *Gödel, Escher, Bach* (1979). One can imagine a system of axioms and theorems, perhaps empirically derived, as might be the case with many generalizations. Imagine, Hofstadter suggests, that these form a kind of knowledge 'tree', the branches of which reach out into the background of the 'truths' that the inquirer seeks to discover. By its nature, the tree will remain connected: twigs to branches to trunk to roots. If the tree is 'seen' against the sky-like background of 'truths', not all truths are reachable from the several branches of the tree. There are finite limits to what can be reached, given the tree's trunk and branches (analogously, the axioms and theorems); the remainder of the 'truths' are unreachable *within this formulation*. Of course, other 'trees' can be planted, two, three, four or more, in the hope that all of the 'unreachable truths' will be touched by some element of some tree. But that is precisely what is meant by the phrase 'consistent formulation'. The planting of several trees may get the job done, but there *are* several trees, not just one; and the trees, being separate entities, each with its own system of axioms, need not conform to any requirement of consistency. To bring the matter home to the level of generalizations [...] not all generalizations that can be imagined need be consistent with one another, in fact, cannot be, if all of 'reality' is to be appreciated. Any single system of generalizations, far from encompassing all elements of some phenomenon, must always fall short, to use Hamilton's phrase, of 'full comprehension'. This fact comes as no surprise to those who are familiar with the Schwartz and Ogilvy 'new' paradigm, which asserts, as one of its major dimensions, that there are always multiple perspectives; that no one perspective can 'tell the full story'; and that all perspectives aggregated do not necessarily sum to the whole of the phenomenon.

Naturalistic generalization as an alternative

The concept of 'naturalistic generalization', which has, on its face, an apparent relevance to the issues we have been discussing, was introduced by Robert Stake in a paper entitled 'The Case Study Method in Social Inquiry', first written in 1976 as part of an assignment for the Organization for Economic Cooperation and Development and later published in *Educational Researcher* (1978; reprinted in this volume, see Chapter 1). Case studies, according to Stake, are often considered non-useful because 'they are not a suitable basis for generalization' (p. 5; see p. 19 above). It seems clear that if generalization is defined in the usual sense of nomic generalization, based upon data representative of some population, the assertion of non-utility is probably correct. But, argues Stake, one must consider the situation from the perspective of the *user* of the generalization: '[C]ase studies will often be the preferred method of research because they may be epistemologically in harmony with the reader's experience and thus to that person *a natural basis for generalization*' (p. 5; see p. 19 above; emphasis added).

Stake's posture seems to be that there are two kinds of generalizations. One kind is rationalistic, propositional, law-like – that is the meaning we usually attach to the term in scientific discourse. The other kind is more intuitive, empirical, based on personal direct and vicarious experience – that is the meaning intended by the term 'naturalistic generalization'. Case studies may not contribute much if the former kind of generalization is desired, but cases are a powerful means for building the latter. Stake points out, 'I believe that it is reasonable to conclude that one of the most effective means of adding to understanding for all readers will be by approximating, through the words and illustrations of our reports the natural experience attained in ordinary personal involvement' (p. 5; see p. 19 above). To put it another way, if you want people to understand better than they otherwise might, provide them information in the form in which they usually experience it. They will be able, both tacitly and propositionally, to derive naturalistic generalizations that will prove to be useful extensions of their understandings.

Some of Stake's readers foundered on the issue of whether naturalistic generalizations were essentially tacit or whether they could be propositional. Were these generalizations things that were felt only 'at gut level' so to speak, or could they be communicated to others in normal language? Hamilton, for example, in an unpublished seminar paper read at the University of Glasgow in 1979, understood Stake to say that naturalistic generalizations were based upon tacit knowledge, that they were the 'pre-verbal, pre-cognitive product of human experience' (p. 1). He argued that there were two 'contrasting accounts' of generalizations, one logical (built, he said, around concepts such as 'sample' and 'population') and one psychological (built around concepts such as 'cognition', 'abstraction' and 'comprehension'). Hamilton indicated that he preferred to equate naturalistic generalization with the psychological version:

> For my part, I would like to keep to a restricted definition of naturalistic generalization. That is, it may be worthwhile to distinguish between (i) making an inside-the-head generalization, and (ii) being able to communicate the reasons for making a generalization. In short, naturalistic generalization should be located within the realm of private knowledge.
>
> Naturalistic generalizations are personal accounts of the external world which, as it were, are held in the form of non-negotiable currency. When persons wish to communicate a naturalistic generalization they must convert their holdings into a shared form of exchange. They must engage upon a key component of scientific practice – public discourse.
>
> From this perspective, naturalistic generalizations and scientific generalizations fit inside each other as 'nested' concepts. They are not the same, yet they are not in opposition to each other.

Stake (1980) objected to this formulation, arguing that 'the key feature is not that naturalistic generalizations cannot be shared', but 'that they reside-in-mind in their natural habitat'. Stake goes on:

> I responded to David Hamilton last summer, from a beach somewhere, musing as follows:
>> I face the water and the breeze cools my face, I am aware of a generalization that breezes blow from water to land. I am not aware of being told or having read it, though in novels and movies I have vicariously experienced incidents that verify the generalization. I have heard people remark on the coolness of the ocean breeze. But *my* generalization I believe is primarily a creation of my own experimental knowing. Even though expressed in propositional form, it is a *naturalistic generalization*.
>> I wonder why breezes blow from water to land. Are people on beaches all *around* a small lake cooled by breezes blowing from the center of the lake? My experience is inadequate. My formal knowledge tells me that heat rises over land. I can recall a drawing in a book, perhaps an explanation of cumulus cloud activity. I know from personal experience and from formal learning that the water is cooler than the land (at least in months I am at the beach). Apparently it is not just heat that is rising but hot air,

and faster over land than over water. So I generalize: the breeze is simply cooler air over water rushing in to replace departed air above land.

Even though I made this generalization in my own mind, it is more the creature of formal knowledge and formal reasoning, modified only slightly by (though given an important confirmation by) experiential learning. It is a formalistic generalizing. (pp. 2–3)

What are we to make of all this? Hamilton and Stake, while apparently disagreeing on whether naturalistic generalization is all in the mind or whether it can be (or should be) shared publicly, nevertheless seem to agree that there are *two* kinds of generalizations: naturalistic (Stake) or psychological (Hamilton), and formalistic (Stake) or logical (Hamilton). Neither is arguing that one is a *replacement* for the other; they exist side by side, and each has its own arena of applicability.

Now it is clear that the kind of generalizations we have been talking about in this chapter tend toward the formalistic or logical (choose your term) rather than toward the naturalistic or psychological. We are not, as some of our critics contend, suggesting that the former have no utility while the latter do. While the idea of naturalistic generalization has for us a great deal of appeal [...] (for we surely agree with Stake that case studies have a great deal of utility in assisting reader understanding by inducing naturalistic generalizations), we do not believe that it is an adequate substitute or replacement for the formalistic or logical generalizations that people usually have in mind when they use the term 'generalization'. Yet we have, as we have tried to show in the earlier portion of this chapter, a serious problem with generalization in the nomic sense intended by Kaplan. We would replace the classic idea of generalization not with naturalistic generalization but with a new formulation proposed by Cronbach (1975): the *working hypothesis*.

The working hypothesis

We have noted that many scientists are committed to the idea of nomic generalization as the be-all and end-all of inquiry; it is these generalizations that become formulated into laws that in turn support theories from which, by hypothetico-deductive means, hypotheses are formulated that form the basis for the next round of inquiry, and so on. What could be the goal of inquiry if not the discovery of generalizable truths? What is left once generalizations are removed?

But of course the issue before us is not of the either/or variety. Between the poles of the most *general* (nomothetic) and the most *specific* (idiographic) is the broad range of the *related*; we are dealing here with a *continuum*, the two ends of which do not begin to encompass all of the possibilities that exist. The issue we pose then is simply this: If broad nomic generalizations, truly universal, unrestricted as to time and space, always and everywhere the same, are not feasible products of inquiry, are there nevertheless some ways of stating outcomes that might hold in Context *B*, although 'discovered' in Context *A*? What are the bases for *transferability*, if not of generalization, from one context to another?

We believe the answer to that question is found in a concept proposed by Lee Cronbach (1975) in his classic paper, 'Beyond the two disciplines' – the *working hypothesis*. Cronbach makes a lengthy case against generalizability in the nomic sense (although he does not use that term); we have already cited a portion of this argument earlier in this chapter. He finally concludes:

> Instead of making generalization the ruling consideration in our research, I suggest that we reverse our priorities. An observer collecting data in the particular situation is in a position to appraise a practice or proposition in that setting, observing effects in context. In trying to describe and account for what happened, he will give attention to whatever variables were controlled, but he will give equally careful attention to uncontrolled conditions, to personal characteristics, and to events that occurred during treatment and measurement. As he goes from situation to situation, his first task is to describe and interpret the effect anew in each locale, perhaps taking into account factors unique to that locale or series of events.... As results accumulate, a person who seeks understanding will do his best to trace how the uncontrolled factors could have caused local departures from the modal effect. That is, generalization comes late, and the exception is taken as seriously as the rule.
>
> ... *When we give proper weight to local conditions, any generalization is a working hypothesis, not a conclusion.* (Cronbach, 1975, pp. 124–5; emphasis added).

There is much in Cronbach's language to which we would take exception. 'Effects', 'variables', 'control', 'treatment', 'measurement', 'modal effect', and the like, are terms that have little place in the naturalistic paradigm. Nevertheless, Cronbach's ideas are powerful; they suggest that there are always factors that are unique to the locale or series of events that make it useless to try to generalize therefrom. But, he notes, inquirers *are* in a position to appreciate such factors and take them into account. And, as the inquirer moves from situation to situation, 'his task is to describe and interpret the effect anew', that is, in terms of the uniqueness found in *each* new situation. Generalization comes late, Cronbach avers – and, we might echo, if at all. For, 'when we give proper weight to local conditions, any generalization is a working hypothesis, not a conclusion'.

Local conditions, in short, make it impossible to generalize. If there is a 'true' generalization, it is that there can be no generalization. And note that the 'working hypotheses' are tentative both for the situation in which they are first uncovered and for other situations; there are always differences in context from situation to situation, and even the single situation differs over time. It is said that a Chinese philosopher, upon being asked whether it is possible to cross the same river twice, replied that it is not possible to cross the same river even once! Constant flux militates against conclusions that are always and forever true; they can only be said to be true under such and such conditions and circumstances.

Transferability and fittingness

How can one tell whether a working hypothesis developed in Context *A* might be applicable in Context *B*? We suggest that the answer to that question must be empirical: the degree of *transferability* is a direct function of the *similarity* between the two contexts, what we shall call '*fittingness*'. Fittingness is defined as the degree of congruence between sending and receiving contexts. If Context *A* and Context *B* are 'sufficiently' congruent, then working hypotheses from the sending originating context *may* be applicable in the receiving context.

Now it is one of the claimed virtues of the nomic generalization that it transcends this fittingness question; one need not know *anything* about either originating and receiving contexts to know the 'truth' of the generalization, assuming only that originating and receiving contexts are in some sense part of the known population of contexts and that the generalization is based upon a study of a representative sample of contexts. But working hypotheses are not that powerful; their transferability depends upon the degree of fittingness. The person who wishes to make a judgement of transferability needs information about *both* contexts to make that judgement well. Now an inquirer cannot know all the contexts to which someone may wish to transfer working hypotheses; one cannot reasonably expect him or her to indicate the range of contexts to which there might be some transferability. But it is entirely reasonable to expect an inquirer to provide sufficient information about the context in which an inquiry is carried out so that anyone else interested in transferability has a base of information appropriate to the judgement. We shall call that appropriate base of information a 'thick description', following the usage introduced by Geertz (1973).

What is described in the 'thick description' of course depends on the focus of the inquiry, or whether it is a research, evaluation or policy analysis inquiry, and on the salient features of the context. The description must specify everything that a reader may need to know in order to understand the findings (findings are *not* part of the thick description, although they must be interpreted in the terms of the factors thickly described). [...]

Holographic generalization

We could not close this chapter without pointing out several implications of the Schwartz and Ogilvy 'new' paradigm that may yet have enormous consequences for the whole idea of generalization. Schwartz and Ogilvy suggest that the metaphor for the world is changing from the machine to the hologram; holograms have characteristics more descriptive of the 'world' as we have come to know it than does the analogue of the machine. If that is so, then one particular characteristic of holograms is of particular significance: the fact that any piece of the hologram contains in it all of the information found in the whole.

A full appreciation of this remarkable fact requires some knowledge of how the process of holography works. The final product – the physical entity in which the hologram is stored – is a piece of film, not unlike that produced by any normal camera. But the image on the film is substantially different from anything produced by a Kodak or a Polaroid; it is not an image of the photographed object (that is, if the film is held to the light one will not 'see' the object, even in negative form), but an image of an 'interference' pattern produced by intersecting, and interacting, light waves.

The discovery of holography was actually made mathematically and not optically; indeed, the possibility of holograms was known for some years before investigators were able to establish the physical conditions needed to carry out the process. For what was needed was a perfectly 'coherent' light source, that is, a light source that emitted 'pure' light of a single wave-length. While Dennis Gabor had worked out the underlying principles in 1947, the physical production of holograms had to await the perfection of lasers, which can emit such coherent light. The first 'real' holograms could not be made until 1964.

Essentially, the hologram is produced by photographing an object using two laser beams that result from the optical splitting of a single original beam, using mirrors. Since they emanate from a single source, these two beams are perfectly coordinated insofar as the peaks and troughs of their waves are concerned. One of the beams is directed at the object to be holographed and allowed to 'bounce' off it; it is then recombined with the other, unimpaired beam. But now some of the peaks and troughs in the two beams are 'out of phase', because of the experience of the first beam in striking the object. 'Interference' patterns of light and dark waves are formed in the interaction of these two beams, and it is these interference patterns that are actually recorded on film. Examination of the film microscopically reveals an intensely fine-grained series of light (at points of wave reinforcement) and dark (at points of wave interference) bands.

To re-create the object, a laser beam is shone through the film, and, as if by magic, the interference pattern is reconverted into an image of the original object. *Frontiers of Photography* comments:

> Since most holograms must be viewed in darkened rooms to be appreciated their effect is doubly impressive – and sometimes chilling. To a viewer who is standing in a dimly lit chamber, the holographic portrait of a man, for

example, has all the stark reality of a living, breathing person, yet the substance of a photograph and the aura of a ghost. The viewer may forget that he is watching a photographic marvel and, with a shiver of recognition, think he is attending a bizarre wake in which the body has been propped up to be seen through a doorway. At that particular moment, holography may seem a breathtaking – and eerie – exercise in necromancy. (Life Library of Photography, 1972, p. 135)

While clearly not necromantic, the holographic image nevertheless possesses some rather remarkable properties:

- It reproduces the object in *three dimensions* – the image looks for all the world to be suspended in space.
- It reproduces an object the appearance of which varies *depending on the perspective of the viewer*. In one well-known demonstration, a man appears to sit at a desk with some papers before him. A magnifying glass is held in one of his hands in such a way that, from one perspective, we see one of the papers magnified in the glass. But if we move our heads slightly, the image in the magnifying glass changes too! Now we may see not the paper magnified but the watch on the man's wrist!
- It reproduces an object that, under certain circumstances, can be viewed from all sides; the observer can actually walk around it and see it front and back!

But it is not only the holographic image that has remarkable properties – the holographic process and the way in which it stores its information also has some unexpected features. Two are of special interest to us with respect to the problem of generalization:

- This information needed to produce an image from the film is stored throughout the *entire* film. When a picture is taken by normal photographic means and stored on a negative, if part of that negative is cut away, the information on that part is lost forever. But if part of a holographic film is cut away, *nothing happens!* The part that remains will produce the *whole object* just as well and as easily as if the entire film were still there. That is, complete information about the whole is stored in each and every part of the hologram, so that even the tiniest bit of the hologram is sufficient to reproduce the whole.
- The process of holography can be used to clarify an otherwise blurred image produced by normal photographic means. The reason for this remarkable capability is that even a blurred image – say a picture taken when the camera was not quite in focus – nevertheless contains *all* of the optical information that would have been contained in a clear picture. The information is simply spread out in a way that is describable mathematically; the blurring can be compensated

for by the use of a holographic filter that effectively applies the mathematics in reverse. To accomplish this seeming miracle, a holographic film is produced of *any* spot in the original blurred picture, since any spot will contain all of the information related to blurring (all parts of the original are blurred in the same way). When a laser beam is passed through a transparency of the original and the holographic film, used as a filter, simultaneously, the image is converted to a more perfectly focused one. All of us are familiar with the fact that blurred images sent back by space probes can be cleared up or 'enhanced'; the process by which this is done is this same holographic reverse filtering.

What are the implications of these facts? Of course, one is immediately on thin ice in attempting to reason from a metaphor, for the metaphor may be imperfect for the use to which it is put. Nevertheless, we may take some comfort from Peircian principles of abduction (retroduction) in asserting that we may come to discover

- that full information about a whole is stored in its parts, if only we knew how to get at it;
- that samples need not be representative in the usual statistical sense to render generalizations warrantable; any part or component is a 'perfect' sample in the sense that it contains all of the information about the whole that one might ever hope to obtain;
- that imperfect (blurred) information from any source can be improved (clarified), if one has the appropriate filters for so doing; and
- that *both* the substantive information about an object *and* the information needed to clarify it are contained in the unclarified versions.

Of course, we are incapable of testing any of these assertions at this point in time; nevertheless they have a ring of credibility about them. Surely we can now at the very least assert that any information found in any part must be characteristic of the whole; to that extent the holographic generalization we are speculating about here is already 'true'.

Notes

1 We find the use of the term 'naturalistic generalization' unfortunate because of the possibility of confusion with the term 'naturalistic paradigm', which we ourselves use. We wish to make clear that the idea of naturalistic generalization is *not* part of our formulation of the naturalistic paradigm.

2 These terms have also been used by one of the authors to describe the two axes of human behaviour in institutional settings, particularly from the perspective of an administrator (see Getzels and Guba, 1956). The spelling 'idiographic' is characteristic of modern usage; Windelband used the spelling 'ideographic' [Windelband, 1998].

3 The problem of describing the range of the population to which the findings of a particular study might be appropriate is of course not limited to naturalistic inquiry. Indeed, the problem comes up very frequently in conventional research, particularly in the social/behavioural sciences, precisely because it is often not possible to select a sample on which to carry out a study that is representative of a defined population. Often the population cannot be delimited adequately, or, even if it can, ethical or political considerations intervene. Thus the sample is often a 'convenience' sample – the sample to which the inquirer happens to have access. The question then arises, given the findings from such a convenience sample of known characteristics, what is the nature of the population to which the findings might be generalized? [In the 1940s] the eminent statistician Palmer O. Johnson provided a complete solution to this problem; unfortunately, however, the predicted parameters of the population were always so broad that sample findings could hold for populations of virtually *any* parameters!

4 An excellent, illustrated, lay treatment of holography can be found in the Life Library of Photography's *Frontiers of Photography* (1972, pp. 134–58).

References

Cronbach, L.J. (1975) 'Beyond the two disciplines of scientific psychology', *American Psychologist*, 30: 116–27.

Dickson, P. (1982) *Words*. New York: Delacorte.

Ford, J. (1975) *Paradigms and Fairy Tales* (2 Vols). London: Routledge & Kegan Paul.

Geertz, C. (1973) 'Thick description: toward an interpretive theory of culture', in C. Geertz (ed.), *The Interpretation of Cultures*. New York: Basic Books.

Getzels, J.W. and Guba, E.G. (1956) 'Social behaviour and the administrative process', *School Review*, 64: 423–41.

Hamilton, D. (1976) 'A science of the singular' (mimeo) Workshop Paper on Case-Study Research, CIRCE, University of Illinois, Urbana.

Hamilton, D. (1979) 'Some more on fieldwork, natural languages, and naturalistic generalisation' (mimeo). Discussion paper, University of Glasgow.

Hesse, M. (1980) *Revolutions and Reconstructions in the Philosophy of Science*. Bloomington: Indiana University Press.

Hofstadter, D.R. (1979) *Gödel, Escher, Bach*. New York: Basic Books.

Kaplan, A. (1964) *The Conduct of Inquiry*. San Francisco: Chandler.

Life Library of Photography (1972) *Frontiers of Photography*. New York: Time-Life Books.

Marceil, J.C. (1977) 'Implicit dimensions of idiography and nomothesis: a reformulation', *American Psychologist*, 32: 1046–55.

Mill, J.S. (1906) *A System of Logic*. London: Longman. (Original work published 1843.)

Reese, W.L. (1980) *Dictionary of Philosophy and Religion*. Atlantic Highlands, NJ: Humanities Press.

Schwartz, P. and Ogilvy, J. (1979) *The Emergent Paradigm: Changing Patterns of Thought and Belief* (Analytical Report 7, Values and Lifestyles Program). Menlo Park, CA: SRI International.

Stake, R.E. (1980) 'Generalizations'. Paper presented at the annual meeting of the American Education Research Association, Boston, April.

Wiles, D.K. (1981) 'The logic of y = f(x) in the study of educational politics', *Educational Evaluation and Policy Analysis*, 3: 67–73.

Windelband, W. (1998) 'History and natural science', *Theory & Psychology*, 8 (1): 5–22.

Wolf, F.A. (1981) *Taking the Quantum Leap*. San Francisco: Harper & Row.

CHAPTER 3

GENERALIZABILITY AND THE SINGLE-CASE STUDY

Robert Donmoyer

Language is a marvellous invention. It helps us think precisely and communicate our thoughts to others. It also helps create culture. A shared way of talking helps ensure not only that the world will be characterized in a similar way but also that it will be perceived similarly.

This latter characteristic has negative as well as positive consequences, of course, for what we cannot say we often cannot see. Nelson (1969), for example, informs us that the Eskimo group he studied had a wide range of terms with which to distinguish different kinds of ice. Our language has no such discriminatory power, and, therefore, we cannot perceive characteristics of ice that Eskimos see clearly.

Our language *is* rich in terminology to characterize colour and texture, however. In contrast, the Hanunoo people of the Phillipines have only four words to describe colour, and each of these words also simultaneously refers to a texture (Conklin, 1955). An art critic in our society would have a considerable advantage over a Hanunoo art critic both because our critic has a richer vocabulary with which to communicate perceptions and because the language used to communicate also enhances those perceptions.

Of course, unlike Eskimos, our survival does not depend on the ability to distinguish different kinds of ice. Similarly, art criticism (as we know it, at least) is not a culturally significant activity for the Hanunoo. It would be wasteful for any society to develop ways of talking that serve no purpose, and should societal conditions change – should, for example, art criticism suddenly become a culturally significant activity among the Hanunoo people – new terminology could be invented and new ways of talking could be developed.

The problem

Research communities have often been likened to exotic cultures, in part because researchers who work within such communities often

From E.W. Eisner and A. Peshkin (eds) (1990) *Qualitative Inquiry in Education: The Continuing Debate.* New York: Teachers College Press.

employ a shared and highly specialized way of talking (Campbell, 1979). Most social scientists in North America, for instance, speak English, but when they are talking with their colleagues about their work, their English is often unintelligible to ordinary citizens.

The terms *generalize, generalization and generalizability*, for example, are not completely alien to ordinary discourse, but when social scientists use these terms, they have highly specialized meanings: the terms become associated with notions of random selection and statistical significance. Although ordinary citizens might talk of generalizing from a single incident, social scientists would be unlikely to talk about such a thing. Indeed, as long as social scientists employ the cant of their 'tribe', they *cannot* talk about such a thing.

In this paper, I want to suggest that social scientists' traditional, restricted conception of generalizability is problematic for applied fields such as education, counselling and social work. I will first argue that thinking of generalizability solely in terms of sampling and statistical significance is no longer defensible or functional. I will argue, in other words, that applied social scientists are currently in the sort of situation that the Hanunoo people would be in should art criticism suddenly become a culturally significant activity for them; in both situations there is a need to expand the way of talking and thinking about a phenomenon. In the second half of the paper I will propose an alternative way of talking and thinking about generalizability, a way of talking and thinking that suggests that single-case studies may be far more useful than has traditionally been believed.

The argument

The argument can be stated simply: social scientists' traditional, restricted conception of generalizability is consistent with traditional views of applied social science but inconsistent with more contemporary views. Furthermore, the traditional, restricted conception is not only out of sync with contemporary epistemology; it is also dysfunctional because it limits our ability to reconceptualize the role social science might play in applied fields such as education, counselling and social work.

The traditional view

Traditionally social scientists have viewed the social universe in a manner similar to the way physical scientists, before Einstein, viewed the physical universe: both the physical and the social world were thought to be places where lawful regularities existed between causes and effects. The role of research, whether in physical science or in social science, was to discover and validate generalizations about these regularities. Practitioners could then link particular situations to general statements about causes and effects and know what to do to produce desired outcomes.

E.L. Thorndike summed up this orientation in 1910 in the lead article of the inaugural issue of *The Journal of Educational Psychology*. 'A complete science of psychology', Thorndike wrote,

> would tell every fact about everyone's intellect and character and behavior, would tell the cause of every change in human nature, would tell the result which every educational force – every act of every person that changed any other or the agent himself – would have. It would aid us to use human beings for the world's welfare with the same surety of the result that we now have when we use falling bodies or chemical elements. In proportion as we get such a science we shall become masters of our own souls as we are now masters of heat and light. Progress toward such a science is being made. (p. 6)

Thorndike's views seem rather quaint and dated today. Two problems have arisen to challenge his conception of the role of social science in applied fields: one challenge relates to the problem of complexity; the other to the problem of paradigms.

The complexity challenge

One of the most convincing presentations of the complexity challenge was made by Cronbach in his 1974 Distinguished Scientific Contribution Award address to the American Psychological Association. In part, the presentation was convincing because of who was making it. Approximately twenty years earlier, Cronbach had stood before the same organization and suggested that Thorndike's dream of 'a complete science of psychology' could be realized if researchers would stop looking at the effects of treatments generally and, instead, begin to study the effects of interactions between treatments and people with different aptitudes (Cronbach, 1957). In 1974, however, after years of frustration brought on by 'inconsistent findings coming from roughly similar inquiries', Cronbach (1975) declared, 'Once we attend to interactions, we enter a hall of mirrors that extends to infinity. However far we carry our analysis – to third order or fifth order or any other – untested interactions of still higher order can be envisioned' (p. 119).

A major part of the problem, according to Cronbach, involves the changeability of culture. He cited as an example Bronfenbrenner's historical look at child-rearing practices of middle- and lower-class parents. Class differences documented in the 1950s were often just the reverse of practices that had been observed in the 1930s. Cronbach (1975) concluded:

> The trouble, as I see it, is that we cannot store up generalizations and constructs for ultimate assembly into a network. It is as if we needed a gross of dry cells to power an engine and could only make one a month. The energy would leak out of the first cells before we had half the battery completed. So it is with the potency of our generalizations. (p. 123)

More recently, Cronbach has taken an even more radical tack with respect to the cultural dimension of human action. Like the symbolic interactionists and ethnomethodologists discussed below, Cronbach has concluded that human action is constructed, not caused, and that to expect Newton-like generalizations describing human action, as Thorndike did, is to engage in a process akin to 'waiting for Godot' (Cronbach, 1982).

Cronbach's arguments have not gone unchallenged, of course. Phillips (1987), for instance, has argued that social phenomena are no more complex than phenomena in the physical world. He notes, for example, that determining where a particular leaf would land when it falls off a tree would be a task no less complex than the tasks social scientists confront.

The problem with Phillips' analysis is that few physical scientists are interested in predicting, much less controlling, where a single leaf falls, just as no engineer employing quantum mechanics is interested in what happens to individual atoms or electrons. Teachers, however, are interested in individual students, and counsellors and social workers are concerned with individual clients. Social phenomena may or may not be more complex than phenomena in the physical world. (Phillips' argument is hardly convincing on this point because he fails even to address the problem of culture raised by Cronbach both in his 1974 address and, even more forcefully, in his more recent and more radical work.) It is obvious, however, that even if social phenomena are not more complex, social purposes are. Given the complexity of social purposes – given the concern with individuals, not just aggregates – it is unlikely that we will ever even approximate Thorndike's (1910) dream of a 'complete science of psychology' (p. 6).

Phillips also indicates that Cronbach overestimates the complexity problem because he adopts an 'unduly inductivist' position and ignores the fact that *a priori* theories help focus social scientists' attention on certain variables while screening out others. While Phillips' criticism of Cronbach is undoubtedly correct, he ignores the fact that the *a priori* theories that inevitably simplify the research process also create a new challenge to the empiricist view of social research articulated by Thorndike. Indeed, because we cannot escape the influence of *a priori* theories or paradigms, because even the most rudimentary acts of perception are influenced by latent *a priori* assumptions about the way the world is and ought to be (see, for example, Neisser, 1976), a second challenge to Thorndike's conception of social science and its role in applied fields has emerged.

The paradigm challenge

The problem posed by paradigms can be demonstrated by considering a term such as *learning*. Few people would disagree with the proposition that schools should promote learning, but the term *learning* will mean different things to a kindergarten teacher influenced by Piaget, a process–product researcher, an art teacher who wants to promote productive idiosyncracy, and a parent who wants the schools to go back to basics. Each of these meanings reflects a different conception of what learning is and what teaching ought to be. Each can be said to reflect a different paradigm of reality.

Before a researcher can determine whether Programme A produces more learning than Programme B, the researcher must choose one of the paradigms – that is, one of the meanings – alluded to above or one of the multitude of other meanings that could be associated with the term *learning*. The meaning selected will influence the researcher's findings at least as much as the empirical reality being described.

The situation is further complicated by the fact that, from certain paradigmatic perspectives, the whole quasi-experimental approach to research becomes problematic. Freire (1970), Buber (1947/1968), peace educators such as Galtung (1974), and a humanist reading of Dewey (see Kleibard, 1975), for example, suggest that educational practice should not be built around predetermined student learning outcomes, no matter what conception of learning the predetermined outcomes reflect. This position suggests that rather than attempting to control students, teachers should engage in dialogue with students, and rather than transmitting a predefined curriculum to students, teachers should work with students to construct jointly the curriculum for the class.

This perspective of what education ought to be is compatible with ethnomethodologists' and symbolic interactionists' view of how human understanding actually develops and how human action actually occurs. Blumer (1969), the father of symbolic interactionism, for example, not only argues that human beings act toward things on the basis of the meanings things have for them and that meanings are a product of social interaction rather than external causes; he also argues that meanings are not static but must constantly be constructed and reconstructed by actors during social interaction. In adopting this later position, Blumer rejects the notion that 'thought objects ... determine ... behavior by motivating it'. Rather, according to Blumer:

A realistic analysis of the human act shows that the tendency to act cannot be taken as moulding or controlling the act. At best the tendency or preparation to act is merely an element that enters into the developing act – no more than an initial bid for a possible line of action ...

Since the act, whether individual or collective, is fashioned, constructed, and directed by the process of definition that goes on in the individual or the group as the case may be, it is this process that should be the central object of study by the psychologist and the sociologist. A knowledge of this process would be of far greater value for prediction, if that is one's interest, than would any amount of knowledge of tendencies or attitudes. (p. 98)

Thus, even if meanings and reasons are allowed to substitute for causes in a cause-and-effect explanatory framework, Blumer is not satisfied. According to him, the explanatory framework itself sends an inaccurate message regardless of its substantive content. In adopting this position, Blumer sides with those continental philosophers who have argued that epistemology can never be completely severed from psychology. According to Blumer, the traditional cause-and-effect approach to explanation, which is at the heart of Thorndike's conception of social science and also at the heart of traditional conceptions of generalizability, carries with it a certain metaphysical model of human beings and human action. It is because of this implicit model and his rejection of it that Blumer refuses to phrase research findings in terms of cause-and-effect generalizations, even probabilistic ones.

Whether or not one accepts Blumer's conception of human action, this conception does provide an alternative to Thorndike's conception of how the social world operates, and, as such, it reminds us once again that Thorndike's conception of the social world is just that, an *a priori* conception. This *a priori* conception is not determined by the facts but rather determines what the facts are.

Furthermore, even if we accept Thorndike's explanatory framework, the words and meanings we fit into that syntax (for example, whether we talk and think of learning in a manner consistent with the process–product researcher or as a Piagetian psychologist does) will still have as significant an impact on our perception and assessment of empirical reality as does the reality itself. Indeed, as Kant concluded long ago, it is impossible to talk of the nature of reality with any sense of certainty because we can never know reality independent of the cognitive structures that influence our perceptions.

Implications

Both of the problems outlined above have implications for the way we think about generalizability. The complexity problem, for example, suggests that it no longer makes sense to think of generalizability as synonymous with the use of large samples and statistical procedures designed to ensure that the large samples accurately represent the population. In the applied fields, social science can never provide the sort of certainty envisioned by Thorndike. Even statistically significant findings from studies with huge, randomly selected samples cannot be applied directly to particular individuals in particular situations; skilled clinicians will always be required to determine whether a research generalization applies to a particular individual, whether the generalization needs to be adjusted to accommodate individual idiosyncrasy, or whether it needs to be abandoned entirely with certain individuals in certain situations.

To be sure, research with large samples can provide clinicians with some idea of a certain strategy's probability for success – it can make teachers and other clinicians more informed gamblers, in other words – but even this advantage has a downside. Researchers' ideal types can easily become stereotypes (Donmoyer, 1987b), and stereotypes, when applied to individuals, can easily become self-fulfilling prophecies (Rist, 1973). For example, findings that poor children will probably have reading difficulties may cause teachers and administrators to behave in ways that will actually create reading difficulties for particular poor children (Heath, 1982).

Thus, for practitioners concerned with individuals, not aggregates, research can never be generalizable in the sense suggested by Thorndike. Research can only function as a heuristic; it can suggest possibilities but never dictate action. It may well be the case that case study research can fulfil this function as well, or possibly even better, than more traditional approaches to research.

While the complexity challenge suggests the need to reconceptualize the notion of generalizability and to rethink the utility of single-case research, the paradigm challenge suggests, in a general way, how the notion of generalizability might be reconceptualized and what the role of case study research might be. Discussion of the role of paradigms in research reminds us that researchers must inevitably rely on *a priori* conceptualization that is not determined by the data but, rather, determines what the data are. In Lather's (1988) words, research is inevitably ideological; it inevitably conceals even as it reveals.

When clinicians utilize social scientists' cause-and-effect findings, for instance, they are also influenced by social scientists' *a priori* conceptions of social action and social relationships. These *a priori* conceptions, these social constructions, can easily become reality for those who employ them. When this occurs, other conceptions of reality are not even considered; indeed, the possibility that alternative conceptions of reality exist is normally not even recognized.

The discussion of paradigms suggests a role that case study research might play: case study research might be used to expand and enrich the repertoire of social constructions available to practitioners and others; it may help, in other words, in the forming of questions rather than in the finding of answers. This role, in turn, suggests that it may be useful to think of generalizability more in psychological terms than in terms of mathematical probability. This is the tack to be taken in the second half of this paper.

The existing literature

Most social scientists have come to accept both that social purposes and social phenomena are too complex for social science to provide definitive answers to practical problems and that *a priori* assumptions or paradigms inevitably influence the conclusions of empirical research. Social scientists, however, have not always thought through the implications of these ideas. From the perspective of history, conceptual shifts in academic disciplines and fields may look like revolutions (Kuhn, 1971); a close-up look at paradigm shifts normally reveals a far more incremental and evolutionary process (Carloye, 1985).

For instance, at the moment, few applied social scientists would disagree with the proposition that social phenomena and/or social purposes are too complex for social science to provide definitive answers to practical problems in fields such as education, counselling and social work. Yet many social scientists continue to distinguish between hypothesis-generating research and verification-oriented research; qualitative studies – particularly qualitative studies of single cases – are relegated to the less prestigious former category. The classic hypothesis generation/verification distinction, however, ignores the fact that in fields such as education, social work and counselling – fields in which there is a concern with individuals, not just aggregates – all research findings are tentative.

Similarly, Weiss (1982) tells us, on the one hand, that the role of social science is not to give policy makers answers but to help them frame policy questions; on the other hand, she recommends that social scientists continue to engage in business as usual. The only procedural change she recommends, in fact, is the allocation of more time, so that social scientists can do what they have always done more thoroughly. Because Weiss remains under the spell of tradition, she fails even to notice that the frames social scientists provide have as much to do with the *a priori* conceptions that make empirical work possible as with the empirical work itself (Gusfield, 1976) and even to consider whether the shift in social science's role from answer-giver to question-framer makes many traditional social science procedures irrelevant. Nor does Weiss consider whether less traditionally accepted forms of research – for example, single-case studies – might serve social science's newly defined purpose as well or even better than more established ways of doing things.

One reason why social scientists often cling uncritically to outdated notions is the absence of an alternative language with which to talk about phenomena. As I indicated earlier, what we cannot say, we often cannot see.

The absence of an alternative language has certainly inhibited our rethinking the notion of generalizability and, consequently, our valuing of single-case studies. For example, when qualitative research first began to be taken seriously in the field of education, Feinberg (1977), at a government-funded conference of researchers sympathetic to qualitative work, offered the following knee-jerk assessment of the limits of qualitative case studies:

> Even though the information collected on a single classroom group over the period of a year or more is extremely rich, the basic fact remains that for a single-classroom study, $N = 1$....
>
> A study such as Rist's may help to generate hypotheses about urban or ghetto schools. It does not allow for generalizations or broad conclusions (perhaps not even narrow ones). (p. 53)

Feinberg's sentiments have been echoed by other advocates and practitioners of qualitative research, including Mishler (1979) and Jackson (1974).

Over the years, others have tried to move beyond the traditional conception of generalizability with varying degrees of success. Hamilton (1976), for example, has talked of creating a 'science of the singular'. Similarly, Stake (1978, 1980) has spoken of 'naturalistic generalizations' that

> develop with a person as a product of experience. They derive from the tacit knowledge of how things are, why they are, how people feel about them, and how these things are likely to be later or in other places with which this person is familiar. They seldom take the form of predictions but lead regularly to expectation. They guide action, in fact they are inseparable from action.... These generalizations may become verbalized, passing of course from tacit knowledge to propositional; but they have not yet passed the empirical and logical tests that characterize formal (scholarly, scientific) generalizations. (1978, p. 6; p. 22 above)

Both the Stake and Hamilton discussions are useful for those who wish to rethink the traditional notion of generalizability, but their utility is limited for two reasons. First, both discussions refer to evaluation research. Stake, for instance, develops the notion of naturalistic generalizations in the course of making the case for qualitative case studies as the method of choice in evaluating a particular programme. (Because qualitative case studies can provide vicarious experiences and, hence, be a source of naturalistic generalizations, Stake argues, ordinary people will be able to better understand evaluation reports and, hence, better understand what is going on in the particular programmes being assessed.) Given this focus on evaluation, the traditional concern associated with the notion of generalizability (that is, how does in-depth knowledge of a single case help us understand and act more intelligently in other potentially different cases) was not even addressed by Stake.

The second problem is that neither Stake nor Hamilton develops his alternative conception in much detail. Stake, for example, makes some quick references to Polanyi's (1958) notion of tacit knowledge and Dilthey's (1961, 1976) notion of experiential understanding, but he fails to develop a theoretical language adequate to talk and think with much specificity about an alternative to the traditional notion of generalizability.

Lincoln and Guba (1985: see Chapter 2 in this volume) have been somewhat more specific in reconceptualizing the notion of generalizability. They have actually shifted terminology; they talk of *transferability* rather than generalizability. They start with the assumption that research findings will always be only working hypotheses, an assumption that, as the above analysis suggests, is defensible whenever the concern is with individuals. (As I have noted in my review of their book [Donmoyer, 1987a], Lincoln and Guba do overlook the possibility that policy makers may find aggregate data sufficient for certain purposes.) They go on to ask, 'How can one tell whether a working hypothesis developed in Context A might be applicable in Context B?' and then answer this question by noting:

> [T]he degree of *transferability* is a direct function of the *similarity* between the two contexts, what we shall call *'fittingness'*. Fittingness is defined as the degree of congruence between sending and receiving contexts. If Context A and Context B are 'sufficiently' congruent, then working hypotheses from the sending originating context *may* be applicable in the receiving context. (Lincoln and Guba, 1985: 124) [see Chapter 2, p. 40 above; emphasis in original – *Editors' Note*]

Later, they add:

> Transferability, far from being established once and for all because certain methodological tenets, such as careful control and random sampling, have been followed, must be reassessed in each and every case in which transfer is proposed. That is to say, an investigator can make no statements about transferability for his or her findings based solely on data from the studied context alone. At best the investigator can supply only that information about the studied site that may make possible a judgement of transferability to some other site; the final judgment on that matter is, however, vested in the person seeking to make the transfer. (Lincoln and Guba, 1985, 217)

Clearly Lincoln and Guba provide a less ethereal, more easily understood alternative to the traditional view of generalizability. The transferability alternative, however, is hardly a radical departure from the traditional view. Although the notion of transferability accommodates the problem of complexity, it still assumes that findings from one setting are only generalizable to another setting if both settings are very similar. My intuition suggests this need not necessarily be the case.

The research community does not currently have a language available to translate my intuition into linguistic form. Indeed, the point of the second half of this paper is to try to develop such a language, or, more precisely, to take an existing, widely accepted theoretical language and apply it to unfamiliar territory: the context of research utilization. Before proceeding with this task, however, let me try to give some sense of where I am heading by relating two personal anecdotes. As I will argue in the next section, stories can often serve as a half-way house between tacit personal knowledge and formal propositional thought.

The first anecdote dates back to the time when I was taking anthropology courses. In one course, I read Eggan's (1974) 'Instruction and affect in Hopi cultural continuity', a paper that contained a rich narrative description of Hopi education. This description of both formal and informal education in a culture radically different from my own provided tremendous insight into schooling in my own culture. Later, when I became a teacher in my own culture, I believe I acted more intelligently – I certainly behaved more thoughtfully – as a result of having read the initiation rite ethnography.

My second story takes us back even further. When I was in my early teens, I had an opportunity to see Arthur Miller's *Death of a Salesman*. Though the Willy Loman on stage and the adolescent who sat in the darkened theatre had little in common, I learned a great deal about myself that night. Despite the many differences between Miller's ageing salesman and the adolescent who watched him – or possibly because of these differences – something, which in ordinary parlance could be called generalization, occurred.

If the sense of generalization referred to in the previous paragraphs is really to impact our thinking, a new theoretical language must be found. This language must be both more detailed than earlier talk of naturalistic generalizations and more radical than Lincoln and Guba's notion of transferability. The next section of the paper presents such a language.

An alternative conceptualization

Like Stake's notion of naturalistic generalization, the conception of generalizability I will articulate here is rooted in a conception of experiential knowledge. I will begin this part of the discussion, therefore, at the experiential level; then suggest why talk of working hypotheses and transferability is inadequate to describe the experience; go on to propose a more adequate theoretical language; and, finally, indicate how all of this relates to questions about the utility of single-case studies.

An experience

My starting point for this discussion of an alternative conception of generalization is the starting point for all inquiry: personal knowledge (Polanyi, 1958). The particular personal knowledge that is relevant here was gleaned from six years of experience as a classroom teacher. I began my teaching career in a ghetto school in the middle of Harlem. Later I taught in an affluent suburb, which was in many ways the antithesis of the ghetto community in which I began my career; my students reflected community differences. Still later I taught a different grade in a rural island community where, once again, my students were quite different from the students I had taught earlier. Despite the differences, however, each year teaching became easier; each year I could more easily anticipate the consequences of my actions; increasingly, I could even control events. Generalization, of one sort or another, occurred.

The language of working hypotheses and transferability

The situation described above is hardly unique; if it were, experience would not be so valued by employers. The sort of experiential knowledge alluded to above, however, could be described in terms of Lincoln and Guba's language of transferability: according to this characterization, an experience in one situation leads to the development of working hypotheses; when a person moves to a new situation, he or she simply compares the sending situation to the receiving situation, determines the degree of fit, and applies those hypotheses that appear to be applicable in the new situation. This way of characterizing the situation, however, seems less than adequate, for at least four reasons.

First, as Stake has suggested, much of the generalizing that occurs at the level of experience occurs tacitly; that is, much experiential knowledge has not been translated into propositional form, the sort of form implied by the term *working hypotheses*. To be sure, it is certainly the case that language is a potent influence on understanding. As I noted at the outset of this paper, what we cannot say, we often cannot see. But it is also the case that language – particularly the propositional language of hypotheses – is too gross a tool to encompass all that we learn from experience.

In addition, mere mortals could never consciously articulate (1) the working hypotheses generated by experience in one situation, (2) the multiple, interacting characteristics at work in that situation,

(3) the multiple, interacting characteristics at work in a second situation, and (4) the similarities and differences between situation one and situation two.

One final point with respect to the tacit knowledge issue: clinicians often encode experiential knowledge in stories and anecdotes, and once such encoding has occurred, tacit knowledge is no longer entirely tacit. We can probably even find hypotheses in embryo form in the stories and anecdotes clinicians use to guide their actions. Much of the understanding engendered by narrative modes of discourse is still at the tacit level, however (Bruner, 1986), and, therefore, it would be inappropriate to characterize even actions engendered by stories and anecdotes as a process of transferring working hypotheses.

There is a second reason why talk of transferring working hypotheses is inadequate for characterizing the sort of experiential learning that occurs when a teacher or clinician in human service fields moves from one setting to another: the relationship of teachers and students – like the relationship of counsellors or social workers and clients – need not necessarily be similar to the relationship of scientist and subject. The relationship is often closer to that captured by Blumer's (1969) notion of 'joint action'. Blumer's notion of 'joint action' refers to the creation, through interaction, of a common set of meanings to describe a situation. The creation of a common set of meanings requires that each participant in an interaction imaginatively 'take on the role' of the other participants. From this perspective, in other words, teachers and clinicians would not be so much concerned with 'acting on' students or clients as with 'interacting with' them.

Please note, I am not suggesting that teachers, counsellors and social workers never behave like applied scientists, that their thoughts can never be characterized by talk of transferring working hypotheses from one situation to another. It is just that skilled clinicians in such fields often play the dual role Powdermaker (1966) defines for anthropologists: they must be not only the stranger who stands outside the action and analyses and acts on subjects; they must also function as a friend who *interacts* with and, in the process, jointly constructs meanings with students or clients. The language of transferability and working hypotheses fails to capture this interactive aspect of experiential learning.

Third, it is not just that talk of working hypotheses and transferability fails to do justice to the process of experiential learning; such talk also provides an inadequate characterization of the knowledge generated by that process. The sort of knowledge gained from experience is not purely intellectual. It is often affect-laden. It is the sort of knowledge that Isaiah Berlin (1966) describes when he talks about the kind of understanding historians need to practise their craft. Berlin describes this sort of knowledge as follows:

> When the Jews are enjoined in the Bible to protect strangers 'For ye know the soul of a stranger, seeing ye were strangers in the land of Egypt' (Exodus, 23: 9), this knowledge is neither deductive nor inductive, nor founded on direct inspection, but akin to the 'I know' of 'I know what it is to be hungry and poor', or 'I know how political bodies function', or 'I know what it is to be a Brahmin'. This is neither (to use Professor Gilbert Ryle's useful classification) 'knowing that' which the sciences provide, nor the 'knowing how' which is the possession of a disposition or skill, nor the experience of direct perception, acquaintance, memory, but the type of knowledge that an administrator or politician must possess of the men with whom he deals. (p. 45)

The sort of knowledge that Berlin suggests is required of administrators, politicians and historians is also required of teachers, counsellors and social workers. Experience can provide such knowledge. When we think of generalizability in terms of the transferability of working hypotheses, however, the sort of visceral knowledge of which Berlin speaks can easily be obscured.

Finally, even when a clinician is not interacting with others and/or attempting to understand others from an insider's perspective, much of the learning that develops experientially can be categorized more as meaning-making than as hypothesis generation and testing. For instance, before I taught in the ghetto, I had been socialized to think of my students as deprived. When I began teaching, however, I discovered that the students I taught were rich in many ways; for example, when I visited my Hispanic students' parents and needed my bilingual students to serve as my translators, it was I who felt deprived. Such experiences forced me to rethink my notion of deprivation and to define it in more than economic terms.

This redefinition process prepared me to work with a very different population of students in affluent suburbia. Here I found children who economically wanted for nothing and who at a very early age had a wealth of mainstream cultural knowledge and skills. Yet some of these same children, these children whose lives were a constant journey from soccer practices to ceramic classes to violin lessons to special math tutoring sessions to library programmes to who knows where, often had been emotionally neglected by professional parents who assumed other professionals (that is, the soccer coach, the ceramics teacher, and so on) would do their parenting for them. I wondered what it was like to spend so much time with paid professionals rather than parents, and I also wondered how successful my students would be outside of class, without an instructor controlling and directing them. Life, after all, is not a series of classes, at least not for most people. These children, at times, seemed much less able than many of the children I had worked with in the ghetto to know their own minds, to direct themselves toward things they wanted, and to function together as a group without the benefit of an adult's direction.

My experience in suburbia, in other words, expanded even further the meaning I attributed to the term *deprivation*. The notions of working hypotheses and transferability hardly do justice to the sort of meaning-making process just described.

The language of schema theory

A far more appropriate way of characterizing how generalizability occurs in experiential learning is provided by schema theory. Here I will employ the notions of assimilation, accommodation, integration and differentiation from the schema theory of Piaget (1971), first to characterize the sort of generalization that occurs in experiential learning and then to rethink the notion of generalizability in the context of research utilization.

Before proceeding, let me acknowledge two caveats with respect to my use of Piaget's terminology. First, Piaget's theory is actually two theories: a stage theory of child development and a more general theory of cognitive functioning. Piaget's stage theory is probably better known; it is also the least defensible part of his work. In employing Piaget's concepts, I in no way endorse his stage theory. Rather, it is his more general description of cognitive processing that I am utilizing here.

Second, Piaget developed his terminology in the process of trying to explain the origin of what he termed 'logico-mathematical knowledge'. Piaget's way of characterizing cognitive functioning need not be limited to this narrow sphere of understanding, however (Cowan, 1978; Turner, 1973). Here I will employ the notions of assimilation, accommodation, integration and differentiation far more liberally and relate schema theory to various sorts of social knowledge, including the sort of visceral, affect-laden knowledge discussed by Berlin.

With these caveats duly noted, let us proceed with a discussion of the notions of assimilation, accommodation, integration and differentiation. According to schema theorists, all knowledge of the empirical world must be filtered through cognitive structures, which shape what we know. Piaget calls this shaping process *assimilation*. Piaget also describes a complementary process, which he calls *accommodation*. This process involves the reshaping of cognitive structures to accommodate novel aspects of what is being perceived. After the dual processes of assimilation and accommodation have occurred, Piaget's theory indicates, a cognitive structure will be both more *integrated* (a particular structure will accommodate more things) and more *differentiated* (a particular structure will be divided into substructures).

A simple example might clarify the Piagetian notions. When I was in graduate school, my oldest son was in kindergarten. He would ask me rather interesting questions. He would ask, for instance, how many recesses I had at my school and when my school had sharing time. In Piagetian terms, my son was *assimilating* my graduate school experience into his very limited cognitive structure of schooling. Over the years, my son's conception of schooling has expanded considerably. He has attended middle and senior high schools as well as elementary schools. He has attended schools throughout the United States and in a foreign country. He has accompanied me to many universities and heard many of my graduate students speak of their experiences. In the process, my son's cognitive structure of schooling has *accommodated* much of the novelty he has seen and heard. As a result, this cognitive structure is both more *integrated* (the terms *school* and *schooling* mean more things) and more *differentiated* (he can now talk about different kinds of school and different aspects of schooling, and he can think about more distinctions related to schooling that he cannot even articulate in language).

I believe I underwent a process similar to my son's when I moved from a Harlem school to schools with very different populations. The sort of generalization that characterized my movement from one school to another was not primarily mediated by working hypotheses transferred from one setting to the next. Rather, the mediating mechanisms are better characterized as cognitive structures that could only partially be coded into language and that, in fact, often functioned at the level of tacit knowledge.

It is important to note that when generalization is thought of in this way, the diversity between school settings becomes an asset rather than a liability: when diversity is dramatic, the knower is confronted by all sorts of novelty, which stimulates accommodation; consequently, the knower's cognitive structures become more integrated and differentiated; after novelty is confronted and accommodated, he or she can perceive more richly and, one hopes, act more intelligently.

Schema theory and case studies

What does all of this have to do with the issue of generalizability and the single-case study? Stake's comment that case studies can provide *vicarious* experiences serves as the linkage.

Those of us who have lost ourselves in a powerful novel or who have been captivated by the superb storyteller around a campfire or who have been transported to another time and place by a powerful narrative history could hardly deny narrative's ability to provide vicarious experience. The following very brief excerpt from Eggan's (1974) ethnography of Hopi cultural life demonstrates how a skilled storyteller can use her direct experience to create a vicarious experience for her readers:

If those who doubt that the forces of nature are powerful in shaping personality and culture were confined for one year on the Hopi reservation – even though their own economic dependence on 'nature' would be negligible – they would still know by personal experience more convincing than scientific experiments the relentless pressure of the environment on their own reaction patterns. They would, for instance, stand, as all Hopis have forever stood, with aching eyes fastened on a blazing sky where thunderheads piled high in promise and were snatched away by 'evil winds,' and thus return to their homes knowing the tension, the acute bodily need for the 'feel' of moisture. (p. 320)

Langer (1953) says that narrative can create a virtual reality, that is, a reality that exists within our imaginations. The above discussion of paradigms reminds us that scientific knowledge is also undergirded by imagination. Indeed, both forms of understanding require symbolic mediation; it is just that the symbolic form we call narrative allows us to symbolize and hence think and communicate about certain aspects of experience – those things Langer (1953) labels the 'ineffable' and Mann (1969) and Vallance (1977) call the 'lived-in' aspects of experience – better than does propositional language. There is a structural equivalence between narrative and real-world experience. Both unfold in time. Both can have multiple things happening simultaneously. Both integrate thought and feeling.

Three advantages of case studies

But why should vicarious experience substitute for the real thing? What can case studies do that direct experience cannot? There are at least three answers to these questions. In the remainder of this paper, I will review each of these answers and, in the process, clarify some other related and salient points.

Accessibility

First, case studies can take us to places where most of us would not have an opportunity to go. As I noted above, my son has had an opportunity to experience schooling in a wide range of settings, and as a result he can now think of schooling much more complexly than he could when he was in kindergarten. It is not likely, however, that he will ever be able to experience a tribal society's approach to schooling. Yet he can read Eggan's (1974) compelling description of Hopi initiation rites and experience vicariously the Hopi process of formal education and the meanings the Hopi attach to this process. I suspect that after reading Eggan's case study, he would have an even more enriched conception of schooling than he has acquired through direct experience. This enriched conception would not only allow him to understand schooling in Hopi culture; it would also help him look at schools in his own society in a new way: he should be able both to see different things and to see differently things he has seen before.

This first benefit does not only apply to learning about exotic cultures. Case studies also allow us to experience vicariously, unique situations and unique individuals within our own culture. They can help us overcome the problem caused by the fact that (1) many [practitioners] learn best by modelling, but (2) there are often not enough truly exceptional models to go around.

Several years ago the Rockefeller Brothers' Fund allowed me to experience (in the role of qualitative researcher) a truly unique and highly effective principal (Donmoyer, 1983, 1985a). One of the many things I learned while interacting with this man was that he and I interpreted his interactions with his staff very differently. My interpretation was influenced by behaviourist psychology and contemporary political science: I coded much of his behaviour as positive social reinforcement and political favour trading. He (and, to a large extent, his staff) was influenced by his own folk paradigm, and he characterized his actions in terms of different kinds of 'personal closeness', a term he had invented.

To the extent that I could understand the principal's perspective and communicate it in the narratives I wrote – and elsewhere, I believe, I have demonstrated the need to use narrative in reporting this particular case, at least (see Donmoyer, 1985a) – readers can experience vicariously an individual whom I had an opportunity to experience directly. In the process, they, too, can begin to see staff relationships in a new light. Their staff relationship schema, in other words, can become enriched as they accommodate the novelty of this particular case.

I should emphasize two points here. First, it does not especially matter whether the principal's folk perspective is more correct than the social science perspectives I brought to the situation. Elsewhere I have suggested that the relative correctness of rival interpretations often cannot be determined (Donmoyer, 1985b). Rival interpretations often reflect the use of alternative theoretical languages, and languages are not true or false, only more or less adequate. Even adequacy can only be assessed in terms of particular purposes in particular contexts, and ultimately it must be the reader who decides whether the principal's interpretation of his interactions with staff serves the reader's purpose in the reader's particular situation.

When generalizability is viewed from the perspective of schema theory, in other words, the role of the research is not primarily to find the correct interpretation. Indeed, the search for the correct interpretation may well be a search for a Holy Grail. Rather, from the schema theory view of generalizability, the purpose of research is simply to expand the range of interpretations available to the research consumer.

The second point I want to make relates to the goal of expanding the range of interpretations available to research consumers. When this is our goal, when, in other words, generalizability is viewed from the perspective of schema theory, uniqueness is an asset rather than a liability. To be sure, it is certainly legitimate to ask questions about typicality – to ask what most principals normally do. When we are interested in expanding cognitive structures, however, this is not the question being asked. To the contrary, when we are interested in expanding cognitive structures, the outlier is prized, for the outlier has great heuristic value.

Seeing through the researcher's eyes

There is a second reason the vicarious experience of case studies might be preferred to direct experience: case studies allow us to look at the world through the researcher's eyes and, in the process, to see things we otherwise might not have seen. When I read Lightfoot's (1983) description of St Paul's School in her book *The Good High School*, I get to see what a private, elite school looks like from the perspective of a black female. When I read Wolcott's (1987) observer-as-participant study 'The teacher as enemy', I get to view cross-cultural-teaching from his highly unique vantage point. It is true that when I read Lightfoot and Wolcott I learn as much about Lightfoot and Wolcott as I do about the phenomena they studied. This is not a liability, however, when our interest is in expanding the reader's cognitive structures. Indeed, given what we know about the mediating influence of cognitive structures on perception, a complete description of a phenomenon is impossible. The best we can hope for is that any individual will have a rich repertoire of schemata through which to view particular events. By viewing a situation vicariously through the eyes of a Lightfoot or a Wolcott, it is likely that a richer repertoire of schemata will develop.

Let me pause here to raise three additional points that are related both to what has just been said and also to one another. First, when we look through a researcher's eyes, we do not necessarily see the world through the researcher's personal, idiosyncratic perspective. The researcher's perspective might be the intersubjectively shared theoretical perspective of a discipline or field of study. When one reads Suransky's (1982) five case studies of early childhood programmes in her book *The Erosion of Childhood*, for example, one does not so much see these programmes through Suransky's eyes alone as through the lenses of the neo-Marxist and feminist theory that influences Suransky's perspective.

In short, case studies can help those who are uninitiated into a particular theoretical viewpoint come to understand that viewpoint.

Second, case study narratives like Suransky's – that is, case study narratives influenced by the perspective of formal theory – are not only useful to those uninitiated in a particular theoretical viewpoint. If the theoretically coloured case studies are well done, they can add depth and dimension to theoretical understanding. By definition, theory simplifies our understanding of reality. At least in this respect, the social scientist's ideal types are no different from stereotypes. Well-done case studies can add nuance and subtlety to the ideal-typical perspective of theory.

Third, let me confront the question that was begged in the previous paragraph: What constitutes a 'well-done case study' when one is viewing generalizability from the perspective of schema theory? The answer to this question is not dramatically different from more traditionally oriented qualitative researchers' definition of quality work (see, for example, Miles and Huberman, 1984). To be sure, those who approach qualitative research from the perspective of schema theory will probably be more open to use of literary discourse, the sort of discourse championed by Eisner (1985) and Barone (1987). Because those influenced by schema theory recognize that all knowledge is symbolically mediated, they should be more receptive to the Eisner/Barone argument that certain aspects of experience can only be accommodated and communicated through literary modes of symbolism. The bottom line for assessing the quality of a case study, however, is still the richness of the data presented.

To be sure, given what has been said in this paper, we can no longer talk of raw data if, by that term, we mean data uncontaminated by the language and the anticipatory schemata of the researcher. We can, however, talk of data that are medium-rare, for example low-inference descriptions of behaviour and excerpts from transcribed interviews. There should be sufficient medium-rare data so that the reader does not simply assimilate the case being described into a theoretical ideal type; rather the reader should have an opportunity to enrich his or her understanding of an ideal type by accommodating the novelty of the particular case. Indeed I think it is reasonable to assume that case studies will provide sufficient medium-rare data so that a reader who starts from a different orientation from the researcher's could fashion an interpretation significantly different from the researcher's narrative.

To put this matter another way, good case studies employ theoretical constructs the way the historian of a particular revolution uses the construct of 'revolution'. In 1957, William Dray, a philosopher of history, noted that a historian who set out to explain the French Revolution

> is just not interested in explaining it as a revolution – as an astronomer might be interested in explaining a certain eclipse as an instance of eclipses; he is almost invariably concerned with it as different from other members of its

class. Indeed, he might even say that his main concern will be to explain the French Revolution's taking a course unlike any other; that is to say, he will explain it as unique in the sense distinguished above. (p. 47)

Decreased defensiveness

There is a third reason why the vicarious experience provided by case studies might be preferable to direct experience: vicarious experience is less likely to produce defensiveness and resistance to learning. One flaw of Piaget's theory is that it assumes that accommodation will inevitably accompany assimilation. We know, however, that human beings socially construct reality and that those with power can often force their social constructions on others. They can – through the exercise of power – make the world change to conform to their conception of it rather than alter their cognitive structures to accommodate those aspects of the world that are disconcerting and threatening. The power of teachers to socially construct reality and create self-fulfilling prophecies, for instance, has been well documented (see, for example, Rist, 1973; Sharp and Green, 1975).

People, of course, can screen out disquieting and psychologically threatening aspects of vicarious experience, just as they screen out aspects of direct experience that make them uncomfortable. When the threat is merely psychological (which is the case when experience is merely vicarious), however, it seems reasonable to assume that resistance to accommodating novelty will not be as great as when a threat is experienced in real life. A teacher reading a narrative description of the self-fulfilling prophecy phenomenon at work in another teacher's classroom, for instance, will likely feel less threatened than if initially asked to confront that phenomenon in his or her own work. For that construct to have impact, of course, the teacher must eventually apply it to him- or herself. If the self-fulfilling prophecy construct is part of the teacher's cognitive repertoire, however, such self-analysis is at least possible.

Conclusion

Philosophers and historians of science talk about scientific revolutions, giant shifts in perspectives and procedures within particular disciplines and fields of study. For those in the midst of such a revolution, however, the 'revolutionary' process can seem slow and laboured, indeed. Giving up sacrosanct notions is a slow and painful process, and time is inevitably required to develop new ways of talking and thinking about the ideas that have guided our thinking and our actions in the past.

Here I have argued that social scientists' traditional way of talking and thinking about generalizability is no longer adequate. I have not suggested the traditional notion is useless. For policy makers who are interested only in aggregates, not individuals, and for whom questions of meaning and perspective have been resolved, the traditional notion of generalizability will do just fine. Practitioners in fields such as education, counselling and social work, however, are concerned with individuals, not aggregates, and, for them, questions about meaning and perspective are central and ongoing. If research is to assist such [practitioners], an alternative way of conceptualizing generalizability is required.

Here I have suggested that schema theory – in particular, the Piagetian notions of assimilation, accommodation, integration and differentiation – provides an alternative way of talking and thinking about generalizability. I have also suggested that when we apply this way of talking and thinking to the area of research, qualitative case studies appear to have far more utility for applied fields such as education, counselling and social work than was traditionally believed.

References

Barone, T. (1987) 'Research out of the shadows: a reply to Rist', *Curriculum Inquiry*, 17: 453–463.

Berlin, I. (1966) 'The concept of scientific history', in W. Dray (ed.), *Philosophical Analysis and History*. New York: Harper & Row.

Blumer, H. (1969) *Symbolic Interactionism: Perspective and Method*. Englewood Cliffs, NJ: Prentice-Hall.

Bruner, J. (1986) *Actual Minds: Possible Worlds*. Cambridge, MA: Harvard University Press.

Buber, M. (1968) 'Education', in M. Buber, *Between Man and Man*. New York: Macmillan. (Original work published 1947.)

Campbell, J. (1979) 'A tribal model of the social vehicle carrying scientific knowledge', *Knowledge: Creation, Diffusion, Utilization*, 1: 181–201.

Carloye, J. (1985) 'Normal science and the extension of theories', *The British Journal of the Philosophy of Science*, 36: 241–56.

Conklin, H. (1955) 'Hanunoo color categories', *Southwestern Journal of Anthropology*, 11: 339–44.

Cowan, P. (1978) *Piaget with Feeling*. New York: Holt, Rinehart & Winston.

Cronbach, L.J. (1957) 'The two disciplines of scientific psychology', *American Psychologist*, 12: 671–84.

Cronbach, L.J. (1975) 'Beyond the two disciplines of scientific psychology', *American Psychologist*, 30: 116–27.

Cronbach, L.J. (1982) 'Prudent aspirations for social inquiry', in W. Kruskal (ed.), *The Social Sciences: Their Nature and Lines*. Chicago: University of Chicago Press.

Dilthey, W. (1961) *Meaning in History*. London: Allen & Unwin.

Dilthey, W. (1976) *Selected Writings*. New York: Cambridge University Press.

Donmoyer, R. (1983) 'The principal as prime mover', *Daedalus*, 112: 81–94.

Donmoyer, R. (1985a) 'Cognitive anthropology and research on effective principals', *Educational Administration Quarterly*, 21: 31–57.

Donmoyer, R. (1985b) 'The rescue from relativism: two failed attempts and an alternative strategy', *Educational Researcher*, 14: 13–20.

Donmoyer, R. (1987a) [Review of *Naturalistic Inquiry.*] *Teachers College Record*, 88: 470–4.

Donmoyer, R. (1987b) 'Why case studies?', *Curriculum Inquiry*, 17: 91–102.

Dray, W. (1957) *Laws and Explanation in History*. London: Oxford University Press.

Eggan, D. (1974) 'Instruction and affect in Hopi cultural continuity', in G. Spindler (ed.), *Education and the Cultural Process*. New York: Holt, Rinehart & Winston.

Eisner, E. (1985) *The Educational Imagination*. New York: Macmillan.

Feinberg, S. (1977) 'The collection and analysis of ethnographic data in educational research', *Anthropology and Education Quarterly*, 8: 50–7.

Freire, P. (1970) *Pedagogy of the Oppressed*. New York: Seabury Press.

Galtung, J. (1974) 'On peace education', in C. Wulf (ed.), *Handbook of Peace Education*. Frankfurt/Main and Oslo: International Peace Research Association.

Gusfield, J. (1976) 'The literary rhetoric of science', *American Sociologist*, 41: 11–33.

Hamilton, D. (1976) 'A science of the singular'. CIRCE, University of Illinois, Urbana.

Heath, S.B. (1982) 'Ethnography and education: defining the essentials', in P. Gilmore and A. Glatthord (eds), *Children in and out of School: Ethnography and Education*. Washington, DC: Center for Applied Linguistics.

Jackson, P. (1974) 'Naturalistic studies of schools and classrooms: one reader's digest', in M. Apple, J. Subpoviak and H. Lufler (eds), *Educational Evaluation: Analysis and Responsibility*. Berkeley, CA: McCutchan.

Kleibard, H. (1975) 'Reappraisal: the Tyler rationale', in W. Pinar (ed.), *Curriculum Theorizing: The reconceptualists*. Berkeley, CA: McCutchan.

Kuhn, T. (1971) *The Structure of Scientific Revolutions*. Chicago: University of Chicago Press.

Langer, S. (1953) *Feeling and Form*. New York: Scribner's.

Lather, P. (1988) 'Ideology and methodological attitude'. Paper presented at the annual meeting of the American Educational Research Association, New Orleans, LA, April.

Lightfoot, S.L. (1983) *The Good High School*. New York: Basic Books.

Lincoln, Y. and Guba, E. (1985) *Naturalistic Inquiry*. Beverly Hills, CA: Sage.

Mann, J. (1969) 'Curriculum criticism', *Teachers College Record*, 71: 27–40.

Miles, M. and Huberman, M. (1984) 'Drawing valid meaning from qualitative data', *Educational Researcher*, 13: 20–30.

Mishler, E. (1979) 'Meaning in context: is there any other kind?', *Harvard Educational Review*, 49: 1–20.

Neisser, U. (1976) *Cognition and Reality: Principles and Implications of Cognitive Psychology*. San Francisco: W.H. Freeman.

Nelson, R. (1969) *Hunters of the Northern Ice*. Chicago: University of Chicago Press.

Phillips, D.C. (1987) *Philosophy, Science and Social Inquiry*. Oxford: Pergamon Press.

Piaget, J. (1971) *Biology and Knowledge*. Chicago: University of Chicago Press.

Polanyi, M. (1958) *Personal Knowledge*. Chicago: University of Chicago Press.

Powdermaker, H. (1966) *Stranger and Friend: The Way of an Anthropologist*. New York: W.W. Norton.

Rist, R. (1973) *The Urban School: Factory for Failure*. Cambridge, MA: MIT Press.

Sharp, R. and Green, A. (1975) *Education and Social Control: A Study in Progressive Primary Education*. London: Routledge & Kegan Paul.

Stake, R. (1978) 'The case-study method in social inquiry', *Educational Researcher*, 7: 5–8. (Reprinted as Chapter 1 in this volume.)

Stake, R.E. (1980) 'Generalizations'. Paper presented at the annual meeting of the American Educational Research Association, Boston, April.

Suransky, V. (1982) *The Erosion of Childhood*. Chicago: University of Chicago Press.

Thorndike, E.L. (1910) 'The contribution of psychology to education', *The Journal of Educational Psychology*, 1: 5–12.

Turner, T. (1973) 'Piaget's structuralism', *American Anthropologist*, 75: 351–73.

Vallance, E. (1977) 'The landscape of "The Great Plains Experience": an application of curriculum criticism', *Curriculum Inquiry*, 7: 87–105.

Weiss, C. (1982) 'Policy research in the context of diffuse decision making', *Journal of Higher Education*, 53: 619–39.

Wolcott, H. (1987) 'The teacher as enemy', in G. Spindler (ed.), *Education and the cultural process*. Prospect Heights, IL: Waveland Press.

CHAPTER 4

INCREASING THE GENERALIZABILITY OF QUALITATIVE RESEARCH

Janet Ward Schofield

Traditional views of generalizability

Campbell and Stanley (1963) laid the groundwork for much current thinking on the issue of generalizability [...] in a groundbreaking chapter in the *Handbook of Research on Teaching*. They wrote, '*External validity* asks the question of *generalizability:* To what populations, settings, treatment variables, and measurement variables can the effect be generalized?' (p. 175; emphasis in original). They then went on to list four specific threats to external validity: the interaction of testing and the experimental treatment; the interaction of selection and treatment; reactive arrangements; and the interference of multiple treatments with one another. Although Campbell and Stanley specifically included populations, settings, treatments and measurement variables as dimensions relevant to the concept of external validity, the aspect of external validity that has typically received the lion's share of attention in textbook and other treatments of the concept is generalizing to and across populations. This may well be due to the fact that, because of advances in sampling theory in survey research, it is possible to draw samples from even a very large and heterogeneous population and then to generalize to that population using the logic of probability statistics.

Campbell and Stanley (1963), as well as many others in the quantitative tradition, see the attempt to design research so that abstract generalizations can be drawn as a worthy effort, although issues connected with internal validity are typically given even higher priority. Thus researchers in the quantitative tradition have devoted considerable thought to the question of how the generalizability of experimental and quasi-experimental studies can be enhanced. Such efforts are consistent with the fact that many quantitatively oriented researchers would agree with Smith (1975) that 'the goal of science is to be able to generalize findings to diverse populations and times' (p. 88).

From E.W. Eisner and A. Peshkin (eds) (1990) *Qualitative Inquiry in Education: The Continuing Debate.* New York: Teachers College Press.

In contrast to the interest shown in external validity among quantitatively oriented researchers, the methodological literature on qualitative research has paid little attention to this issue, at least until quite recently. For example, Dobbert's (1982) text on qualitative research methods devotes an entire chapter to issues of validity and reliability but does no more than mention the issue of generalizability in passing on one or two pages. Two even more recent books, Kirk and Miller's *Reliability and Validity in Qualitative Research* (1986) and Berg's *Qualitative Research Methods for the Social Sciences* (1989), ignore the issue of external validity completely. The major factor contributing to the disregard of the issue of generalizability in the qualitative methodological literature appears to be a widely shared view that it is unimportant, unachievable, or both.

Many qualitative researchers actively reject generalizability as a goal. For example, Denzin (1983) writes:

> The interpretivist rejects generalization as a goal and never aims to draw randomly selected samples of human experience. For the interpretivist every instance of social interaction, if thickly described (Geertz, 1973), represents a slice from the life world that is the proper subject matter for interpretive inquiry.... Every topic ... must be seen as carrying its own logic, sense or order, structure, and meaning. (pp. 133–4)

Although not all researchers in the qualitative tradition reject generalization so strongly, many give it very low priority or see it as essentially irrelevant to their goals. One factor contributing to qualitative researchers' historical tendency to regard the issue of external validity as irrelevant and hence to disregard it is that this research tradition has been closely linked to cultural anthropology, with its emphasis on the study of exotic cultures. This work is often valued for its intrinsic interest, for showing the rich variety and possible range of human behaviour, and for serving a historical function by describing traditional cultures before they change in an increasingly interconnected and homogeneous world. For researchers doing work of this sort, the goal is to describe a specific group in fine detail and to explain the patterns that exist, certainly not to discover general laws of human behaviour.

Practically speaking, no matter what one's philosophical stance on the importance of generalizability, it is clear that numerous characteristics that typify the qualitative approach are not consistent with achieving external validity as it has generally been conceptualized. For example, the traditional focus on single-case studies in qualitative research is obviously inconsistent with the requirements of statistical sampling procedures, which are usually seen as fundamental to generalizing from the data gathered in a study to some larger population. This fact is often cited as a major weakness of the case study approach (Bolgar, 1965; Shaughnessy and Zechmeister, 1985).

However, the incompatibility between classical conceptions of external validity and fundamental aspects of the qualitative approach goes well beyond this. To give just one example, the experimental tradition emphasizes replicability of results, as is apparent in Krathwohl's (1985) statement: 'The heart of external validity is replicability. Would the results be reproducible in those target instances to which one intends to generalize – the population, situation, time, treatment form or format, measures, study designs and procedures?' (p. 123). Yet at the heart of the qualitative approach is the assumption that a piece of qualitative research is very much influenced by the researcher's individual attributes and perspectives. The goal is *not* to produce a standardized set of results that any other careful researcher in the same situation or studying the same issue would have produced. Rather it is to produce a coherent and illuminating description of and perspective on a situation that is based on and consistent with detailed study of that situation. Qualitative researchers have to question seriously the *internal* validity of their work if other researchers reading their field notes feel the evidence does not support the way in which they have depicted the situation. However, they do not expect other researchers in a similar or even the same situation to replicate their findings in the sense of conceptualization. As long as the other researchers' conclusions are not inconsistent with the original account, differences in the reports would not generally raise serious questions related to validity or generalizability.

In fact, I would argue that, except perhaps in multi-site qualitative studies, which will be discussed later in this paper, it is impractical to make precise replication a criterion of generalizability in qualitative work. Qualitative research is so arduous that it is unlikely that high-quality researchers could be located to engage in the relatively unexciting task of conducting a study designed specifically to replicate a previous one. Yet studies not designed specifically for replication are unlikely to be conducted in a way that allows good assessment of the replicability issue. Of course it is possible, even likely, that specific ideas or conclusions from a piece of qualitative work can stimulate further research of a qualitative or quantitative nature that provides information on the replicability of that one aspect of a study. However, any piece of qualitative research is likely to contain so many individual descriptive and conceptual components that replicating it on a piece-by-piece basis would be a major undertaking.

The increasing interest in generalizability in the qualitative tradition

[Recently], interest in the issue of generalizability has increased markedly for qualitative researchers involved in the study of education.

Books by Patton (1980), Guba and Lincoln (1981) and Noblit and Hare (1988), as well as papers by Stake (1978) [see Chapter 1 above – *Editors' Note*], Kennedy (1979) and others, have all dealt with this issue in more than a cursory fashion. Two factors seem to be important in accounting for this increase in attention to the issue of generalizability. First, the uses of qualitative research have shifted quite markedly in [recent times]. In the area of education, qualitative research is not an approach used primarily to study exotic foreign or deviant local cultures. Rather it has become an approach used widely in both evaluation research and basic research on educational issues in our own society. The issue of generalizability assumes real importance in both kinds of work.

The shift in the uses of qualitative work that occurred during the 1970s was rapid and striking. The most obvious part of this shift was the inclusion of major qualitative components in large-scale evaluation research efforts, which had previously been almost exclusively quantitative in nature (Fetterman, 1982; Firestone and Herriott, 1984). The acceptance of qualitative research as a valid and potentially rich approach to evaluation progressed to the point that Wolcott (1982) wrote, with only some exaggeration, 'By the late 1970s the term "ethnography" ... had become synonymous with "evaluation" in the minds of many educators' (p. 82). Evaluations are expensive and time-consuming undertakings. Although formative evaluations are usually site-specific, the worth of a summative evaluation is greatly enhanced to the extent it can inform programme and policy decisions relating to other sites. In fact, as Cronbach (1982) points out, when summative evaluations are reported, no more than a fraction of the audience is interested primarily in the specific programme and setting that was the object of the study. Even at the study site itself, by the time the evaluation is completed, changes may well have occurred that have important consequences for programme functioning and goal achievement. Thus the question of whether an evaluation's findings can usefully be generalized to a later point in time at the site at which the evaluation was conducted is an issue that, although often ignored, requires real consideration.

The issue of generalizability is also salient for more basic qualitative research on educational issues [...]. Funding agencies providing resources for qualitative studies of educational issues are presumably interested in shedding light on these issues generally, not just as they are experienced at one site. For example, I am currently directing a qualitative study of computer usage in an urban high school. It is clear that the impetus for the funding of this study by the Office of Naval Research derived from concerns about the Navy's own computer-based education and training efforts, not from concerns about the public schools. Quite apart from the goals of funding agencies, many qualitative researchers themselves hope to accomplish more than describing the culture of the specific school or classroom that they have chosen to study. For example, Peshkin (1982) writes of his study of school and community in a small town in Illinois, 'I hoped ... to explicate some reality which was not merely confined to other places just like Mansfield' (p. 63), a hope tellingly reflected in the title of his book, *Growing Up American* (1978), as opposed to 'Growing Up in Illinois' or 'Growing Up in Mansfield'. This desire to have one's work be broadly useful is no doubt often stimulated by concern over the state of education [...]. It is also clearly reinforced by the fact that, unlike most readers of ethnographic reports of exotic cultures, most readers of qualitative reports on American education have had considerable exposure during their own school years to at least one version of the culture described. Thus, unless the researcher chooses a very atypical site or presents an unusually insightful analysis of what is happening, the purely descriptive value of the study may be undercut or discounted.

So far I have argued that qualitative research's [...] shift in both purpose and locale [...] has contributed to an increased interest in generalizability among qualitative researchers. There is yet one other factor contributing to this trend – the striking rapprochement between qualitative and quantitative methodologies that has occurred [recently] (Cronbach et al., 1980; Filstead, 1979; Reichardt and Cook, 1979; Spindler, 1982). Exemplifying this trend is the shift in the position of Donald Campbell. Campbell and Stanley (1963) at one point contended that the 'one-shot case study', which is one way of describing much qualitative research, has 'such a total absence of control as to be of almost no scientific value' (p. 176). However, more recently Campbell (1979) wrote a paper to 'correct some of [his] own prior excesses in describing the case study approach' (p. 52) in which he takes the, for many, rather startling position that when qualitative and quantitative results conflict, 'the quantitative results should be regarded as suspect until the reasons for the discrepancy are well understood' (p. 52).

One result of the rapprochement that has occurred is that qualitative and quantitative researchers are more in contact with each other's traditions than had typically been the case heretofore. As is often the case when a dominant tradition makes contact with a minority one, the culture and standards of the dominant group make a significant impact on the members of the minority group. This trend has most likely been reinforced by the fact that a great deal of the qualitative research on education conducted [recently] has been embedded within multimethod evaluation projects undertaken by private research firms that have traditionally specialized in quantitative research. Thus the concept of external validity and the associated issue of generalizability have been made salient for qualitative researchers, whose own tradition has not predisposed them to have given the issue a great deal of thought.

Reconceptualizing generalizability

Although many qualitative researchers have begun to recognize the importance of dealing with the issue of generalizability, it is clear that the classical view of external validity is of little help to qualitative researchers interested in finding ways of enhancing the likelihood that their work will speak to situations beyond the one immediately studied – that is, that it will be to some extent generalizable. The idea of sampling from a population of sites in order to generalize to the larger population is simply and obviously unworkable in all but the rarest situations for qualitative researchers, who often take several years to produce an intensive case study of one or a very small number of sites. Thus most of the work on generalizability by qualitative researchers […] has dealt with developing a *conception* of generalizability that is useful and appropriate for qualitative work.

A second approach to the issue of generalizability in qualitative research has been very different. A number of individuals have worked on ways of gaining generality through the synthesis of pre-existing qualitative studies. For example, Noblit and Hare (1988) have published a slim volume on meta-ethnography. Substantially earlier, Lucas (1974) and Yin and Heald (1975) had developed what they call the 'case survey method'. Ragin (1987) has presented yet another way of synthesizing qualitative studies, one that employs Boolean algebra. I will discuss these approaches to generalizing from qualitative case studies briefly at the end of this chapter. At the moment, I would like to focus on issues connected with the first approach – that is, with transforming and adapting the classical conception of external validity such that it is suitable for qualitative work.

Important and frequently cited discussions of conceptions of generalizability appropriate in qualitative work can be found in Guba and Lincoln (1981, 1982), Goetz and LeCompte (1984) and Stake (1978). Guba and Lincoln's stance on the issue of generalizability is aptly summarized in two excerpts of their own words:

> It is virtually impossible to imagine any human behavior that is not heavily mediated by the context in which it occurs. One can easily conclude that generalizations that are intended to be context free will have little that is useful to say about human behavior. (Guba and Lincoln, 1981, p. 62)

They go on to say:

> The aim of [naturalistic] inquiry is to develop an idiographic body of knowledge. This knowledge is best encapsulated in a series of 'working hypotheses' that describe the individual case. Generalizations are impossible since phenomena are neither time- nor context-free (although some transferability of these hypotheses may be possible from situation to situation, depending on the degree of temporal and contextual similarity). (Guba and Lincoln, 1982, p. 238)

Given these views, Guba and Lincoln call for replacing the concept of generalizability with that of 'fittingness' [see Chapter 2 – *Editors' Note*]. Specifically, they argue that the concept of 'fittingness', with its emphasis on analysing the degree to which the situation studied matches other situations in which one is interested, provides a more realistic and workable way of thinking about the generalizability of research results than do more classical approaches. A logical consequence of this approach is an emphasis on supplying a substantial amount of information about the entity studied and the setting in which that entity was found. Without such information, it is impossible to make an informed judgement about whether the conclusions drawn from the study of any particular site are useful in understanding other sites.

Goetz and LeCompte (1984) place a similar emphasis on the importance of clear and detailed description as a means of allowing decisions about the extent to which findings from one study are applicable to other situations. Specifically, they argue that qualitative studies gain their potential for applicability to other situations by providing what they call 'comparability' and 'translatability'. The former term

refers to the degree to which components of a study – including the units of analysis, concepts generated, population characteristics, and settings – are sufficiently well described and defined that other researchers can use the results of the study as a basis for comparison. (p. 228)

Translatability is similar but refers to a clear description of one's theoretical stance and research techniques.

Stake (1978) starts out by agreeing with many critics of qualitative methods that one cannot confidently generalize from a single case to a target population of which that case is a member, since single members often poorly represent whole populations. However, he then goes on to argue that it is possible to use a process he calls 'naturalistic generalization' to take the findings from one study and apply them to understanding another *similar* situation. He argues that through experience individuals come to be able to use both explicit comparisons between situations and tacit knowledge of those same situations to form useful naturalistic generalizations.

Several major themes can be found in the work of qualitative researchers who have written recently on the concept of generalizability. Whether it is Guba and Lincoln (1981, 1982) writing of fittingness, Goetz and LeCompte (1984) writing of translatability and comparability, or Stake (1978) discussing naturalistic generalizations, the emerging view shared by many qualitative researchers appears to involve several areas of consensus. First of all, there is broad agreement that generalizability in the sense of producing laws that apply universally is not a useful standard or goal for qualitative research. In fact, most qualitative researchers would join Cronbach (1982) in arguing that this is not a useful or obtainable goal for any kind of research in the social sciences. Second, most researchers writing on generalizability in the qualitative tradition agree that their rejection of generalizability as a search for broadly applicable laws is not a rejection of the idea that studies in one situation can be used to speak to or to help form a judgement about other situations. Third, as should be readily apparent from the preceding discussion, current thinking on generalizability argues that thick descriptions (Ryle, cited in Geertz, 1973) are vital. Such descriptions of both the site in which the studies are conducted and of the site to which one wishes to generalize are crucial in allowing one to search for the similarities and differences between the situations. As Kennedy (1979) points out, analysis of these similarities and differences then makes it possible to make a reasoned judgement about the extent to which we can use the findings from one study as a 'working hypothesis', to use Cronbach's (1982) term, about what might occur in the other situation. Of course, the generally unstated assumption underlying this view is that our knowledge of the phenomena under study is sufficient to direct attention to important rather than superficial similarities and differences. To the extent that our understanding is flawed, important similarities or differences may inadvertently be disregarded.

Three targets of generalization

Given the growing emphasis on generalizability in qualitative research and the emerging consensus about how the concept of generalizability might most usefully be viewed by qualitative researchers, two questions present themselves:

1 To what do we want to generalize?
2 How can we design qualitative studies in a way that maximizes their generalizability?

It is to these two questions that I will devote the majority of the rest of this chapter. Although I will use the term *generalize* here and elsewhere, it is important that the reader recognize that I am not talking about generalization in the classical sense. Rather, I use it to refer to the process as conceptualized by those qualitative researchers to whose work I have just referred.

I believe that it is useful for qualitative researchers interested in the study of educational processes and institutions to try to generalize to three domains: to *what is*, to *what may be*, and to *what could be*. I will deal with these possibilities one at a time, providing the rationale for striving to generalize to each of these kinds of situations and then suggesting some ideas on how studies can actually be designed to do this.

Studying what is

From one perspective the study of any ongoing social situation, no matter how idiosyncratic or bizarre, is studying *what is*. But when I use the phrase *studying what is*, I mean to refer to studying the typical, the common or the ordinary. The goal of describing and understanding cultures or institutions as they typically are is an appropriate aim for much current qualitative research on educational institutions and processes. If policy makers need to decide how to change a programme or whether to continue it, one very obvious and useful kind of information is information on how the programme usually functions, what is usually achieved, and the like. Thus the goal of studying *what is* is one important aim for many kinds of summative evaluations. It is also appropriate outside of the area of evaluation for researchers hoping to provide a picture of the current educational scene that can be used for understanding or reflecting on it and possibly improving it. Classic works of this type that focus primarily on *what is* are Wolcott's *The Man in the Principal's Office* (1973) and Jackson's *Life in the Classrooms* (1968). If one accepts the goal of designing research to maximize the fit between the research site and *what is* more broadly in society, an obvious question that arises is how this can be accomplished within the context of the qualitative tradition.

Studying the typical

One approach sometimes used is to study the typical (Bogdan and Biklen, 1981; Goetz and LeCompte, 1984; Patton, 1980; Whyte, 1984). Specifically, I would argue that choosing sites on the basis of their fit with a typical situation is far preferable to choosing on the basis of convenience, a practice that is still quite common.

The suggestion that typicality be weighed heavily in site selection is an idea that needs to be taken both more and less seriously than it currently is. When I say that it needs to be taken more seriously than it currently is, I am suggesting that researchers contemplating selecting a site on the basis of convenience or ease of access need to think more carefully about that decision and to weigh very carefully the possibility of choosing on the basis of some other criterion, such as typicality. When I say that the strategy of selecting a typical site needs to be taken less seriously than it may sometimes be, I intend to point out that choosing a typical site is not a 'quick fix' for the issue of generalizability, because what is typical on one dimension may not be typical on another. For example, Wolcott (1973) chose to focus his ethnographic study of a principal on an individual who was typical of other principals in gender, marital status, age, and so forth. This choice most likely substantially enhanced the range of applicability or generalizability of his study. Yet such a typical principal operating in an atypical school or an atypical system or even an atypical community might well behave very differently from a typical principal in a typical school in a typical system. The solution to this dilemma cannot be found in choosing typicality on every dimension. First of all, not too many typical principals operate in environments that are typical in every way. So this strategy gains less in the realm of generalizability or fittingness than it might appear to at first glance. More important, even if one could achieve typicality in all major dimensions that seem relevant, it is nonetheless clearly true that there would be enough idiosyncracy in any particular situation studied so that one could not transfer findings in an unthinking way from one typical situation to another.

Carried to extremes or taken too seriously, the idea of choosing on the basis of typicality becomes impossible, even absurd. However, as a guiding principle designed to increase the potential applicability of research, it is, I believe, useful. This is especially true if the search for typicality is combined with, rather than seen as a replacement for, a reliance on the kind of thick description emphasized by Guba and Lincoln (1981, 1982), Goetz and LeCompte (1984) and Stake (1978). Selection on the basis of typicality provides the potential for a good 'fit' with many other situations. Thick description provides the information necessary to make informed judgements about the degree and extent of that fit in particular cases of interest.

In arguing that qualitative researchers would do well to seek to study the typical, I am not suggesting that we study the typical defined solely by national norms. Research that followed this prescription would greatly increase our knowledge of typical situations, but in a nation as diverse as the United States, it would provide too restricted, pallid and homogeneous a view of [the] educational system. My emphasis on typicality implies that the researcher who has decided on the kind of institution or situation he or she wants to study – an urban ghetto school, a rural consolidated school or a private Montessori school – should try to select an instance of this kind of situation that is, to the extent possible, typical of its kind. Such an approach suggests, for example, that a researcher interested in studying mathematics teaching chooses to observe classrooms that use a popular text and generally accepted modes of instruction, rather than falling for convenience's sake into the study of classrooms that may well do neither of these. Furthermore, to the extent preliminary investigation of possible sites suggests that some or all are atypical in certain regards, careful thought about the possible implications of this atypicality for the topic under study may help to aid in site selection.

In sum, the point of my argument here is that choosing a site for research on the basis of typicality is far more likely to enhance the potential generalizability of one's study than choosing on the basis of convenience or ease of access – criteria that often weigh more heavily than they should. However, even if one chooses on the basis of typicality, one is in no way relieved of the necessity for thick description, for it is foolhardy to think that a typical example will be typical in all important regards. Thus thick description is necessary to allow individuals to ask about the degree of fit between the case studied and the case to which they wish to generalize, even when the fit on some of the basic dimensions looks fairly close.

Performing multi-site studies

An alternate approach to increasing the generalizability of qualitative research was evident in the sudden proliferation in the 1970s of multi-site qualitative studies. Such studies were almost always part of federally funded evaluation efforts focusing on the same issue in a number of settings, using similar data collection and analysis procedures in each place. Well-known examples of this approach include the Study of Dissemination Efforts Supporting School Improvement (Crandall et al., 1983; Huberman and Miles, 1984) and the study of Parental Involvement in Federal Educational Programs (Smith and Robbins, 1984). One of the primary purposes of conducting such multi-site studies is to escape what Firestone and Herriott (1984) have called the 'radical particularism' of many case studies and hence to provide a firmer basis for generalization.

The multi-site studies conducted in the 1970s were extremely varied, although they were all quite expensive and tended to take several years to complete. At least two kinds of variation have special implications for the extent to which this approach actually seems likely to produce results that are a good basis for generalization to many other situations. The first of these is the number of sites studied. Firestone and Herriott's (1984) survey of twenty-five multi-site case study efforts found major variation on this dimension, with one study including as few as three sites and another covering sixty. All other things being equal, a finding emerging repeatedly in the study of numerous sites would appear to be more likely to be a good working hypothesis about some as yet unstudied site than a finding emerging from just one or two sites.

A second dimension on which multi-site studies vary, which is also likely to affect the degree of fit between these studies and situations to which one might want to generalize, concerns the heterogeneity of the sites chosen for study. Generally speaking, a finding emerging from the study of several very heterogeneous sites would be more robust and thus more likely to be useful in understanding various other sites than one emerging from the study of several very similar sites (Kennedy, 1979). Heterogeneity can be obtained by searching out sites that will provide maximal variation or by planned comparisons along certain potentially important dimensions. An example of the second strategy can be found in the parental-involvement study previously mentioned. The sites chosen for study were selected to allow comparison between urban and rural settings, between those with high and low reported degrees of involvement, and so forth (Smith and Robbins, 1984). This comparative strategy is potentially quite powerful, especially if there is heterogeneity among cases within each of the categories of interest. For example, if several rather different rural cases all share certain similarities that are not found in a heterogeneous group of urban cases, one has some reasonable basis for generalizing about likely difference between the two settings. Although the most obvious comparative strategy is to select cases that initially differ on some variable of interest as part of the research design, it is also possible to group cases in an *ex post facto* way on the basis of information gathered during the field-work. For example, if one were studying numerous very different classrooms and found that student achievement gains were quite high in some and quite low in others, one could compare these two sets of classrooms as a strategy for trying to suggest factors that contribute to high or low gains.

In sum, the possibility of studying numerous heterogeneous sites makes multi-site studies one potentially useful approach to increasing the generalizability of qualitative work to *what is*. Yet I am very hesitant to see this approach as the only or even the best solution to the problem. First, such studies can be quite expensive, and the current lull in their funding highlights the extent to which such research is dependent on federal dollars that may or may not be forthcoming. Second, as Firestone and Herriott (1984) point out, budget constraints make it likely that studies including very large numbers of sites are less likely than studies of a relatively small number of sites to be able to devote intensive and prolonged care to studying the details of each site. Thus there is typically a trade-off to be made between the increased potential for generalizability flowing from studying a large number of sites and the increased depth and breadth of description and understanding made possible by a focus on a small number of sites. In suggesting that an increased number of sites leads to increased generalizability, I am assuming that enough attention is paid to each site to ensure that problems of internal validity do not arise. To the extent such problems do arise, generalizability is obviously threatened, since one cannot speak meaningfully of the generalizability of invalid data. The fact that roughly 40 per cent of the multi-site studies surveyed by Firestone and

Herriott (1984) involved just one or two short visits to the research site raises serious questions about whether such studies can appropriately be categorized as qualitative research in the usual sense of that term. The term *qualitative research,* and more especially the word *ethnography,* usually implies an intensive, ongoing involvement with individuals functioning in their everyday settings that is akin to, if not always identical with, the degree of immersion in a culture attained by anthropologists, who live in the society they study over a period of one or more years (Dobbert, 1982; Spindler, 1982; Wolcott, 1975). Thus it is conceivable, though not logically necessary, that attempts to gain generalizability through studying large numbers of sites undercut the depth of understanding of individual sites, which is the hallmark of the qualitative approach as it has come to be understood.

Studying what may be

The goal of portraying typical schools – or, for that matter, typical instances of federal educational programmes as they now exist – is, I believe, worthwhile. Yet accepting this as our only or even primary goal implies too narrow and limited a vision of what qualitative research can do. I would like to suggest that we want to generalize not only to *what is* but also to *what may be.* Let me explain. Here I am proposing that we think about what current social and educational trends suggest about likely educational issues for the future and design our research to illuminate such issues to the extent possible. Let me use some of my own current research to illustrate this possibility, without implying that it is the best or only example of such an approach.

One very obvious and potentially important trend in education recently has been the increasing utilization of microcomputers in instruction. In fact, microcomputers are being adopted in schools at an almost frantic pace (Becker, 1986) in spite of tight educational budgets and a generally acknowledged tendency on the part of educational institutions to resist rapid change. There is a clear division of opinion about the likely consequences of this trend. At one extreme are those who see computers as having the capability to revolutionize education in absolutely fundamental ways. Proponents of this school of thought make the rather startling claim that 'the potential of computers for improving education is greater than that of any prior invention, including books and writing' (Walker, 1984, p. 3). Others take quite a different stance, emphasizing the inherent conservativism of the teaching profession with regard to pedagogical change and the failure of other highly touted educational innovations to bring about far-reaching changes. Thus it seemed important to me to design a research project focused on understanding the impact of computer usage on students and classrooms (Schofield and Evans-Rhodes, 1989; Schofield and Verban, 1988). One could approach this issue with an emphasis on what is. For example, it would be possible to choose a school that is presently typical in terms of the uses it makes of computers in instruction. But this strategy encounters an immediate problem if one's goal is to speak to what may be. Changes both in microcomputer technology and in individuals' level of experience with computers have been so rapid [...] that a study of what is today could arguably be a study of primarily historical interest by the time it gets conducted, written and published. In hopes of not just documenting the present, which is rapidly becoming the past, but of speaking to the future, I have made a number of methodological decisions that, in their abstract form, may be of use to others interested in making their work applicable to what may be.

Studying the 'leading edge' of change

First, since it is hard to know what kinds of computer usage will become most typical or popular in the future, I have made a point of studying a broad array of uses rather than just one particular kind. More important, I have not looked only for heterogeneity of usage but for types of usage that are now in their infancy but that many informed observers see as likely to be common in the future. Thus I consciously chose to study a school that not only uses computers as they are currently employed around the country to teach computer programming and word processing in fairly typical ways but that also was the field test site for the kind of artificially intelligent computer-based tutor that researchers in a number of centres around the [United States] are currently developing for classroom use (Feigenbaum and McCorduck, 1983; Lawler and Yazdani, 1987). I see this choice as a step in the direction of increasing the chances that this work will 'fit' or be generalizable to the educational issues important at the time the work is published. But this is only a mere first step.

Probing factors likely to differentiate the present from the future

One of the big problems in trying to make one's work applicable to even the fairly near future is, as Cronbach (1975) has so eloquently argued, that people and institutions change. Thus it is logically impossible to see the future even when studying futuristic uses of artificial intelligence, because one is studying that future technology in the context of a present-day institution peopled with individuals who are shaped by the era in which they live.

There is no completely satisfactory solution to this situation, but a partial one emerged as I grappled with the issue. It is to think through how the present and the future are likely to differ. Then the research can be structured in a way that explicitly probes the impact of things that are likely to change over time. Of course, if the analysis of the likely differences between present and future is wrong, this approach will not be particularly useful. But if the analysis is accurate, this strategy has the potential to enhance greatly the usefulness of the study.

Let me illustrate in concrete terms how I have done this. Given the rapidity with which computers are being adopted for use in widely varying arenas of life, especially in schools, it seems a reasonable expectation that one major difference between now and five to ten years in the future is what might be called the 'novelty factor'. Specifically, many of today's high school students are having their first real introduction to the computer, or at least to its use for educational purposes, in their high school classrooms. However, in ten years it is rather unlikely that high school students will be having their first exposure to educational computing in the tenth or eleventh grade. I have used this assumption, which is, I think, relatively uncontroversial, to influence the shape of my study in a way that will allow it to speak more adequately to the future. For example, in interviews students were specifically asked about the impact of novelty on their reactions to the computer and its importance in shaping their feelings about computer usage. Similarly, observers in the study carefully looked for reactions that appeared to be influenced by students' unfamiliarity with the computers. Moreover, I have been careful to find out which students have had prior computer experience and what kind of experience this has been in order to see as clearly as possible whether these students differ from those for whom computer use is a completely novel experience. The fact that students were observed during the full course of the school year allowed assessment of whether any initial differences in students' reactions due to prior experience were transitory or relatively long-lasting. To the extent that novelty is crucial in shaping students' reactions, I will be forced to conclude that my study may not help us understand the future as well as it might otherwise. To the extent that students' reactions appear to be more heavily influenced by things that are unlikely to change in the near future, such as adolescents' striving for independence from adult control, the likely applicability of the findings of the study to the near future is clearly increased.

Considering the life cycle of a phenomenon

The preceding discussion of the possible impact of novelty on students' reactions to educational computing brings up an important point regarding qualitative work and the issue of generalizability. The ethnographic habit of looking at a phenomenon over substantial time periods allows assessment of one aspect of generalizability that quantitative research usually does not – of where a particular phenomenon is in its life cycle and what the implications of this are for what is happening. Qualitative research, when studying a dynamic phenomenon, is like a movie. It starts with one image and then moves on to others that show how things evolve over time. Quantitative research, in contrast, is more typically like a snapshot, often taken and used without great regard for whether that photograph happened to catch one looking one's best or looking unusually dishevelled. This point can be illustrated more substantively by briefly discussing a study that I carried out in a desegregated school during its first four years of existence (Schofield, 1989). The study tracked changes in the school by following two different groups of students from the first day they entered the school to graduation from that school three years later. Important changes occurred in race relations over the life of the institution and over the course of students' careers in the school. Such findings suggest that in asking about what happens in desegregated schools and what the impact of such schools is on students, it is important to know where both the students and the institution are in their experience with desegregation. Yet virtually all quantitative studies of desegregation, including, I must admit, some of my own, tend to ignore these issues completely. In fact, as I discovered in reviewing the desegregation literature (Schofield and Sagar, 1983), many do not even supply bare descriptive information on the life-cycle issue. Paying attention to where a phenomenon is in its life cycle does not guarantee that one can confidently predict how it will evolve. However, at a minimum, sensitivity to this issue makes it less likely that conclusions formed on the basis of a study conducted at one point in time will be unthinkingly and perhaps mistakenly generalized to other later points in time to which they may not apply.

Studying what could be

As mentioned previously, I would like to argue that qualitative research on education can be used not only to study *what is* and *what may be* but also to explore possible visions of *what could be*. By studying what could be, I mean locating situations that we know or expect to be ideal or exceptional on some *a priori* basis and then studying them to see what is actually going on there.

Selecting a site that sheds light on what could be

When studying what could be, site selection is not based on criteria such as typicality or heterogeneity. Rather it is based on information either about the *outcomes* achieved in the particular site studied or on the *conditions* obtaining there. Perhaps the best-known example of site selection based on outcomes is choosing to study classrooms or schools in which students show unusual intellectual gains, as has been done in the voluminous literature on effective schools (Bickel, 1983; Dwyer et al., 1982; Phi Delta Kappan, 1980; Rutter et al., 1979; Weber, 1971). For an example of site selection based on the conditions obtaining at the site, a less common approach, I will again make reference to my own work on school desegregation.

When thinking about where to locate the extended study of a deseg-regated school mentioned previously, I decided not to study a typical desegregated school. First, given the tremendous variation in situations characterized as desegregated, it is not clear that such an entity could be found. Second, there is a body of theory and research that gives us some basis for expecting different kinds of social processes and outcomes in different kinds of interracial schools. In fact, in the same year in which the *Brown* v. *Board of Education* decision laid the legal basis for desegregating educational institutions, Gordon Allport (1954) published a classic analysis of racial prejudice in which he argued that interracial contact can either increase or decrease hostility and stereotyping, depending on the kind of conditions under which it occurs. Specifically, he argued that in order to ameliorate relations between groups such as blacks and whites three conditions are espe-cially important: equal status for members of both groups within the contact situation; a cooperative rather than a competitive goal struc-ture; and support for positive relations from those in authority. A substantial amount of empirical and theoretical work stemming from Allport's basic insight has been carried out [...], most of which sup-ports his emphasis on the crucial importance of the specific conditions under which intergroup contact occurs (Amir, 1969; Aronson and Osherow, 1980; Cook, 1978; Pettigrew, 1967, 1969; Schofield, 1979; Schofield and Sagar, 1977; Slavin, 1980; Stephan, 1985).

It is clear that desegregating school systems often take little if any heed of the available theory and research on how to structure desegre-gated schools in a way likely to promote positive intergroup relations, perhaps at least partly because much of this work is laboratory-based and hence may seem of questionable use in everyday situations. Thus selecting a site for study on the basis of typicality might be expected to yield a site potentially rich in sources of insight about the problems of desegregated education but weak in shedding light on what can be accomplished in a serious and sophisticated effort to structure an environment conducive to fostering positive relations between stu-dents. Since both scholars in the area of intergroup relations and the public are well aware of the potential for difficulties in desegregated schools, the task of seeing whether and how such difficulties can be overcome seems potentially more informative and useful than that of documenting the existence of such difficulties. Thus I chose to study a site that at least approximated a theoretical ideal. My goal was not to generalize to desegregated schools as a class. Rather it was to see what happens under conditions that might be expected to foster relatively positive outcomes. If serious problems were encountered at such a site, there would be reason to think that problems would be encountered in most places or, alternatively, to revise or reject the theory that led to the site selection. However, if things went well at such a site, the study would then provide an opportunity to gain some insight into how and why they go well and into what the still-intractable problems are.

Of course, the strategy of choosing a site based on some *a priori* theoretical viewpoint or, for that matter, any seriously held expectation about it raises a difficult problem. If one is unduly committed to that viewpoint, one's analysis of both what happens and why may be heavily influenced by it, and one may not ask whether other more fruitful perspectives might emerge from a more dispassionate approach to studying the situation. This is the very danger that has led to the development of such elaborate safeguards in the quantitative tradition as the double-blind experiment. Although such procedures are rarely used in the qualitative tradition, a substantial literature on the issue of internal validity in qualitative research offers assistance with this problem to the researcher who pays it close heed (Becker, 1958; Bogdan and Biklen, 1981; Glaser and Strauss, 1967; Goetz and LeCompte, 1984; Guba, 1981; Guba and Lincoln, 1981; Kirk and Miller, 1986; Miles and Huberman, 1984a, 1984b; Patton 1980; Strauss, 1987). Furthermore, if one's purpose is not to support or reject a specific *a priori* theory but to discover, using an approach that is as open as possible, what is actually happening in a site that was chosen with the assistance of a particular theory, problems related to internal validity are somewhat mitigated. For example, the fact that I chose to study a school that theory suggested might be conducive to positive relations did not keep me from exploring in considerable depth problems that occurred there (Sagar and Schofield, 1980; Schofield, 1981, 1982, 1989).

One characteristic of the school chosen [...] was especially helpful in assessing [...] the theory on which [it] was chosen [...]. Specifically, for various reasons, conditions in two of the three grades in this school came much closer than conditions in the remaining grade to meeting those that theory suggests are conducive to producing positive relations. Thus it was possible to assess intergroup relations as the children went from one kind of environment to another within the school (Schofield, 1979, 1982, 1989; Schofield and Sagar, 1977). This suggests one very useful strategy for studying what may be – selecting an 'ideal' case and a comparative case that contrasts sharply on the relevant dimensions.

Generalizing from an unusual site to more typical ones

Although I indicated above that my goal was to learn about the possibilities and problems associated with a *certain kind* of desegregated education, I would like to argue that studying a site chosen for its special characteristics does not necessarily restrict the application of the study's findings to other very similar sites. The degree to which this is the case depends on the degree to which the findings appear to be linked to the special characteristics of the situation. Some of the findings from the study I have been discussing were clearly linked to unusual aspects of the school and hence have very limited generalizability to other situations, although they may nonetheless be important in demonstrating what is possible, even if not what is generally likely. For example, I found very low levels of overt racial conflict in the school studied (Schofield and Francis, 1982). It would obviously be misguided to conclude on the basis of this study that intergroup conflict is unlikely in all desegregated schools, since the school's emphasis on cooperation, equal status and the like, did actually appear to play a marked role in reducing the likelihood of conflict.

However, other findings that emerged from the study [which] were also related to atypical aspects of the situation may have a greater degree of applicability or generalizability than the finding discussed above. For example, I found the development of a colour-blind perspective and of an almost complete taboo against the mention of race in the school studied (Schofield, 1986, 1982/1989). Since the emergence of the colour-blind perspective and the accompanying taboo appeared to be linked to special characteristics of the school, I would not posit them as phenomena likely to occur in most desegregated schools. But I feel free to argue that *when* they do develop, certain consequences may well follow because these consequences are the logical outcomes of the phenomena. For example, with regard to the taboo against racial reference, if one cannot mention race, one cannot deal with resegregation in a straightforward way as a policy issue. Similarly, if one cannot mention race, there is likely to be little or no effort to create or utilize multicultural curricular materials. Thus, although the taboo against racial reference may not occur in a high proportion of desegregated schools, when it does occur the study I carried out gives a potentially useful indication of problems that are likely to develop.

I would now like to turn to a third finding of the study, one so unrelated to the atypical aspects of the situation studied that it is a reasonable working hypothesis that this phenomenon is widespread. After I observed extensively in varied areas of the school and interviewed a large number of students, it became apparent that the white children perceived blacks as something of a threat to their physical selves.

Specifically, they complained about what they perceived as black roughness or aggressiveness (Schofield, 1981, 1982, 1989). In contrast, the black students perceived whites as a threat to their social selves. They complained about being ignored, avoided and being treated as inferior by whites, whom they perceived to be stuck-up and prejudiced (Schofield, 1982, 1989). Such findings appear to me to be linked to the black and white students' situation in the larger society and to powerful historical and economic forces, not to special aspects of the school. The consequences of these rather asymmetrical concerns may well play themselves out differently in different kinds of schools, but the existence of these rather different but deeply held concerns may well be widespread.

I have gone into some detail with these examples because I think they raise a crucial point for judging the applicability or generalizability of qualitative work. One cannot just look at a study and say that it is similar or dissimilar to another situation of concern. A much finer-grained analysis is necessary. One must ask what aspects of the situation are similar or different and to what aspects of the findings these are connected.

Generalizing through aggregation or comparison of independent studies

This paper has argued that, by following some of the design suggestions above, it is possible to achieve greater generalizability of qualitative research to situations of interest than is often now the case. [...] However, there is another approach to increasing the generalizability of qualitative case studies that should not be ignored. This other strategy aims not at increasing the generalizability of one study or a set of studies planned in conjunction with each other but at finding ways to aggregate, compare or contrast already existing studies. One of these strategies was first laid out some time ago by Yin and Heald (1975). Another promising approach is suggested by Ragin's (1987) recent work on a strategy that he calls the 'qualitative comparative method'. A third very different approach has been outlined recently by Noblit and Hare (1988).

The case survey method

Yin and Heald (1975) point out that case studies, whether qualitative or quantitative, are very prevalent in many fields. The nub of the problem from their perspective is that while 'each case study may provide rich insights into a specific situation, it is difficult to generalize about the studies as a whole' (p. 317). Their solution to this problem is to propose a method for aggregating the information from separate studies. They call the method they developed 'the case survey method'. Basically this method consists of several steps. First, the literature relevant to one's interest is located. Then these studies are subjected to close scrutiny, so that those failing to meet certain crucial methodological requirements can be removed from the set to be analysed. Then coders go through each of the remaining case studies with the goal of using the information contained therein to complete a set of closed-ended questions. These questions pertain to the topic of one's study and constitute the dataset ultimately used in the case survey approach. For example, Yin and Heald (1975) discuss a study of the effectiveness of urban decentralization efforts in which the closed-ended questions covered (1) the nature of the case study itself, (2) the context in which the decentralization effort occurred, (3) the characteristics of the specific effort at decentralization, and (4) five possible outcomes of decentralization. One then uses the material in the questionnaires to search for patterns on which generalizations can be based. The strategy for producing these generalizations is the use of statistical tests of association between different variables. For example, Yin and Heald report a statistically significant positive association between their judgements of the quality of specific case studies and the degree to which the study concluded that decentralization succeeded. The case survey procedure is parallel in some respects to the procedures suggested more recently by Miles and Huberman (1984a, 1984b) for aggregating data from multi-site studies. However, Miles and Huberman tend not to emphasize statistical significance, perhaps because the number of studies in many multi-site qualitative endeavours is so small as to preclude attaining statistical significance unless the effects are of extraordinary strength.

As Yin and Heald (1975) acknowledge, there are clear limitations to the approach they suggest. First, of course, there must be a substantial body of literature available relevant to a particular topic for this procedure to work well. For example, Yin and Yates (1975) aggregated data from more than 250 studies of urban decentralization. When the number of available cases is small, statistical techniques lack power, since each case study must be treated as a single observation. Also, in such cases the number of variables worthy of coding may well be large compared to the number of sampling points (that is, case studies), which also poses statistical problems. Second, the case survey method, with its emphasis on reducing the rich descriptive material provided in many case studies to uniform quantifiable data, risks ignoring unique factors that may be crucial to understanding specific cases or kinds of cases. Third, as Yin and Heald (1975) note, the case survey method may be more suited to inquiries focusing on outcomes rather than on process. Because of the numerous limitations of the case survey method, Yin (1981) has concluded that the 'case-survey method should be used in highly selective situations' (p. 63) and that other methods for comparing across cases may ultimately prove more fruitful.

Unfortunately, the development of other methods for comparing and aggregating across cases, especially cases that have not been planned as part of a unified multi-site effort, are not well developed. Although the work of Miles and Huberman (1984a, 1984b) and Yin (1984) provides many useful design and analysis suggestions for investigators planning multi-site studies, relatively little methodological guidance is available to researchers who wish to compare studies that were designed and executed independently. A crucial difference between these two cases, of course, is that in the former one can obtain some degree of uniformity in the information gathered. This is crucial for the kinds of pattern-producing techniques suggested by Miles and Huberman and by Yin. There are other important differences as well. For example, in a multi-site study with central direction it is at least theoretically possible, if not eminently practical, for one individual to have access to the raw data from all the different sites. However, such is generally not the case when one is trying to conduct comparisons of previously published case studies or ethnographies. Thus, at this point in time, our ability to achieve generalizations through the comparison of independently conducted pieces of qualitative work on a particular topic is quite limited.

The qualitative comparative method

One promising new strategy for aggregating case studies has recently been developed by Ragin (1987). Ragin starts with the premise that two of the distinctive traits of case studies, and of case-oriented comparative research more generally, are their attention to cases as wholes and to the possibility that several different sets of circumstances can lead to the same outcome. He argues that most attempts to aggregate numerous case studies using quantitative approaches tend not to make use of these strengths and thus do not make full use of the data-bases on which they are built. To remedy this situation, Ragin proposes an approach that he calls the 'qualitative comparative method'. This approach is based on Boolean algebra, the algebra of sets and logic. Although a full discussion of this technique is beyond the scope of this paper, since it would require introducing readers to the basics of Boolean algebra, it is possible briefly to discuss Ragin's general approach without becoming unduly technical.

First, Ragin's techniques can be used with widely varying numbers of case studies as one's raw data. In this regard it is more flexible than the case survey method, which is suitable only when relatively large numbers of case studies are available because of its dependence on the concept of statistical significance. Second, the techniques can be used with either pre-existing case studies or with multi-site studies planned with the qualitative comparative strategy in mind. All that is necessary are data that allow one to build truth tables – that is, categorial information on the variables of major interest to the analysis. Ragin argues that his approach allows one to examine complex and multiple patterns of causation, to produce parsimonious explanations, to study cases both as wholes and as parts, and to evaluate competing explanations. Ragin presents several extended and sharply contrasting examples of the varied ways in which the approach he uses can be applied. Although his approach seems better suited in many ways to aggregating qualitative case studies than the case survey method, since a Boolean approach allows one to take better advantage of the characteristic strengths of case studies, it is too early to understand completely either its full potential or the various problems that individuals using this approach will face.

Meta-ethnography

Consideration of the techniques discussed above suggests that both the case survey method and attempts at case comparison are often based on a logic that seeks to generalize by aggregating studies. Noblit and Hare (1988) suggests that such an effort is misdirected, arguing that efforts at aggregation tend to ignore the interpretive nature of qualitative research and to miss much of what is most important in each study. They believe it is possible to systematically compare very diverse cases in order to draw cross-case conclusions. However, they see such an effort as best conceptualized as the *translation* of studies into one another rather than as their aggregation. They call this translation 'meta-ethnography'.

Noblit and Hare argue that studies of similar topics can be seen as directly comparable, as essentially refutational, or as together suggesting a new line of argument. Once a preliminary look at the material to be synthesized suggests which of the above is the case, a translation and synthesis is attempted. This process may refute the initial assumption about the relation between the cases, but it would generally be expected not to do so.

In order to perform the translation and synthesis, Noblit and Hare suggest a focus on and a listing of the concepts, themes and metaphors that the author of each study utilizes. The meta-ethnographer lists and organizes these themes and then attempts to relate them to one another. This somewhat abstract process is perhaps best clarified by a brief example. Noblit and Hare exemplify the idea of a reciprocal translation of studies by comparing Collins and Noblit's (1978) research in a desegregated school to Wolcott's study *The Man in the Principal's Office* (1973). The comparison makes sense and, in fact, is only possible because Collins and Noblit's study laid great emphasis on the role of the principal in the desegregated school they studied. Noblit and Hare list the terms used in both studies to describe the context in which the principal functioned, the principal's behaviour, and the like. The meta-ethnography then consists of a discussion of the ways in which the two situations and studies appear to be similar and different and, more important, of the extent to which the themes developed in each are adequate to handle the other ethnography as well. These judgements are based on attributes of the themes, such as their economy, cogency and scope. For example, Wolcott describes the conduct of the principal he studied as characterized by patience and prudence. Collins and Noblit compare two different principals in a particular school. The first was said to have created negotiated order in the school. His successor, with a far different style, created what Collins and Noblit characterized as a bureaucratic order. After discussing the particulars of the two studies, Noblit and Hare (1988) conclude that a translation between them is possible but that Wolcott's metaphors are more adequate to this task than those of Collins and Noblit. This means that Wolcott's concepts were able to capture what occurred in the Collins and Noblit study in a fuller and more adequate way than the Collins and Noblit themes fitted the Wolcott study. Of course, it is possible in a meta-ethnography that none of the studies compared will have characterized its themes in a way that adequately fits all others, even though there are many parallels. In such a case, the hope is that the individual doing the meta-ethnography may be able to produce new, more inclusive concepts that work better than those from any particular study.

Summary and conclusions

Although qualitative researchers have traditionally paid scant attention to the issue of attaining generalizability in research, sometimes even disdaining such a goal, this situation has changed noticeably in [recent decades]. Several trends, including the growing use of qualitative studies in evaluation and policy-oriented research, have led to an increased awareness of the importance of structuring qualitative studies in a way that enhances their implications for the understanding of other situations.

Much of the attention given to the issue of generalizability in recent years on the part of qualitative researchers has focused on redefining the concept in a way that is useful and meaningful for those engaged in qualitative work. A consensus appears to be emerging that for qualitative researchers generalizability is best thought of as a matter of the 'fit' between the situation studied and others to which one might be interested in applying the concepts and conclusions of that study. This conceptualization makes thick descriptions crucial, since without them one does not have the information necessary for an informed judgement about the issue of fit.

This paper argues that three useful targets for generalization are *what is, what may be* and *what could be* and provides some examples of how qualitative research can be designed in a way that increases its ability to fit with each of these situations. Studying *what is* refers to studying the typical, the common and the ordinary. Techniques suggested for studying *what is* include choosing study sites on the basis of typicality and conducting multi-site studies. Studying *what may be* refers to designing studies so that their fit with future trends and issues is maximized. Techniques suggested for studying *what may be* include seeking out sites in which one can study situations likely to become more common with the passage of time and paying close attention to how such present instances of future practices are likely to differ from their future realizations. Studying *what could be* refers to locating situations that we know or expect to be ideal or exceptional on some *a priori* basis and studying them to see what is actually going on there. Crucial here is an openness to having one's expectations about the phenomena disconfirmed.

A very different approach to increasing the generalizability of qualitative research is evident in the work of some scholars who have focused on how to achieve generalizability through the aggregation or comparison of extant independently designed case studies or ethnographies. The case survey approach suggested by Yin and Heald (1975) is promising in a limited number of cases in which comparable information is available from a relatively large number of studies. Case comparison strategies, such as the qualitative comparative method suggested by Ragin (1987), may be more realistic and fruitful in many areas of research; but these comparative techniques are still in the early stages of development. Noblit and Hare (1988) suggest a kind of comparison they call 'meta-ethnography', which focuses on the reciprocal translation rather than the aggregation of studies. Although such an approach may have promise, [...] its ultimate fruitfulness is still quite untested.

Acknowledgements

Much of the research on which this paper is based was funded by the Office of Naval Research, Contract Number N00 14-85-K-0664. Other research utilized in this paper was funded by Grant Number NIE-G-78-0126 from the National Institute of Education. However, all opinions expressed herein are solely those of the author, and no endorsement by ONR or NIE is implied or intended. My sincere thanks go to Bill Firestone and Matthew Miles for their constructive comments on an earlier draft of this paper.

References

Allport, G.W. (1954) *The Nature of Prejudice*. Cambridge: Cambridge University Press.

Amir, Y. (1969) 'Contact hypothesis in ethnic relations', *Psychological Bulletin*, 71: 319–42.

Aronson, E. and Osherow, N. (1980) 'Cooperation, prosocial behavior, and academic performance: experiments in the desegregated classroom', in L. Bickman (ed.), *Applied Social Psychology Annual* (Vol. 1). Beverly Hills, CA: Sage.

Becker, H.J. (1986) 'Instructional uses of school computers', *Reports from the 1985 National Survey* (Issue No. 1). Baltimore, MD: Center for Social Organization of Schools, Johns Hopkins University.

Becker, H.S. (1958) 'Problems of inference and proof in participant observation', *American Sociological Review*, 23: 652–9.

Berg, B.L. (1989) *Qualitative Research Methods for the Social Sciences*. Boston: Allyn & Bacon.

Bickel, W.E. (1983) 'Effective schools: knowledge, dissemination, inquiry', *Educational Researcher*, 12 (4): 3–5.

Bogdan, R.C. and Biklen, S.K. (1981) *Qualitative Research for Education: An Introduction to Theory and Methods*. Boston: Allyn & Bacon.

Bolgar, H. (1965) 'The case study method', in B.B. Wolman (ed.), *Handbook of Clinical Psychology*. New York: McGraw-Hill.

Brown v. Board of Education (1954) 347 U.S. 483.

Campbell, D.T. (1979) 'Degrees of freedom and the case study', in T.D. Cook and C.S. Reichardt (eds), *Qualitative and Quantitative Methods in Evaluation Research*. Beverly Hills, CA: Sage.

Campbell, D. and Stanley, J. (1963) 'Experimental and quasi-experimental designs for research on teaching', in N. Gage (ed.), *Handbook of Research on Teaching*. Chicago: Rand McNally.

Collins, T. and Noblit, G. (1978) *Stratification and Resegregation: The Case of Crossover High School*. Final report of NIE contract #400-76-009.

Cook, S.W. (1978) 'Interpersonal and attitudinal outcomes in cooperating interracial groups', *Journal of Research and Development in Education*, 12: 97–113.

Crandall, D.P., et al. (1983) *People, Policies and Practices: Examining the Chain of School Improvement* (Vols 1–10). Andover, MA: The Network.

Cronbach, L.J. (1975) 'Beyond the two disciplines of scientific psychology', *American Psychologist*, 30: 116–27.

Cronbach, L.J. (1982) *Designing Evaluations of Educational and Social Programs*. San Francisco: Jossey-Bass.

Cronbach, L.J., Ambron, S.R., Dornbusch, S.M., Hess, R.D., Hornik, R.C., Phillips, D.C., Walker, D.F. and Weiner, S.S. (1980) *Toward Perform of Program Evaluation*. San Francisco: Jossey-Bass.

Denzin, N.K. (1983) 'Interpretive interactionism', in G. Morgan (ed.), *Beyond Method: Strategies for Social Research*. Beverly Hills, CA: Sage.

Dobbert, M.L. (1982) *Ethnographic Research: Theory and Application for Modern Schools and Societies.* New York: Praeger.

Dwyer, D.C., Lee, G.V., Rowan, B. and Bossert, S.T. (1982) 'The Principal's Role in instructional management: five participant observation studies of principals in action.' Unpublished manuscript, Far West Laboratory for Educational Research and Development, San Francisco.

Feigenbaum, E.A. and McCorduck, P. (1983) *The Fifth Generation: Artificial Intelligence and Japan's Computer Challenge to the World.* Reading, MA: Addison-Wesley.

Fetterman, D.M. (1982) 'Ethnography in educational research: the dynamics of diffusion', in D.M. Fetterman (ed.), *Ethnography in Educational Evaluation.* Beverly Hills, CA: Sage.

Filstead, W.J. (1979) 'Qualitative methods: a needed perspective in evaluation research', in T.D. Cook and C.S. Reichardt (eds), *Qualitative and Quantitative Methods in Evaluation Research.* Beverly Hills, CA: Sage.

Firestone, W.A. and Herriott, R.E. (1984) 'Multisite qualitative policy research: some design and implementation issues', in D.M. Fetterman (ed.), *Ethnography in Educational Evaluation.* Beverly Hills, CA: Sage.

Geertz, C. (1973) 'Thick description: toward an interpretive theory of culture', in C. Geertz (ed.), *The Interpretation of Cultures.* New York: Basic Books.

Glaser, B. and Strauss, A. (1967) *The Discovery of Grounded Theory.* Chicago: Aldine Publishing.

Goetz, J.P. and LeCompte, M.D. (1984) *Ethnography and Qualitative Design in Education Research.* Orlando, FL: Academic Press.

Guba, E.G. (1981) 'Criteria for assessing the trustworthiness of naturalistic inquiry', *Educational Communication and Technology Journal,* 29: 79–92.

Guba, E.G. and Lincoln, Y.S. (1981) *Effective Evaluation: Improving the Usefulness of Evaluation Results Through Responsive and Naturalistic Approaches.* San Francisco: Jossey-Bass.

Guba, E.G. and Lincoln, Y.S. (1982) 'Epistemological and methodological bases of naturalistic inquiry', *Educational Communication and Technology Journal,* 30: 233–52.

Huberman, A.M. and Miles, M.B. (1984) *Innovation Up Close: How School Improvement Works.* New York: Plenum Press.

Jackson, P.W. (1968) *Life in Classrooms.* New York: Holt, Rinehart & Winston.

Kennedy, M.M. (1979) 'Generalizing from single case studies', *Evaluation Quarterly,* 3 (4): 661–78.

Kirk, J. and Miller, M.L. (1986) *Reliability and Validity in Qualitative Research.* Beverly Hills, CA: Sage.

Krathwohl, D.R. (1985) *Social and Behavioral Science Research: A New Framework for Conceptualizing, Implementing, and Evaluating Research Studies.* San Francisco: Jossey-Bass.

Lawler, R.W. and Yazdani, M. (eds) (1987) *Artificial Intelligence and Education: Learning Environments and Tutoring Systems* (Vol. 1). Norwood, NJ: Ablex Publishing.

Lucas, W. (1974) *The Case Survey Method: Aggregating Case Experience.* Santa Monica, CA: Rand.

Miles, M. and Huberman, A. (1984a) 'Drawing valid meaning from qualitative data: toward a shared craft', *Educational Researcher,* 13: 20–30.

Miles, M. and Huberman, A. (1984b) *Qualitative Data Analysis: A Sourcebook of New Methods.* Newbury Park, CA: Sage.

Noblit, G.W. and Hare, R.D. (1988) *Meta-ethnography: Synthesizing Qualitative Studies.* Beverly Hills, CA: Sage.

Patton, M.O. (1980) *Qualitative Evaluation Methods.* Beverly Hills, CA: Sage.

Peshkin, A. (1978) *Growing Up American: Schooling and the Survival of Community.* Chicago: University of Chicago Press.

Peshkin, A. (1982) 'The researcher and subjectivity: reflections on an ethnography of school and community', in G. Spindler (ed.), *Doing the Ethnography of Schooling: Educational Anthropology in Action.* New York: Holt, Rinehart & Winston.

Pettigrew, T. (1967) 'Social evaluation theory: convergences and applications', in D. Levine (ed.), *Nebraska Symposium on Motivation* (Vol. 5). Lincoln: University of Nebraska Press.

Pettigrew, T. (1969) 'Racially separate or together?', *Journal of Social Issues,* 25: 43–69.

Phi Delta Kappan (1980) *Why Do Some Urban Schools Succeed? The Phi Delta Kappa Study of Exceptional Urban Elementary Schools.* Bloomington: Phi Delta Kappa and Indiana University.

Ragin, C.C. (1987) *The Comparative Method: Moving beyond Qualitative and Quantitative Strategies.* Berkeley: University of California Press.

Reichardt, C.S. and Cook, T.D. (1979) 'Beyond qualitative *versus* quantitative methods', in T.D. Cook and C.S. Reichardt (eds), *Qualitative and Quantitative Methods in Evaluation Research.* Beverly Hills, CA: Sage.

Rutter, M., Maughan, B., Mortimore, P., Ouston, J. and Smith, A. (1979) *Fifteen Thousand Hours: Secondary Schools and Their Effects on Children.* Cambridge, MA: Harvard University Press.

Sagar, H.A. and Schofield, J.W. (1980) 'Racial and behavioural cues in black and white children's perceptions of ambiguously aggressive acts', *Journal of Personality and Social Psychology,* 39: 590–598.

Schofield, J.W. (1979) 'The impact of positively structured contact on intergroup behavior: does it last under adverse conditions?', *Social Psychology Quarterly,* 42: 280–4.

Schofield, J.W. (1981) 'Competitive and complementary identities: images and interaction in an interracial school', in S. Asher and J. Gottman (eds), *The Development of Children's Friendship.* New York: Cambridge University Press.

Schofield, J.W. (1986) 'Causes and consequences of the colorblind perspective', in S. Gaertner and J. Dovidio (eds), *Prejudice, Discrimination and Racism: Theory and Practice.* New York: Academic Press.

Schofield, J.W. (1989) *Black and White in School: Trust, Tension, or Tolerance?* New York: Teachers College Press. (Original work published 1982).

Schofield, J.W. and Evans-Rhodes, D. (1989) 'Artificial intelligence in the classroom: the impact of a computer-based tutor on teachers and students'. Paper presented at the 4th International Conference on Artificial Intelligence in Education, Amsterdam, The Netherlands, May.

Schofield, J.W. and Francis, W.D. (1982) 'An observational study of peer interaction in racially-mixed "accelerated" classrooms', *The Journal of Education Psychology,* 74: 722–32.

Schofield, J.W. and Sagar, H.A. (1977) 'Peer interaction patterns in an integrated middle school', *Sociometry,* 40: 130–8.

Schofield, J.W. and Sagar, H.A. (1983) 'Desegregation, school practices and student race relations', in C. Rossell and W. Hawley (eds), *The Consequences of School Desegregation.* Philadelphia, PA: Temple University Press.

Schofield, J.W. and Verban, D. (1988) 'Computer usage in the teaching of mathematics: issues which need answers', in D. Grouws and T. Cooney (eds), *Effective Mathematics Teaching.* Hillsdale, NJ: Erlbaum.

Shaughnessy, J.J. and Zechmeister, E.B. (1985) *Research Methods in Psychology.* New York: Knopf.

Slavin, R.E. (1980) 'Cooperative learning', *Review of Educational Research,* 50: 315–42.

Smith, A.G. and Robbins, A.E. (1984) 'Multimethod policy research: a case study of structure and flexibility', in D.M. Fetterman (ed.), *Ethnography in Educational Evaluation.* Beverly Hills, CA: Sage.

Smith, H.W. (1975) *Strategies of Social Research: The Methodological Imagination.* Englewood Cliffs, NJ: Prentice-Hall.

Spindler, G. (1982) 'General introduction', in G. Spindler (ed.), *Doing the Ethnography of Schooling: Educational Anthropology in Action.* New York: Holt Rinehart & Winston.

Stake, R.E. (1978) 'The case-study method in social inquiry', *Educational Researcher,* 7: 5–8.

Stephan, W.J. (1985) 'Intergroup relations', in G. Lindzey and E. Aronson (eds), *The Handbook of Social Psychology* (Vol. 2). New York: Random House.

Strauss, A.L. (1987) *Qualitative Analysis for Social Scientists.* Cambridge: Cambridge University Press.

Walker, D.F. (1984) 'Promise, potential and pragmatism: computers in high school', *Institute for Research in Educational Finance and Governance Policy Notes,* 5: 3–4.

Weber, G. (1971) *Inner-City Children Can be Taught to Read: Four Successful Schools.* Washington, DC: Council for Basic Education.

Whyte, W.F. (1984) *Learning from the Field: A Guide from Experience.* Beverly Hills, CA: Sage.

Wolcott, H.F. (1973) *The Man in the Principal's Office: An Ethnography.* New York: Holt, Rinehart & Winston.

Wolcott, H.F. (1975) 'Criteria for an ethnographic approach to research in schools', *Human Organization,* 34: 111–27.

Wolcott, H.F. (1982) 'Mirrors, models, and monitors: educator adaptations of the ethnographic innovation', in G. Spindler (ed.), *Doing the Ethnography of Schooling: Educational Anthropology in Action.* New York: Holt Rinehart & Winston.

Yin, R.K. (1981) 'The case study crisis: some answers', *Administrative Science Quarterly,* 26: 58–64.

Yin, R.K. (1984) *Case Study Research: Design and Methods.* Beverly Hills, CA: Sage.

Yin, R.K. and Heald, K.A. (1975) 'Using the case survey method to analyze policy studies', *Administrative Science Quarterly,* 20: 371–81.

Yin, R.K. and Yates, D. (1975) *Street-level Governments: Assessing Decentralization and Urban Services.* Lexington, MA: D.C. Heath.

CHAPTER 5

CASE STUDY AND GENERALIZATION

Roger Gomm, Martyn Hammersley and Peter Foster

Case study research has often been criticized on the grounds that its findings are not generalizable, especially by comparison with those of survey research. The response of some case study researchers to this criticism has been to deny that their work is designed to produce scientific generalizations. Thus, Stake argues that case studies facilitate learning on the part of those who use them; and that this involves 'naturalistic generalization', a quite different kind of generalization from that which is characteristic of science (Stake, Chapter 1). Following much the same line, Lincoln and Guba question the appropriateness of law-like generalizations in social science, and argue that what case studies offer are 'working hypotheses' whose appropriateness for understanding other cases (that is, their 'transferability') can only be assessed by comparing the 'fit' – the similarities – between source and target cases (Lincoln and Guba, Chapter 2).[1]

In this paper we will begin by examining the arguments for naturalistic generalization and transferability. We will conclude that while these notions capture one way in which case study research may be used – by other researchers as well as by lay people – they do not offer a substitute for the drawing of general conclusions in research reports. Indeed, we will suggest that to deny the possibility of case studies providing the basis for empirical generalizations is to accept the views of their critics too readily. We also point out that, in practice, much case study research has in fact put forward empirical generalizations. Indeed, we suggest that in at least one respect this is unavoidable. We draw a distinction between generalization across and within cases, though we also note the similarities between the two; and we outline the strategies case study researchers can use to make reasonably secure generalizations of each kind. At the same time, we emphasize that the necessary precautions have not always been taken, and that the danger of error in drawing general conclusions from a small number of cases must not be underestimated. We will illustrate these points with examples from case study research in education; but we claim that our arguments are applicable more widely!

Are general conclusions necessary?

As we have noted, some case study researchers suggest that the goal of their work is not the production of general conclusions, and that this does not detract from its value. In this spirit, Stake (1994) argues for what he calls 'intrinsic case study', which involves the investigation of particular cases for their own sake.[2] There is some justification for this argument. Sometimes, the case(s) researchers study are of sufficient interest in themselves to a target audience for the findings to have intrinsic value. For instance, with much evaluation research, a central concern is with whether a policy or programme implemented in a particular place achieved its goals or produced desirable effects. Furthermore, case study research that is not evaluative can also have intrinsic interest. This is true where cases are significant enough, or large enough, to be of widespread national or international relevance. For example, a study of decision-making procedures in the Cabinet room of the British government would surely have sufficient intrinsic relevance, obviating any need to try to generalize the findings to other governments.

However, it seems to us that there are severe limits on the applicability of this justification for case study research. Thus, most evaluation research is concerned not just with whether the policy or programme studied has worked in the case investigated, but also with whether it would work elsewhere. Furthermore, most of the cases investigated by social researchers do not have intrinsic interest for more than a very small potential audience. Indeed, in most studies cases are anonymized, which undermines any claim about their intrinsic interest. As a result, one way or another, most case study researchers appeal to the general relevance of the cases they study in order to establish the value of their work.

There are several different ways in which they do this. One is the argument that the case investigated is a microcosm of some larger system or of a whole society: that what is found there is in some sense symptomatic of what is going on more generally. In one of its forms, this is what Geertz (1973) refers to, dismissively, as the 'Jonesville-is-the-USA' model. Lincoln and Guba's appeal to the metaphor of holographic film also seems to imply this idea (see Chapter 2). And it is analogous to the figure of speech that literary theorists refer to as synechdoche – the use of a part of something to stand for the whole – which is frequently used in qualitative research (see Atkinson, 1990, pp. 51–3). This idea is presented explicitly in Denzin's account of 'interpretive interactionism'. In this approach: 'Each person, and each relationship, studied is assumed to be a *universal singular*, or a single instance of the universal themes that structure the postmodern period' (Denzin, 1989, p. 139). Yet, while this idea of the case as microcosm has a long history, it has never been supplied with a convincing justification (Hammersley, 1992, pp. 16–19). After all, any social phenomenon occurs in a specific context, and is likely to be the product of multiple causal processes. While it may well exemplify general patterns, establishing that it does – *and what these are* – requires comparative investigation; its universal significance cannot be taken for granted.

A different argument for the general relevance of case study findings calls on what Stake (see Chapter 1) refers to as 'naturalistic generalization' or what Lincoln and Guba (see Chapter 2) call 'transferability' (see also Walker, 1978: 166–7; Connolly, 1998). What these ideas imply is that readers of case study reports must themselves determine whether the findings are applicable to other cases than those which the researcher studied. Here, as Lincoln and Guba comment, the burden of proof is on the user rather than on the original researcher; though the latter is responsible for providing a description of the case(s) studied that is sufficiently 'thick' to allow users to assess the degree of similarity between the case(s) investigated and those to which the findings are to be applied (Guba and Lincoln, 1989, p. 241).

The idea of naturalistic generalization is an important one. There are good reasons to think that we all engage in this routinely in everyday life. Donmoyer (see Chapter 3) underlines the point by seeking to clarify what is involved through appeal to a theory which was designed to represent the essential nature of children's learning: Piaget's schema theory. Furthermore, case study research is clearly capable of contributing to the resources available for naturalistic generalization by providing vicarious experience. As Donmoyer notes, 'case study research might be used to expand and enrich the repertoire of social constructions available to practitioners and others' (pp. 51–2). At the same time, it seems to us that two questions must be answered before we can conclude that facilitating naturalistic generalization should replace the more conventional function of research in producing general knowledge – knowledge about broad categories, or populations, of social phenomena. First, it needs to be shown that such conventional, general knowledge is out of the reach of case study work. If it is not, then case studies may be able to serve both functions. Second, it is necessary to establish that case study research can provide an effective basis for readers themselves to draw conclusions about other cases, and that it can do this better than alternative sources of vicarious experience, such as practitioners' reports of their own experience or fictional accounts.

In our view, the advocates of naturalistic generalization and transferability have not dealt effectively with either of these issues. As regards the first, Lincoln and Guba (see Chapter 2) reject the possibility of generalization by researchers, on the grounds that it involves unacceptable assumptions: determinism; the possibility of inductive logic; the idea that the validity of accounts can be context-free; the existence of exception-less laws; and reductionism. In short, they deny that the social world is governed by laws, and therefore rule out the possibility of generalization. Yet, much depends on what is meant by 'law' and 'generalization' here. Indeed, the concept of transferability itself assumes that the social world is lawful, in the sense that there is some order in it. Lincoln and Guba argue that transferability depends on similarity: in other words, a pattern of events that occurred in one case recurs in the other. Moreover, for this to be possible, the pattern must be a stable feature of the world, or of some specific part of it. If this were not so, the original situation could tell us nothing about the new one. Of course, such lawfulness does not have to be deterministic, in the sense that everything which happens could not have been otherwise; nor does it imply reductionism. But these features are not essential for researchers to draw more conventional kinds of generalization either.

A further problem with transferability as a substitute for the pursuit of general conclusions is that it provides no guidance for researchers about *which* cases to study (in effect, it implies that any case may be as good as any other in this respect).[3] Similarly, it cannot supply much guidance to potential users of case study research, who will need to know *which* of the very large number of studies available can illuminate the particular problems with which they are concerned. Moreover, transferability is said to depend on 'fit', but there are difficult questions about how this is to be assessed. And these are exacerbated by Donmoyer's argument that difference can be as important as similarity in making one case significant for another (see Chapter 3).

There are also problems about the nature of the 'thick description' that is believed to be necessary in order to facilitate naturalistic generalization or transferability. In its original sense, derived from the philosopher Gilbert Ryle, thick description was contrasted with the thin descriptions put forward by those who believed that human actions could be represented exhaustively through description of physical behaviour (Ryle, 1971a, 1971b). Ryle shows that some activities are 'intention parasitic': for instance, we can only distinguish between a twitch and a wink in terms of some notion of intention. Furthermore, it would be quite wrong to describe a wink as twitch-plus-intention; or, by implication, any other action as a composite of behaviour plus meaning. Geertz uses this argument against those social scientists who would seek to understand human behaviour as the product of laws; but in the process he extends the meaning of 'thick description', suggesting that actions can only be understood in the context of narrative accounts which draw on the whole culture in which the actions occur. This indicates that thickness is a matter of degree. And Lincoln and Guba recognize this, suggesting that the issue of what constitutes proper thick description has not been completely resolved, and that it may never be resolved because 'the criteria which separate relevant from irrelevant descriptors are still largely undefined' (Guba and Lincoln, 1989, p. 241). More to the point, what are and are not relevant descriptors for facilitating transferability depends on assumptions about the respects in which other cases are likely to be similar to or different from the one(s) studied. Here, implicit generalizations are being smuggled in via the back door. In the same way, as soon as one argues that there are reasons for studying one case rather than another (reasons that go beyond personal preference or convenience), assumptions are being made about the relationship between that case and others; assumptions that ought at some point to be subjected to empirical test. *Ad hoc* judgements of usability are no substitute for this.[4]

Another way of formulating this problem is by looking at the question of what a case is. Some writers, such as Stake, argue that cases exist independently of, and prior to, the process of investigation. Indeed, Stake argues that what case study amounts to is a commitment to studying cases in their own terms, rather than in terms of prior categorizations: to documenting their uniqueness. Yet there is a semantic problem here; and it points to a deeper methodological one. The very meaning of the word 'case' implies that what it refers to is a *case of* something.[5] In other words, we necessarily identify cases in terms of general categories. Of course, those categories may be relatively mundane ones, rather than abstractly theoretical in character; but the idea that somehow cases can be identified independently of our orientation to them is false. It is also misleading to talk of the uniqueness of cases without being clear about what this term means. Sometimes it is used to refer simply to particularity; but in this sense all individual phenomena are unique. Moreover, while we may argue that some particulars are more distinctive than others, we can only identify their distinctiveness on the basis of a notion of what is typical or representative of some categorial group or population.

In summary, then, while *some* case study research may be able to avoid 'the problem of generalization' because the case(s) studied have sufficient intrinsic relevance, this is not true of most of it. Nor are we convinced by the justifications for case study research which rely on ideas about microcosms and universal singulars. Furthermore, while naturalistic generalization and transferability point to one way in which case studies – and indeed other kinds of research – may be used, they do not provide a sound basis for the design, or justification, of case study research. Indeed, these notions seem to relax the requirements on researchers to proceed in principled ways, transferring this responsibility to readers. In our view, then, most case study research must be directed towards drawing general conclusions. In the next section we will examine how this can be done.

Two ways of drawing general conclusions

There seem to us to be just two effective strategies for drawing conclusions from some smaller set of cases to a larger set. Furthermore, these are the ones used by experimental and survey researchers. We shall refer to these as theoretical inference and empirical generalization, respectively.[6] We believe that a great deal of confusion has been caused by a failure to make this distinction.

Theoretical inference involves reaching conclusions about what always happens, or what happens with a given degree of probability, in a certain type of theoretically defined situation. For example, teacher expectation theory holds that, other things being equal, where a teacher has high expectations of a child's academic performance, and these expectations are communicated to the child, the latter's performance will be enhanced by comparison with that of children to whom the teacher has conveyed lower expectations (see Rogers, 1982). So, the aim in research directed towards drawing conclusions on the basis of theoretical inference is to identify a set of relationships among variables that are universal, in the sense of occurring everywhere that specified conditions hold, other things being equal (that is, wherever there are not countervailing or overdetermining factors). The experimental method facilitates achievement of this by creating cases in which the focal variables take contrasting values, and where the values of other relevant variables are held constant. And, if and when a relationship is found, there will usually be subsequent attempts to replicate it, so as to ensure that it was not a methodological artefact.

By contrast, survey researchers typically rely on what we shall call empirical generalization in order to produce general findings. This involves drawing inferences about features of a larger but finite population of cases from the study of a sample drawn from that population. At its simplest, this amounts to reaching conclusions about the *distribution* of particular features within a population. For example, the concern might be with the relative prevalence of mixed-ability grouping, setting, streaming or tracking in a particular population of secondary schools. However, survey researchers also frequently investigate the extent to which there is *co-occurrence* or *co-variation* of particular features within cases belonging to a population; generalizing on the basis of information about the co-occurrence or co-variation of these features within a sample drawn from that population. Co-occurrence/co-variation is of interest, of course, because it may be evidence of a causal relationship, and hence the basis for theoretical inference.

As we have seen, many case study researchers explicitly reject empirical generalization as an inappropriate goal. Yet, if one looks at examples of case study research, it is not uncommon to find that generalizations of this kind are presented (see Hammersley, 1992, Chaps 1 and 5). Furthermore, while it is possible for case study work to have general relevance without empirical generalization across cases, through reliance on theoretical inference, there is one respect in which all case study research tends to involve empirical generalization: cases are often so large that it is not possible to collect data about them as a whole. Instead, parts of them are investigated and the findings generalized to the whole case.

We shall look first at empirical generalization from case(s) studied to a larger population; and then at generalization within cases. (We discuss theoretical inference in Chapter 12.)

Empirical generalization from studied to unstudied cases

Denial of the capacity of case study research to support empirical generalization often seems to rest on the mistaken assumption that this form of generalization requires statistical sampling. This restricts the idea of representation to its statistical version; it confuses the task of empirical generalization with the use of statistical techniques to achieve that goal. While those techniques are a very effective basis for generalization, they are not essential. After all, as noted earlier, we all engage in naturalistic generalization routinely in the course of our lives, and this may take the form of empirical generalization as well as of informal theoretical inference. Given this, there is no reason in principle why case study research should not provide the basis for empirical generalization. What is also true, though, is that our everyday generalizations are often subject to high levels of error (Sadler, 1981); whereas statistical techniques, if properly applied, guarantee a relatively high and known level of probable accuracy. The questions that arise, then, are as follows. First, are there ways in which case study researchers can improve significantly on the typical accuracy of informal empirical generalizations, even if this still does not match the performance of statistical techniques? And, second, do case study researchers use these strategies?

It is important to recognize that the greater the heterogeneity of a population the more problematic are empirical generalizations based on a single case, or a handful of cases. If we could reasonably assume that the population were composed of more or less identical units, then there would be no problem. However, this seems not to be true of most of the phenomena that interest social researchers.[7] Of course, it is not so much heterogeneity in general that is a problem here, but any heterogeneity which is likely to have consequences for what is the focus of the research. Simple random sampling is an attempt to solve this problem by taking account of *all* forms of heterogeneity. The large number of data points, and their random distribution across the population, produces a high probability that major forms of heterogeneity within the population will be reflected more or less accurately in the sample.[8] By contrast, case studies take a great deal of data from a few data points in a population, perhaps just one. Even if these data points, or this data point, were chosen at random, the chances are that the data collected would not be representative of the population as a whole. Indeed, as Schofield (Chapter 4) points out, it is actually very unlikely that any case study will be close to the norm on a number of dimensions concurrently. Nevertheless, it is possible for case study researchers to try to take account of probable relevant heterogeneity within the population with which they are concerned in at least two, complementary, ways: by using theoretical ideas and information about the case and the population in their analyses; and by selecting cases for study on the basis of such ideas and information.[9]

Collecting and presenting information about the case and the population

One way in which case study researchers can seek to check and improve the quality of their empirical generalizations, and provide evidence in support of them for readers, is to consider the relevant respects in which the target population might be heterogeneous. In other words, we need to think about how the case(s) we are studying might be typical or atypical in relevant respects – or, indeed, of what population it (or they) could be typical; and to use what is actually known about the cases and the wider population to get a fix on where the former fits in terms of the diversity likely to be present in the latter. In short, it is necessary to compare the characteristics of the case(s) being studied with available information about the population to which generalization is intended. Very often, of course, information about that population concerning the specific focus of the research will not be available; but information may be available about what seem likely to be related dimensions of heterogeneity.[10]

In order to illustrate this point, we will take the example of case study research on inequalities in educational performance among ethnic minority groups in Britain. Most of the studies in this area present themselves, and have usually been interpreted, as documenting processes going on in the whole school system. A common claim is that differential treatment by teachers of pupils from different 'racial' groups has produced inequalities in educational performance among these groups at the national level. This is the conclusion of Gillborn and Gipps' (1996) review of research in this field, which provides substantial information about national and local differences in performance among ethnic groups, and links these to case studies that have claimed to document differential treatment of ethnic groups within schools.

While by no means all the information that would be useful for addressing this issue is available, a substantial body of relevant secondary data can be found in government- and Local Education Authority-produced statistics on schools and educational performance (see Mackinnon et al., 1995; Skellington and Morris, 1992); and in the reports of surveys, such as the Youth Cohort Study (Drew and Gray, 1990; Drew, 1995), those covering the Inner London Education Authority area

(ILEA, 1987; Kysel, 1988; Mortimore et al., 1988), and Smith and Tomlinson's work on *The School Effect* (1989). Although these data are not all statistically representative of schools or students, even in England, they contain enough data to enable judgements to be made about how representative particular schools might be in some relevant respects, such as the social class and ability profiles of their intake or the level of their pupils' educational achievement; or at least about whether the school (or schools) studied are likely to be significantly atypical in these respects.

Yet, if we look at the studies of school process and ethnic inequality referred to by Gillborn and Gipps, we find that they make little or no use of this information to assess representativeness; do not provide much detail about the schools and pupils studied in terms of relevant, likely dimensions of heterogeneity; and do not show much awareness of the dangers of generalization. Nor do Gillborn and Gipps themselves address the typicality of the schools subjected to case study as regards the whole population of schools in England. In particular, they do not explore the issue of whether differences in outcome across ethnic groups are a product of between-school rather than within-school processes (see Foster, 1990, Chaps 9 and 10). Moreover, what information is supplied suggests that most of the schools studied are ones in which there is higher than average representation of working-class children, and/or are schools whose overall levels of pupil achievement are below the national average. To the extent that this is true, generalization from the findings of these studies to the population of schools in England and Wales as a whole involves substantial risk of error (see Gomm et al., 1998).

The points we have made here about case study research on ethnic minority pupils apply to work in many other fields as well. Without knowledge of the location of the cases studied in terms of relevant dimensions of likely heterogeneity in the target population, we cannot know how far empirical generalizations drawn from them will be sound. Such information is often not provided in case studies that nevertheless seek to justify their relevance on the basis of empirical generalization. So, we are suggesting that where information about the larger population (or about overlapping populations) is available, it should be used. If it is not available, then the potential risks involved in generalization still need to be noted, preferably via specification of likely types of heterogeneity that could render the findings unrepresentative.

Systematic selection of cases

A complementary approach that case study researchers can use to deal with the problem of empirical generalization is systematic selection of cases for study. Several sampling strategies are available here. An obvious one is to select a case that is, as far as possible, typical in relevant respects. Whether this is possible, even in principle, will depend on the focus of the research, on the level of relevant heterogeneity in the population, and on the availability of information about this. So, this is not a strategy that is always feasible, nor is it easy to implement. However, as Schofield has noted (Chapter 4, pp. 77–8), far too often cases seem to be selected solely on the basis of convenience, and turn out to be atypical in important respects.[11] Another strategy is to study a small sample of cases that have been selected to cover the extremes of expected relevant heterogeneity within the population. It is worth noting that here cases do not all have to be studied in the same depth: one or two may be investigated in detail, with others examined more superficially to check the likely generalizability of findings from the main case study. We should also remember that it is possible to combine case study work with surveys that are designed to provide some assessment of the typicality, in relevant respects, of the cases that *have* been investigated in depth. Equally, the survey could come first, providing a basis for the selection of cases.

Furthermore, while the simultaneous investigation of multiple, systematically selected cases will often be difficult, it is possible for subsequent investigations to build on earlier ones by providing additional cases, so as to construct a sample over time that *would* allow effective generalization. At present, this kind of cumulation is unusual. Even when case studies are concerned with generalizing to the same (or a similar) population as earlier ones, the cases are not usually selected in such a way as to complement previous work, and the research is often pursued in a manner that is sufficiently different to make comparison impossible because relevant data are missing. Furthermore, as already mentioned, information that would enable readers to carry out meta-analysis is often not supplied.[12]

Schofield has also pointed out that the population that is the target for empirical generalization can take different forms. It may be an actually existing population of cases, but it could also be a population that seems likely to, or might, exist in the future. Which of these is the target will clearly have implications for the cases that should be selected for study, if one wishes the findings to be generalizable. As regards studying what *may* or *could* be, Schofield identifies a number of case selection strategies. One of these is to investigate a case which represents the 'leading edge' of change. A classic example of this is Cicourel and Kitsuse's (1973) study of Lakeside High, a school that they point out was unrepresentative of US high schools at the time they studied it. This was true not just because it served an exclusively high-income neighbourhood, but also because of its large size, bureaucratic structure and professionalized counselling service. However, they argued that this school was in the vanguard of changes that were taking place among US high schools, so that more and more schools would become similar to it in important respects in the future. Thus, they claimed, it offered a good basis for generalization to a future population.[13]

A related strategy also involves the selection of a case where a particular kind of development is unusually advanced, but here the illumination desired is retrospective rather than prospective. Studying a case that is likely to display the highest (or the lowest) incidence or intensity of some feature in a population, we can assume that the rest of the population is below (or above) the level identified. An example of this strategy is Foster's (1990) investigation of multicultural/anti-racist education, in which Milltown School was selected because it was in the forefront of policy in this field. The assumption seems to have been that, whatever the level of racism found in this school, it would be even higher elsewhere.[14] Of course, the illumination provided by this strategy is heavily dependent on what is found. In the case of Foster's work, he discovered little evidence of teacher racism, and this undercut the basis for generalization in these terms.[15]

It is important to underline, then, that to the extent that there is substantial heterogeneity in the target population, no case within it preserves all the features of the whole. It is a fragment, with a distinctive location that shapes its character.[16] Only if this is taken into account can case study research serve as an opportunity to understand what goes on elsewhere. In order to draw sound empirical generalizations on the basis of case studies, it is essential to use what information is available about the cases studied and the target population; to recognize and signal possible risks to sound generalization of the findings; and to organize the selection of cases for investigation in such a manner as to allow for relevant heterogeneity.

Generalization within the case

We turn now to generalization *within* the case. As we noted earlier, the cases studied by case study researchers are often sufficiently large that they cannot be studied comprehensively. Instead, investigation has to be selective, and reliance is thereby placed on internal generalization.[17] This can occur along several dimensions.

One dimension is time (see Ball, 1983, pp. 81–3). It is not uncommon for researchers who have studied processes going on within a particular site to treat their case as if it were identical with that site. This is potentially misleading, however. For one thing, cases are never identical with the settings to which they relate: they involve emphasis only on those aspects of these that are relevant to the research focus. Another important point is that the temporal boundaries of a case will rarely be identical to the 'life' of the setting concerned. Furthermore, very often, the temporal scope of the case will be longer than the period about which data have actually been collected. For instance, when a case study researcher collects data in a school for a few months, he or she usually treats those data as holding true for the relevant aspects of the school for a longer time period than this; perhaps treating them as stable over a period of several years, or as characteristic of that school in some deeper sense. In fact, case study researchers rarely make clear what they take to be the temporal boundaries of the cases they have studied.

To the extent that the duration of the case extends beyond the period about which data are collected, generalization over time is involved; and evidence may be necessary to support this. Yet, this is rarely provided. Thus, it is not unusual for case studies of schools to focus on one year-group or cohort of students and to assume that the experience of these students is representative of other cohorts, past and future. For instance, studies of the early years of secondary schooling may proceed as if the cohort of pupils studied will achieve the same pattern of results as the contemporary (and unstudied) final year-group have done. Yet, it cannot be assumed that one cohort will adequately represent others, in this or other respects. School effectiveness researchers have cautioned against assuming that the relative exami- nation performance of schools is stable over time. Indeed, they have shown that there is some year-on-year variation in league-table posi- tioning (Thomas et al., 1995). The same body of research also indicates that variation in performance in particular subjects is even more labile between years (Sammons et al., 1995). And, given that different kinds of students seem to achieve differentially in different subjects, the pat- tern of achievement for one cohort of students may be very different from that of another in the same school *even when each cohort achieves the same overall examination score*. Of course, teachers themselves also frequently note substantial differences between cohorts of students year-on-year in this and in other respects; and these differences may relate to matters that are relevant to the research focus.

Another aspect of generalization within cases is that it often relies on observations that took place at a number of sampling points, rather than on continuous observation over a lengthy period. And, unless the temporal organization of settings is taken into account, there is a dan- ger of error here too. A classic illustration is provided by Berlak et al.'s study of progressive primary school practice in Britain in the 1970s (Berlak and Berlak, 1981; Berlak et al., 1975). They argued that previ- ous American accounts had been inaccurate because observation had been brief and had tended to take place in the middle of the week, not on Mondays or Fridays. On the basis of these observations, the inference had been drawn that in progressive classrooms children simply chose what they wanted to do and got on with it. As Berlak et al. document, however, what typically happened was that the teachers set out the week's work on Mondays, and on Fridays they checked that it had been completed satisfactorily. Thus, earlier studies were based on false temporal generalizations within the cases they investigated.[18]

So, unless case study researchers take account of the temporal organization of the cases they are investigating, there is a danger of erroneous inferences from what they observe (or from information received) about what goes on routinely in those cases. The longer the period of time spent in the field the better, of course; but it may also be necessary to collect and present data about points in time that cover some of the internal temporal heterogeneity operating in the case. Also, it may be possible to check findings against information about what occurred before the fieldwork began, or to return to the situation briefly after the main period of fieldwork is ended to check that the analysis still holds in key respects.

Time is only one dimension across which there is often generalization within cases. Even within the period of data collection, the researcher cannot be everywhere at once. In other words, there is a synchronic as well as a diachronic dimension to generalization within the case. One example of this is where statements are made about all the teachers in a school on the basis of data that relate to only some, often a minority, of them. And, putting these two dimensions of generalization together, case studies may rely on information about a small number of teachers within a school, relating to a relatively short period, and generalize from this to the behaviour of all of them over a long period. Needless to say, the narrower the base for such generalization, and the more relevant heterogeneity there is within the case, the less likely it is to be accurate.[19]

The problem of synchronic generalization is, if anything, even more significant in relation to pupils: since there are a greater number of them than teachers in any school. It is not uncommon for conclusions to be drawn about a whole year-group on the basis of data relating to a minority of its members. An example is Willis's (1977) study of boys in the fourth year of a secondary modern school. This was based very largely on data from around twelve 'lads', and most of the data reported in the book come from a sub-sample of these. Willis does not seem to have given sufficient attention to the dangers of generalizing from this sample, nor does he provide readers with the information about his research that would enable them to judge whether his internal generalizations were sound. Thus, it is difficult to decide whether his account is an accurate portrayal of all the pupils who form part of the case studied; indeed, it seems rather unlikely that it is. Ball's (1981) *Beachside Comprehensive* raises the same problem, but he provides information that allows the reader to check the extent to which the two case study classes he studied over two years are representative of the whole year-group in relevant respects (see Gomm, 1996). It is therefore possible to make a much better judgement about the validity of this aspect of his study than is true of some other case study research.

There is also likely to be variation in the behaviour of both teachers and pupils across different contexts within a school. While most contacts between members of the two groups probably occur in classrooms, they also meet one another in other places as well: in assembly halls, dining rooms, corridors, on games fields, and so on. Thus, in order to generalize about staff–student (and, indeed, student–student) relationships, it may be necessary to sample across these contexts (see Thorne, 1993). Nor should we assume that all classrooms are the same in relevant respects. Teacher–pupil relationships are likely to vary across mathematics classrooms, drama studios and science laboratories, for example.

Generalization within the case is often unavoidable, then; and it can be an uncertain business. Moreover, often it does not seem to be given the attention it deserves. Certainly, it is rare for sufficient information to be provided about the boundaries of the case studied, and about the data collected, for readers to make a reasonable assessment of the likely validity of the internal generalization that has taken place.

Conclusion

We have argued in this paper that generalization is not an issue that can be dismissed as irrelevant by case study researchers. It can be of significance for their work in two respects. First of all, it is one means by which they may seek to argue for the general relevance of the findings they have produced. Second, much case study research involves generalization within the case(s) investigated. In both respects case study researchers do not always meet what would seem to be the necessary methodological requirements. As regards the first form of generalization, they are often not very clear about the basis on which they are claiming the general relevance of their findings; or, when empirical generalization is involved, about what population is the target. Furthermore, effective use is not always made of relevant information that is available about the population to which generalization is being made. It is also rare for cases to be selected in such a way as to cover significant likely dimensions of heterogeneity in the population; or for much evidence to be provided in support of claims that the case(s) studied are typical (or atypical) in relevant respects. As regards generalization *within* the case, there is often a lack of clarity about the boundaries of the case, and sometimes the evidential base used for internal generalization is obscure, and/or seems likely to be inadequate. In our view, in all these respects more attention needs to be given to the requirements of empirical generalization in case study research.

Notes

1 Other advocates of case study research have responded to the challenge about generalizability by arguing that the focus of such research is the development and testing of theories. This argument is to be found in several of the chapters in the second half of this book, and is discussed by us in Chapter 13.

2 There is some ambiguity in Stake's position. He also recognizes that case studies can be instrumental rather than intrinsic, and in an outline of the 'major conceptual responsibilities' of case study inquiry he lists the final one as 'developing assertions or generalizations about the case' (Stake, 1994, p. 244).

3 This defect is analogous to a problem that Rescher (1978) has identified with Popper's view that any falsifiable hypothesis is worth testing. The question arises: What are the chances that scientists will select productive ones from the infinite number of possible hypotheses available?

4 Tripp (1985) recognizes this problem and advocates the development of a comprehensive theory in terms of which 'fit' can be determined. This effectively reduces transferability to what we will refer to in the next section as theoretical inference.

5 The terms 'instance' and 'example' have the same logical grammar.

6 This terminology may be potentially misleading, given that 'generalization' and 'inference' have largely overlapping domains of reference. And this is reflected in the terminology used by others to label more or less the same distinction. Thus, Yin (1994) distinguishes between 'statistical' and 'analytic' generalization. Our terminology here is closer to that of Mitchell (Chapter 7); though he refers to 'logical' rather than to theoretical inference. Formulating the distinction in the way that we have is designed to underline the very different character of the two strategies. It is also worth noting that this is a distinction that relates not only to case study research but also to debates about the relevance of the concept of external validity to experiments (see Mook, 1983).

7 In contrast with those phenomena of concern to natural scientists. H.L. Mencken once commented on the Lynds' study of Middletown that most of the American cities of Middletown's size were 'as alike as peas in a pod', thereby implying that the findings of this study could be generalized to that population unproblematically. This is a comment which those who carried out the Middletown III restudy dismiss as 'hyperbole', with considerable justification (Bahr and Caplow, 1991, p. 84).

8 The extent to which statistical sampling can accurately capture population heterogeneity is a function of sample size. Thus, a sample which is large enough to produce an adequate representation of the sex ratio of a population may be too small for an adequate representation of the frequency distribution of different types of ethnicity in the population. And a sample which is adequate in size for the latter purpose may still be too small adequately to represent the sex ratio within smaller ethnic groups. Moreover, even very large samples may fail to be representative with regard to all forms of relevant heterogeneity.

9 Survey researchers also do this when they use quota sampling or stratified rather than simple random sampling. Of course, there are limitations on what can be concluded about a large population on the basis of a small sample of cases, even when this is designed to capture relevant heterogeneity. Case study work cannot provide sound information about the *distribution* of features across the population. At best, it can only show features that seem likely to be modal, given that they are observed within all or most of the sample cases irrespective of their other differences.

10 See Kennedy (1979, p. 666–8) for a discussion of this.

11 This is not to suggest that convenience is an unimportant consideration, especially given the constraints under which research is carried out. And the increasing problems faced in getting access to some types of setting (Troman, 1996) may make strategic selection of cases more and more difficult in the future. Nevertheless, such selection is often essential for general conclusions to be drawn with justification.

12 See, for instance, the various studies of male anti-school subcultures in English secondary schools (Aggleton, 1987; Ball, 1981; Corrigan, 1979; Hargreaves, 1967; Turner, 1983; Willis, 1977; Woods, 1979). For a discussion of meta-analysis in relation to case studies, see Schofield, Chapter 4. See also Noblit and Hare (1988).

13 The selection of cases from the cutting edge points to another kind of heterogeneity in populations: across time periods. It is worth underlining that there is no good reason to expect that the population to which generalization is being made will remain the same in relevant respects indefinitely. In other words, the validity of empirical generalizations is subject to erosion over time in a way that the validity of theories is not.

14 The school was selected on this basis prior to Foster's employment on the project.

15 Some critics have sought to argue that Foster overlooked evidence of teacher racism, thereby preserving the basis for this type of generalization. On the tendentious character of this criticism, see Hammersley (1998).

16 In other words, contrary to what Lincoln and Guba suggest, case studies are not like fragments of hologram film, in the sense that each is capable of projecting the whole picture.

17 Generalization within the case is often involved in case study research whose conclusions do not extend beyond the case studied or depend on theoretical inference, as well as in research whose conclusions entail empirical generalization across cases.

18 Of course, Berlak et al's argument itself involves a retrospective temporal generalization: the results of a current study are being used to issue a corrective to earlier ones.

19 See our discussion of the work of Wright (1992a, 1992b) on differential treatment of ethnic minority children in primary schools (Foster et al., 1996, pp. 113–16).

References

Aggleton, P. (1987) *Rebels Without a Cause*. London: Falmer.

Atkinson, P.A. (1990) *The Ethnographic Imagination*. London: Routledge.

Bahr, H.M. and Caplow, T. (1991) 'Middletown as an urban case study', in J.R. Feagin, A.M. Orum and G. Sjoberg (eds), *A Case for the Case Study*. Chapel Hill: University of North Carolina Press.

Ball, S.J. (1981) *Beachside Comprehensive*. Cambridge: Cambridge University Press.

Ball, S.J. (1983) 'Case study research in education: some notes and problems', in M. Hammersley (ed.), *The Ethnography of Schooling*. Driffield: Nafferton Books.

Berlak, H. and Berlak, A. (1981) *Dilemmas of Schooling*. London: Methuen.

Berlak, A., Berlak, H., Bagenstos, N.T. and Mikel, E. (1975) 'Teaching and learning in English primary schools', *School Review*, 83 (2): 215–43.

Cicourel, A.V. and Kitsuse, J.I. (1973) *The Educational Decision-Makers*. Indianapolis: Bobbs-Merrill.

Connolly, P. (1998) '"Dancing to the wrong tune": ethnography, generalization, and research on racism in schools', in P. Connolly and B. Troyna (eds), *Researching Racism in Education*. Buckingham: Open University Press.

Corrigan, P. (1979) *Smash Street Kids*. London: Paladin

Denzin, N.K. (1989) *Interpretive Interactionism*. Newbury Park, CA: Sage.

Drew, D. (1995) *'Race', Education and Work: The Statistics of Inequality*. Aldershot: Avebury.

Drew, D. and Gray, J. (1990) 'The first-year examination achievements of black young people in England and Wales', *Educational Research*, 32 (2): 107–17.

Foster, P. (1990) *Policy and Practice in Multicultural and Anti-Racist Education: A Case Study of a Multi-ethnic Comprehensive School*. London: Routledge.

Foster, P., Gomm, R. and Hammersley, M. (1996) *Constructing Educational Inequality*. London: Falmer.

Geertz, C. (1973) 'Thick description: toward an interpretive theory of culture', in C. Geertz, *The Interpretation of Culture*. New York: Basic Books.

Gillborn, D. and Gipps, C. (1996) *Recent Research on the Achievements of Ethnic Minority Pupils*. London, Office for Standards in Education. London: HMSO.

Gomm, R. (1996) 'Quantitative research', in Open University, E835, *Educational Research in Action*. Milton Keynes: Open University Press.

Gomm, R., Foster, P. and Hammersley, M. (1998) 'From one to many, but how? Theory and gener-alisation in case study research', paper given at a conference on Case Study Research in Education, Centre for Development and Appraisal in Education, University of Warwick.

Guba, E. and Lincoln, Y.S. (1989) *Fourth Generation Evaluation*. Newbury Park, CA: Sage.

Hammersley, M. (1992) *What's Wrong with Ethnography?* London: Routledge.

Hammersley, M. (1998) 'How *not* to engage in academic discussion: a commentary on Gillborn's "Racism and Research"'. Unpublished paper.

Hargreaves, D.H. (1967) *Social Relations in a Secondary School*. London: Routledge & Kegan Paul.

ILEA (1987) 'Ethnic background and examination results, 1985 and 1986', *Research and Statistics Report*, London: ILEA.

Kennedy, M.M. (1979) 'Generalizing from single case studies', *Evaluation Quarterly*, 3 (4): 661–78.

Kysel, F. (1988) 'Ethnic background and examination results', *Educational Research*, 30 (2): 83–9.

Mackinnon, D., Statham, J. and Hales, M. (1995) *Education in the UK: Facts and Figures*. London: Hodder & Stoughton.

Mook, D.G. (1983) 'In defense of external invalidity', *American Psychologist*, 38 (4): 379–87.

Mortimore, P., Sammons, P., Stoll, L., Lewis, D. and Ecob, R. (1988) *School Matters: The Junior Years*. Wells: Open Books.

Noblit, G.W. and Hare, R.D. (1988) *Meta-ethnography: Synthesizing Qualitative Studies*. Beverly Hills, CA: Sage.

Rescher, N. (1978) *Peirce's Philosophy of Science*. South Bend, IN: University of Notre Dame Press.

Rogers, C. (1982) *The Social Psychology of Schooling*. London: Routledge & Kegan Paul.

Ryle, G. (1971a) 'Thinking and reflecting', in G. Ryle, *Collected Papers* (Vol. 2). London: Hutchinson.

Ryle, G. (1971b) 'The thinking of thoughts', in G. Ryle, *Collected Papers* (Vol. 2). London: Hutchinson.

Sadler, D. (1981) 'Intuitive data processing as a potential source of bias in naturalistic evaluations', *Educational Evaluation and Policy Analysis*, 3: 25–31.

Sammons, P., Thomas, S., Mortimore, P., Cairns, R., Bausor, J. and Walker, A. (1995) 'Understanding school and departmental differences in academic effectiveness'. Paper presented at the International Congress for School Effectiveness and Improvement, Leeuwarden, Netherlands.

Skellington, R. and Morris, P. (1992) *'Race' in Britain Today*. London: Sage.

Smith, D. and Tomlinson, S. (1989) *The School Effect: A Study of Multi-racial Comprehensives*. London: Policy Studies Institute.

Stake, R.E. (1994) 'Case studies', in N.K. Denzin and Y.S. Lincoln (eds), *Handbook of Qualitative Research*. Thousand Oaks, CA: Sage.

Thomas, S., Sammons, P., Mortimore, P. and Smees, R. (1995) 'Stability and consistency in secondary school effects on students' GCSE outcomes over 3 years'. Paper presented at the
International Congress for School Effectiveness and Improvement, Leeuwarden, Netherlands.

Thorne, B. (1993) *Gender Play: Girls and Boys in School.* Buckingham: Open University Press.

Tripp, D.H. (1985) 'Case study generalization: an agenda for action', *British Educational Research
Journal,* 11 (1): 33–43.

Troman, G. (1996) 'No entry signs: educational change and some problems encountered in nego-
tiating entry to educational settings', *British Educational Research Journal,* 22 (1): 71–88.

Turner, G. (1983) *The Social World of the Comprehensive School.* London: Croom Helm.

Walker, R. (1978) 'The conduct of educational case studies: ethics, theory and procedures', in
B. Dockrell and D. Hamilton (eds), *Rethinking Educational Research.* London: Hodder &
Stoughton.

Willis, P. (1977) *Learning to Labour.* Farnborough: Saxon House.

Woods, P. (1979) *The Divided School.* London: Routledge & Kegan Paul.

Wright, C. (1992a) 'Early education: multiracial primary school classrooms', in D. Gill, B. Mayor and
M. Blair (eds), *Racism and Education.* London: Sage.

Wright, C. (1992b) *Race Relations in the Primary School.* London: David Fulton.

Yin, R. (1994) *Case Study Research: Design and Methods* (2nd edn). Thousand Oaks, CA: Sage.

CASE STUDY AND THEORY

CHAPTER 6

CASE STUDY AND THEORY IN POLITICAL SCIENCE

Harry Eckstein

[...] Case studies run the gamut from the most microscosmic to the most macrocosmic levels of political phenomena. On the micro level, we have many studies of conspicuous political personalities (political leaders such as Lincoln, Stalin, Gandhi), and of particular leadership positions and small leadership groups (the American presidency, the British Cabinet, the prime minister in British government, the operational code of the Soviet leadership, and so on). [...] Beyond that level, one finds a similar profusion of case studies of transnational phenomena: specific processes of and organizations for transnational integration, particular 'systems' of international politics, particular crises in international relations, and the like. [...]

This plenitude of case studies is not associated with any perception that they are a particularly useful means for arriving at a theoretical understanding of the subject matter of political study. [...] One might explain this apparent paradox by holding that political scientists do not place a high value on theory building. No doubt this is true for many of them. But it is much less true nowadays than it used to be, and the volume, or proportion, of case studies in the field has not notably decreased.

It is in order, therefore, to raise three questions: What general role can the case study play in the development of theories concerning political phenomena? How useful is the case method at various stages of the theory-building process? And how is case study best conducted for purposes of devising theories? [...]

Case studies, I will argue, are valuable at all stages of the theory-building process, but most valuable at that stage of theory building where least value is generally attached to them: the stage at which candidate theories are 'tested'. Moreover, the argument for case studies as a means for building theories seems strongest in regard to precisely those phenomena with which the subfield of 'comparative' politics is most associated: macropolitical phenomena, that is, units of political

From H. Eckstein (1992) *Regarding Politics: Essays on Political Theory, Stability and Change.* Berkeley: University of California Press.

study of considerable magnitude or complexity, such as nation-states and subjects virtually coterminous with them (party systems or political cultures). More precisely, the abstract brief in favour of the case study as a means of building theories seems to me to hold regardless of level of inquiry, but at the macrocosmic level practical research considerations greatly reinforce that brief. [...]

Definitions

Case study and comparative study

1.   The conception of case study commonly held in the social sciences is derived from, and closely similar to, that of clinical studies in medicine and psychology. Such studies are usually contrasted dichotomously (as if they were antitheses) to experimental ones, which furnish the prevalent conception of comparative study. Contrasts generally drawn between the two types of study cover virtually all aspects of inquiry: range of research; methods and techniques; manner of reporting findings; and research objectives (see Riley, 1963, pp. 32–75).

As to *range of research*: experimental studies are held to be conducted with large numbers of cases, constituting samples of populations, while clinical studies deal with single individuals, or at most small numbers of them not statistically representative of a populous set. Experimental studies thus are sometimes said to be 'extensive' and clinical ones 'intensive'. These adjectives do not refer to numbers of individuals alone, but also involve the number of variables taken into account. In experimental studies that number is deliberately and severely limited, and pre-selected, for the purpose of discovering relationships between traits abstracted from individual wholes. Clinical study, to the contrary, tries to capture the whole individual – 'tries to' because it is, of course, conceded that doing so is only an approachable, not an attainable, end.

As for *methods and techniques*: the typical experimental study, first of all, starts with, and adheres to, a tightly constructed research design, whereas the typical clinical study is much more open-ended and flexible at all stages. The clinical researcher may have (probably must have) in mind some notions of where to begin inquiry, a sort of checklist of points to look into during its course, or perhaps even a preliminary model of the individual being studied; but actual study proceeds more by feel and improvisation than by plan. Second, the techniques most commonly associated with such inquiry in the case of 'collective individuals' (that is, social units) are the loose ones of participant observation (simply observing the unit from within, as if a member of it) and *Verstehen* (that is, empathy: understanding the meaning of actions and interactions from the members' own points of view). The typical techniques of experimental inquiry, *per contra*, are those rigorous and routinized procedures of data processing and data analysis concocted to ensure high degrees of 'non-subjective' reliability and validity – the techniques of the statistics texts and research methods primers.

Reports of the findings of clinical study are generally characterized as narrative and descriptive: they provide case histories and detailed portraiture. Such reporting might therefore also be termed synthetic, while that of experimental studies is analytic, since it presents not depictions of 'whole' individuals but rather of relations among components, or elements, of them. Beyond description, clinical studies present 'interpretation'; beyond raw data, experimental ones present rigorously evaluated 'findings'.

It follows that the *objectives* of the two types of study also differ. That of experimental study is generalized knowledge: theoretical propositions. These may certainly apply to individuals but never exhaust the knowledge it is possible to have of them. Being general they necessarily miss what is particular and unique, which may or may not be a lot. The objective of clinical study, however, is precisely to capture the particular and unique, for if anything about an individual whole is such, so must be the whole *per se*. It is conceded that in describing an individual configuration we may get hunches about the generalizability of relations not yet experimentally studied, but only hunches, and even these only by serendipity (Merton, 1962, p. 103). Clinical study is therefore associated more with action objectives than those of pure knowledge. In the case of single individuals, it aims at diagnosis, treatment and adjustment; in that of collective individuals, at policy. This association of clinical study with adjustive action is based on the assumption that therapy and policy can hardly proceed without something approximating full knowledge of its subjects, however much general propositions may help in proceeding from clinical knowledge of a case to the appropriate manipulation of a subject. Clinical and experimental objectives draw near, asymptotically, as 'pure' knowledge becomes 'applied' (that is, in engineering models), but application is merely a possible extension of experimental knowledge while generally being an intrinsic objective of clinical research. [...]

2.   However, while the distinction between clinical and experimental studies is useful for contrasting the old and new comparative politics, it does not serve nearly so well in distinguishing the case study from other modes of research. At best, it can provide an initial inkling (but only an inkling) of the differences among them. [...] The distinction offers a useful denotative definition of case studies in the social

sciences (that is, what people usually mean by the term) but a far from useful connotative and generic one (how the term ought to be used if it is not to raise serious difficulties of meaning and classification and not to define merely one of numerous types of case study).

3.   The essential objections to equating case study with clinical and comparative study with experimental inquiry all revolve on one basic point: nothing compels the clustering (hence, dichotomization) of the various characteristics used to distinguish clinical and experimental studies. Although that clustering in fact occurs very frequently in the social sciences, it does so chiefly because of dubious beliefs and assumptions. At most, the characteristics have a certain practical affinity; for example, the fewer the cases studied, the more intensive study may be, other things being equal. But no logical compulsion is at work, and the practical considerations often are not weighty.

We may certainly begin with the notion that case studies, like clinical studies, concern 'individuals', personal or collective (and, for tidiness of conceptualization, assume that only one individual is involved). From this, however, it does not follow that case studies must be intensive in the clinician's sense: nothing like 'wholistic' study may be attempted, and the researcher may certainly aim at finding relationships between pre-selected variables – unless he assumes, *a priori*, that this is foolish. The research may be tightly designed and may put to use all sorts of sophisticated research techniques. (An excellent example is Osgood and Luria's [1954] 'blind analysis', using the semantic differential, of a case of multiple personality.) Its results need not be cast in narrative form, and its objective can certainly be the development of general propositions rather than portraiture of the particular and unique; nor need case studies be concerned with problems of therapeutic action when they go beyond narration, depiction and subjective interpretation. […]

These points of overlap and ambivalence in the distinction between the clinical and experimental have led to a concerted attack on the dichotomy in psychology itself. One typical attack argues that the dichotomy originates in an archaic and absurd *Methodenstreit* between 'mechanistic' and 'romantic' views of human nature (Holt, 1962). Another argues that experimental modes of study can also be used profitably in research into single cases; this is the theme of a notable book of essays, *N = 1* (Davidson and Costello, 1969). This work implies the most important definitional point of all: if case study is defined as clinical study in the traditional sense, then we not only construct a messy generic (not necessarily classificatory) concept, but also foreclose the possibility of useful argument about case study as a tool in theory building. The definition answers the question: case study and theory are at polar opposites, linked only by the fortuitous operation of serendipity.

4. This attack on the conventional idea of case study serves a constructive as well as destructive purpose. It provides ammunition for later arguments against highly restrictive views concerning the role of case study in theory building and also points the way toward a better, and simpler, definition of what case studies are.

An unambiguous definition of case study should proceed from the one sure point that has been established: case study is the study of individuals. That is about as simple as one can get – but, because of one major problem, it is too simple. The problem is that one person's single individual may be another's numerous cases. Take an example: in order to help break down the dichotomy between the clinical and experimental, Davidson and Costello (1969, pp. 214–32) reprint a study by Chassan on the evaluation of drug effects during psychotherapy. Chassan argues for the greater power of single-case study over the usual 'treatment group' versus 'control group' design – in this case, for determining the relative effects of tranquillizers and placebos. Readers can catch the flavour of his argument through two of his many italicized passages:

> The intensive statistical study of a single case can provide more meaningful and statistically significant information than, say, only end-point observations extended over a relatively large number of patients.
>
> The argument cited against generalization to other patients, from the result of a single case intensively studied, can actually be applied in a more realistic and devastating manner against the value of inferences ... drawn from studies in which extensive rather than intensive degrees of freedom are used.

And so on, in the same vein. The whole paper is an object lesson to those who seek theoretical safety only in numbers. But there is a catch. Chassan studied only one patient, but used a large number of treatments by drug and placebo: 'frequent observations over periods of sufficiently long duration'. The individuals here are surely not the patients, although they may be for other purposes; it is each treatment, the effects of which are being compared. It is easy enough to see the advantages of administering different treatments to the same person over a long period (hence, safety in small numbers of a sort), as against using one patient per observation (although it is to Chassan's credit that he pointed them out in contrast to the more usual procedure). But N, despite the title of the book, in this case is not one.

If this problem arises with persons, it arises still more emphatically with 'collective individuals'. A study of six general elections in Britain may be, but need not be, an $N = 1$ study. It might also be an $N = 6$ study. It can also be an $N = 120{,}000{,}000$ study. It depends on whether the subject of study is electoral systems, elections or voters.

What follows from this is that ambiguity about what constitutes an 'individual' (hence 'case') can only be dispelled by looking not at concrete

entities but at the measures made of them. On this basis, a *'case' can be
defined technically as a phenomenon for which we report and interpret only a
single measure on any pertinent variable.* This gets us out of answering
insoluble metaphysical questions that arise because any concrete entity
can be decomposed, at least potentially, into numerous entities (not
excluding 'persons': they differ almost from moment to moment, from
treatment to treatment, and consist of highly numerous cells, which
consist of highly numerous particles, and so on). It also raises starkly the
critical problem of this essay: What useful role can single descriptive
measures (not measures of central tendency, association, correlation,
variance or covariance, all of which presuppose numerous measures of
each variable) play in the construction of theory? [...]

Theory and theory building

We will be concerned with the utility of case studies in the development
of theories in macropolitics – their utility both in themselves and, to an
extent, relative to comparative (N = many) studies. While nearly
everyone in the field at the present time agrees that the development of
good theories is the quintessential end of political inquiry, conceptions
of theory, and of the processes by which it may be developed, vary
extremely in our field. This makes unavoidable a definitional exercise
on theory and a review of the normal steps in theory building.

1.   Two polar positions on what constitutes theory in our field can be
identified. While positions range between them, they have recently
been rather polarized, more often on, or very near, the extremes than
between them.
    On one extreme (the 'hard' line on theory) is the view that theory
consists solely of statements like those characteristic of contemporary
theoretical physics (or, better, considered to be so by influential
philosophers of science). A good summary of this view, tailored to the
field of political science, is presented in Holt and Richardson's (1968)
discussion of the nature of 'paradigms', but even better sources are the
writings of scientist-philosophers such as Kemeny (1959), Popper
(1959) and Hempel (1965).
    Theories in this sense have four crucial traits: (1) The concepts used
in them are defined very precisely, usually by stating definitions in
terms of empirical referents, and are less intended to describe
phenomena fully than to abstract from them characteristics useful for
formulating general propositions about them. (2) The concepts are used
in deductively connected sets of propositions that are either axioms
(assumptions) or theorems deduced from them. (3) The object of the
propositions is both logical consistency and 'empirical import', that is,

correspondence to observations of phenomena. And (4) empirical import is determined by tests themselves deduced from the propositions, and these are designed to make it highly probable that the propositions will flunk the tests because confidence in propositions is proportionate to the stiffness of the tests they manage to survive. In [political science], theories of this type are sometimes called 'formal theories', mainly because of the large role of formal deduction in their elaboration; and economics is generally taken as the nearest social science model for them, not only in general form but also in regard to substantive 'rationality' axioms (Buchanan and Tullock, 1967; Curry and Wade, 1968; Downs, 1965; Riker, 1962).

On the other pole (the 'soft' line), theory is simply regarded as any mental construct that orders phenomena or inquiry into them. This qualifies as theory many quite diverse constructs, including classificatory schemes that assign individual cases to more or less general classes; 'analytic' schemes that decompose complex phenomena into their component elements; frameworks and checklists for conducting inquiry (for example, the 'systems' approach to macropolitics, or 'decision-making' checklists for the study of foreign policy formation); any empirical patterns found in properly processed data, or anything considered to underlie such patterns (for example, learning processes or class position).

2. If the term *theory* were always prefaced by an appropriate adjective, wrangling about these, and less extreme, positions could be avoided. But this would not take us off the hook of having to specify how 'good theory' as an objective of inquiry in our field should be conceived. The best position on this issue, it seems to me, is neither hard nor soft but does come closer to the hard than the soft extreme. It rests on two major premises.

The first is that it makes no sense whatever to call any mental construct a theory. Such constructs differ vastly in nature and purpose, so that they can hardly be considered to be of the same species. With some of them, not much more can be done than to assign names to phenomena or to order one's filing cabinets. And it can be demonstrated that, strictly speaking, the soft position compels one to regard as theory any statement whatever in conventional or technical discourse.

Second, it makes little more sense to restrict the term to constructs like those of theoretical physics, or those abstracted from that field by philosophers of science. While such constructs have proved extremely powerful in certain senses, one may doubt that they alone possess power (even in these senses). If constructs like them are not attainable in a field such as [political science] at its present stage of development (which is at least an open question, since constructs like them have in fact not been attained), commitment to theory in such a narrow sense may induce one to forego theoretical inquiry altogether. Most important, theories in the 'hard' sense are a particular form developed, over considerable time, to realize the purposes – the motivating goals, *animus, telos* – of an activity; and while they do this very well, it does not follow that they are absolutely required for realizing these purposes.

Consequently, even if the constructs of theoretical physics are taken as a model, it seems unwise to restrict the notion of theory entirely to such constructs. It seems better to label as theory any constructs designed to realize the same ends and formulated with the same *animus* as those that characterize the fields in which hard theory has been developed – leaving open, anyway provisionally, the forms such constructs may take consistent with reasonable achievement of the ends. On this basis, theory is characterized by a *telos*, or *animus*, of inquiry rather than by the particular form of statements. The only requirement (which, however, is far from soft) is that the forms of theoretical statements must be conducive to the goals of theoretical activity. […]

Theories can, of course, be more or less powerful, or 'good', depending on the rulefulness of regularity statements, the amount of reliability and validity they possess, the amount and kinds of foreknowledge they provide, and how parsimonious they are.[1] The *animus* of theoretical inquiry is constantly to increase their power to some unattainable absolute in all these senses. And while that absolute might have a unique ideal form to which the forms of theoretical physics might provide a discerning clue, it should be evident that it can be approached through many kinds of formulations, and always only approached. This is why 'theory' is better conceived of as a set of goals than as statements having a specified form.

At the same time, no mental construct qualifies as theory unless it satisfies the goals in some minimal sense. This minimal sense is that it must state a presumed regularity in observations that is susceptible to reliability and validity tests, permits the deduction of some unknowns, and is parsimonious enough to prevent the deduction of so many that virtually any occurrence can be held to bear it out. If these conditions are not satisfied, statements can still be interesting and useful; but they are not 'theory'.

These are the sort of constructs we want about macropolitics. It should be evident that the pivotal point in the whole conception is that regarding foreknowledge: validity is held to depend on it, parsimony is mainly required for the sake of establishing validity, and regularity statements are not an end unless valid. Any general appraisal of the utility of a method of inquiry must therefore also pivot on that point, as will my brief for the case study method.[2]

3.   It should also be evident that foreknowledge is most closely bound up with the testing of theories and that the process of theory building

involves much that precedes testing and some activities subsequent to it as well. It follows that modes of inquiry might be highly serviceable at one stage of the process but not at others, and this also must be considered in arguments about them.

(a) The process of theory building, needless to say, always begins with *questions* about experience for which answers are wanted – and raising questions, especially penetrating ones, is anything but a simple matter; indeed it is perhaps what most distinguishes the genius from the dullard (for whom common sense, the sense of ordinary people, leaves few mysteries). It is also an ability that, conceivably, could be sharpened or dulled by various modes of inquiry.

(b) Questions, to be answered by theories, must usually be restated as *problems* or *puzzles*. This is a complex process that I have discussed elsewhere (Eckstein, 1964), and it consists essentially of stating questions so that testable rules can answer them (which is not the case for any and all questions) and determining what core-puzzles must be solved if questions are to be answered. A familiar example is the subtle process by which Weber arrived at the conclusion that the question of his *Protestant Ethic* ('Why did modern capitalism as an economic system develop spontaneously only in the modern West?') boils down to the problem 'What engenders the (unlikely) attitude of continuous, rational acquisition as against other economic orientations?'

(c) The next step is *hypothesis*: formulating, by some means, a candidate-solution of the puzzle that is testable in principle and sufficiently plausible, *prima facie*, to warrant the bother and costs of testing. Like the formulation of theoretical problems this initial step toward solving them generally first involves a 'vision', then the attempt to state that vision in a rigorous and unambiguous form, so that conclusive testing becomes at least potentially possible. The candidate-solution need not be a single hypothesis or integrated set of hypotheses. In fact, a particularly powerful alternative is what Platt (1966) calls 'strong inference' (and considers characteristic of the more rapidly developing 'hard' sciences, such as molecular biology and high-energy physics): developing a set of competing hypotheses, some or most of which may be refuted by a single test.

(d) After that, of course, one searches for and carries out an appropriate, and if possible definitive, *test*. Such tests are rarely evident in hypotheses themselves, especially if questions of practicability are added to those of logic.

Testing is, in a sense, the end of the theory-building process. In another sense, it is not: if a test is survived the process of theorizing does not end. Apart from attempting to make pure knowledge applied, one continues to keep an eye out for contradictory or confirmatory observations, continues to look for more definitive tests, and continues to look for more powerful rules that order larger ranges of observations, or the same range more simply, or subsume the tested rule under one of a higher order, capable of subsuming also other tested rules. [...]

Options on the utility of case studies: an overview of the argument

The options

In taking positions on the value of case studies for theory building, both in themselves and relative to comparative studies, one can choose between six, not all mutually exclusive, options. These have been derived from a review of actual political case studies, the scant methodological literature about them (and counterparts in other social and behavioural sciences), and my own reflections on unconsidered possibilities. They are listed in order of the value seen in case studies, especially as one progresses along the path of theory building – a progression in which, arguably, intuitive vision plays a constantly decreasing role relative to systematic procedure.

Option 1 holds case studies and comparative studies to be wholly separate and unequal. They are separate in that the two modes of inquiry are considered to have so little in common that case studies are unlikely to provide more than a severely limited and crude basis for systematic comparisons (for example, variables of major importance in 'N = many' studies might be wholly ignored in studies of pertinent cases or might not be treated in readily comparable ways, and so on). The two modes of study are unequal in that only comparative studies are associated with the discovery of valid theories; case studies are confined to descriptions and intuitive interpretations.

Option 2 desegregates case studies and comparative studies, but hardly lessens their inequality. It holds that the two modes of inquiry draw near (asymptotically) in the interpretation of cases, because such interpretations can be made only by applying explicit or implicit theoretical generalizations to various cases. Case study, however, remains highly unequal because it is certainly not required, nor even especially useful, for the development of theories. There is an exception to this principle, but it is very limited. One never, or at least very rarely, has all the theories needed to interpret and treat a case; hence, something in the process of case interpretation must nearly always be left incomplete or to intuitive insight (which is why the two modes may approach closely but not intersect). Any aspects of case interpretation in regard to which theory is silent may be regarded as questions on the future agenda of theory building, as any intuitive aspects of interpretation may be regarded as implicit answers to the questions.

Option 3 grows out of the exception to Option 2. It holds that case studies may be conducted precisely for the purpose of discovering questions and puzzles for theory and discovering candidate-rules that might solve theoretical puzzles. The idea is simply that, if subjects and insights for comparative study are wanted, case study can provide them, and that case study might be conducted precisely for that purpose; and perhaps satisfy it by something less chancy than serendipity, or at least by affording larger scope to serendipitous discovery than studies that sacrifice intensive for extensive research. This still confines the utility of case study to the earlier stages of theorizing and makes it a handmaiden to comparative study. But it does tie case study into the theory-building process by something less contingent than possible feedback flowing from the 'clinician' to the 'experimentalist'.

Option 4 focuses on the stage in theory building at which one confronts the question whether candidate-rules are worth the costs (time, effort, ingenuity, manpower, funds, and so on) of testing. It holds that, although in the final analysis only comparative studies can really test theories, well-chosen case studies can shed much light on their plausibility, hence whether proceeding to the final, generally most costly, stage of theory building is worthwhile. This clearly involves something more than initial theoretical ideas. It begins to associate case study with questions of validity, if only in the grudging sense of *prima facie* credibility.

Option 5 goes still another step further, to the testing (validation) stage itself. It might be held (no revelation forbids it) that in attempting to validate theories, case studies and comparative studies generally are equal, even if separate, alternative means to the same end. The choice between them may then be arbitrary or may be tailored to such non-arbitrary considerations as the particular nature of theories, accessibility of evidence, skills of the researcher, or availability of research resources. A corollary of this position is, of course, that case studies may be no less systematic in procedure and rigorous in findings than comparative studies.

Option 6 is the most radical from the comparativist's point of view. It holds that case studies are not merely equal alternatives at the testing stage, but, properly carried out, a better bet than comparative studies. It might even be extended to hold that comparative studies are most useful as preliminary, inconclusive aids to conclusive studies: that is, the former may suggest probabilities and the latter clinch them. (Beyond this, of course, lies the still more radical possibility that comparative studies are good for nothing, case studies good for everything. But all inquiry suggests that this is wrong, and while the history of ideas also suggests that the unthinkable should be thought, there is no point in doing so unless a good case can be made for Option 6.)

Arguments on the options: an overview

The options discussed above tell us how we might answer the first two questions posed in the introduction to this chapter, while the answer to the third depends on the others. Since the answers to be proposed are complex and the manner of the presentation is far from simple (being intended to present others' views as well as my own), I will outline them before arguing them, as a sort of map to the discussion.

1.   First of all, a taxonomic point should be emphasized. This is that 'case study' is in fact a very broad generic concept, whether defined technically as 'single-measure' study or by the simpler 'single-individual' criterion. The genus can and, for our purposes, must be divided into numerous species, some of which closely resemble, some of which differ vastly from, the model of clinical study. The species that need distinction are: *configurative-idiographic studies, disciplined-configurative studies, heuristic case studies, case studies as plausibility probes* and *crucial case studies*. There may be still other types, but these five occur most frequently or are of most consequence to us.

Two things are notable about these species. They are intimately associated with the options on the utility of case studies in theory building: each option is linked to a special type of case study (except that Options 5 and 6 make no difference to the type of case study used). And as the utility attributed to case study increases, especially in progression through the phases of theory building, the associated type of case study increasingly departs from the traditional mode of clinical research and, except for numbers of individuals studied, increasingly resembles that of experimental inquiry.

2.   As for choice among the options, and associated types of case study, it seems that the modal preference of contemporary political scientists is the third and/or second (not so different, except in nuance, that they preclude being chosen in conjunction); that few choose the fourth (more for reasons of unfamiliarity than methodological conviction); that Options 5 and 6 are not chosen by anyone, or at least by very few. The evidence for this is mostly what political scientists actually write, reinforced by reactions to a preliminary version of this paper by a pretty fair cross-section of fellow professionals and a desultory poll among colleagues and students (only one of whom chose any option beyond the third, and that only because he reckoned that no one would list other possibilities unless up to tricks).

The prevailing preferences seem worth challenging on behalf of the options more favourable to case study. The latter appear to be rejected (better, not considered) for reasons other than full methodological deliberation, more as a result of overreaction against one weak type of case study than because of full consideration of the whole range of alternatives. In consequence, potentially powerful types of case study are neglected, and case studies are carried out less rigorously than they might be. Arguably, as well, this incurs liabilities in the conclusiveness of theories and the definitiveness of findings.

I propose to conduct the argument to this effect by evaluating each option, and associated type of case study, *seriatim*. In gist, my argument runs as follows:

(a) Option 1 is hardly worth arguing against. Its basic premise – that comparative and case studies are, for all intents and purposes, antithetical – has been exploded for good and all by Verba (1967) in [political science], and has been widely attacked in other social sciences as well (Davidson and Costello, 1969; Holt, 1962). Nevertheless, it is worth discussing because the type of case study associated with it was once dominant (and is still fairly common), and still provides the most widely prevalent notion of what case study is all about and of its potential for theory building.

(b) All the other options are tenable, but only because there are different types of case study that have different power in regard to theory building, and because the utility of case studies is not fully determined by logic (abstract methodology) but depends also on practical considerations (for example, characteristics of one's subject matter).

(c) Options 2 and 3 identify perfectly legitimate uses of case study and methods of carrying them out. They are implicit in a host of meritorious political studies, but these studies do not come near exhausting the utility of case study for theory building. Case studies may be used not merely for the interpretive application of general ideas to particular cases (that is, after theory has been established) or, heuristically, for helping the inquirer to arrive at notions of problems to solve or solutions worth pursuing, but may also be used as powerful means of determining whether solutions are valid.

(d) Option 4 deserves special consideration, for two reasons. It identifies an objective for which case study of a particular type is eminently serviceable and which can be of vast importance in theory building, but which is rarely pursued, by case study or other means. In addition, the utility of case study for that objective prepares the ground for arguing the case for the more radical options remaining.

(e) Option 5 will be held to state the logically most defensible position: to attain theory in political inquiry, comparative studies and case studies should be considered, by and large, as alternative strategies at all stages, with little or nothing to choose (logically) between them. Since that argument will be most difficult to sustain – at least against the conventional wisdom – for the testing stage, the argument will concentrate on the type of case study suitable to it.

(f) When practical considerations are added to logic, Option 6 seems still more sensible, at least for studies of politics on the macro level.

Case study is generally a better choice than comparative study for testing theories in macropolitics, but the type of case study useful for this purpose requires a kind of prior knowledge for which preliminary comparative study (of a limited kind) may often be useful or even necessary. This amounts to saying that comparative study can, in some circumstances, be treated as a handmaiden to case study, not vice versa, and thus, in a sense, stands the popular Option 3 on its head.

Before working through all this in detail, I want particularly to emphasize two points. First, nothing that follows should be regarded as an attack on the utility of comparative study in theory building, simply because case studies are defended. [...] Second, it is not to be inferred that just any case study will do for the purposes of theory building. Some readers of a draft of this essay concluded that it constituted a defence of 'traditional' political studies against the 'behaviouralists'. This is ludicrous, but it occurred. *The discussion presents an argument both for case studies and for carrying them out in a particular way.* Since the type of case study for which it argues is very demanding, implying great rigour of thought and exactitude of observation, it is hardly 'anti-behaviouralist'; and since that type of case study, to my knowledge, is as yet virtually non-existent in [political science], the argument can hardly be 'traditionalist'.

Types and uses of case study

Configurative-idiographic study

1.   In philosophy and psychology a distinction has long been drawn between nomothetic (generalizing, rule-seeking) and idiographic (individualizing, interpretive) types of, or emphases in, science. The philosophic progenitor of this terminology (and, in part, the ideas that underlie it) is Windelband ([1982]/1998), the most notable contemporary defender of the distinction is Gordon Allport.[3] Idiographic study is, in essence, what was earlier described as clinical study, and configurative-idiographic study is its counterpart in fields, like macropolitics, that deal with complex collective individuals. (Verba calls them configurative-idiosyncratic studies, but the difference in terminology is of no consequence.)

The configurative element in such studies is their aim to present depictions of the overall *Gestalt* (that is, configuration) of individuals: polities, parties, party systems, and so on. The idiographic element in them is that they either allow facts to speak for themselves or bring out their significance by largely intuitive interpretation, claiming validity on the ground that intensive study and empathetic feel for cases provide authoritative insights into them.

If configurative-idiographic studies are made from philosophic conviction, then the following assumptions usually are at work (see Holt, 1962, pp. 388–97): (a) In the study of personalities and the collectivities they form, one cannot attain prediction and control in the natural-science sense, but only 'understanding' (*Verstehen*) – and thus, from understanding, limited, non-deductive conceptions of probable futures and prudent policy. (b) In attaining understanding, subjective values and modes of cognition are crucial, and these resist quantification. (c) Each subject, personal or collective, is unique, so generalizations can at most be only about their actions (persons) or interactions (collectivities). And (d) the whole is lost or at least distorted in abstraction and analysis – the decomposition of the individual into constituent traits and statements of relations among limited numbers of these; it is 'something more' than an aggregate of general relations, rather than 'nothing but' such an aggregate. [...]

2. Configurative-idiographic studies are certainly useful, and, at their best, have undeniably considerable virtues. They may be beautifully written and make their subjects vivid. They may pull together and elegantly organize wide and deep researches. The intuitive interpretations they provide may be subtle and persuasive and suggest an impressive feel for the cases they treat.

Their most conspicuous weakness is that, as Verba puts it, 'they do not easily add up' – presumably to reliable and valid statements of regularity about sets of cases, or even about a case in point (Kaufmann, 1958; Lowi, 1964). This is plain in regard to sets of cases; the summation regarding them is at most factual (information about similar subjects, for example, legislatures, parties, and so on, in different contexts) and, because of idiosyncrasies in fact collecting and presentation, rarely involving even the systematic accumulation of facts. Anyone who has used secondary sources for compiling comparable data on numerous cases knows this to his pain, and, even more painfully, that inventories of interpretive propositions culled from case studies usually contain about as many distinguishable items as studies. The point is less plain, but just as true, for regularity statements concerning individual cases. The interpretations, being idiosyncratic, rarely come to an agreed position, or even to a point of much overlap. For example, in the configurative-idiographic literature on France there seems to be overlap on the position that there are 'two Frances', but nearly everyone has his own conception of what they are and where they are found. This situation is hardly surprising: in configurative-idiographic study the interpreter simply considers a body of observations that are not self-explanatory, and, without hard rules of interpretation, may discern in them any number of patterns that are more or less equally plausible.

The criticism that configurative-idiographic study does not add up to theory, in our sense, is mitigated by the fact that its capability to do so was never claimed by its exponents; in fact it is often explicitly repudiated. What is really troublesome about configurative-idiographic study is the repudiation itself (that is, the claim that case study in the behavioural and social sciences can only be idiographic) and its consequences for the way in which the nomothetic utility of case studies in these fields is regarded.

For a thorough refutation of the idiographer's position, and a broad attack on the distinction between the nomothetic and idiographic itself, readers should consult Holt (1962). His argument, in gist, is (a) that both the position and distinction have 'peculiar origins' – misunderstandings of Kant by lesser German philosophers and 'romantic' assumptions prevalent during the early nineteenth century ('Teutonic ghosts' raised against classical ideas and styles) that led to unreasonably sharp lines between nature and mechanisms, on one hand, and behaviour and organisms, on the other; and, more important, (b) that none of the postulates of idiographic study, as outlined above, withstands examination. As for the consequences of the claims of idio-graphers, the most stultifying has been the association of nomothetic study in macropolitics with study different from that favoured by idiographers in all respects: not only study based on more systematic methods of collecting and processing data and on explicit frameworks of inquiry intended to make for cumulation, but 'comparative' (that is, multi-case, cross-national, cross-cultural) studies.

If case study could only be configurative-idiographic in character, then the conclusions that case studies and comparative studies are wholly antithetical and that theories about politics require comparative study, or are unattainable, could not be avoided. But case study need not have that character, and the comparativists themselves have pointed the way to other varieties – without, however, overcoming a fundamental bias against case study of any kind in theory construction, largely anchored to the archetype of such studies in our field.

Disciplined-configurative study

1. The comparativist's typical reaction to the theoretical poverty of configurative-idiographic studies is to hold that, while theories cannot be derived from case interpretations, such interpretations can, and should, be derived from theories. 'The unique explanation of a particular case', says Verba (1962, p. 114), 'can rest on general hypotheses'. Indeed, it *must* rest on them, since theoretical arguments about a single case, in the last analysis, always proceed from at least implicit general laws about a class or set to which it belongs or about universal attributes of all classes to which the case can be subsumed.

The logic involved has been succinctly stated in Hempel's discussion of 'scientific' explanation, the essence of which is the explanation of particular phenomena (in my terms 'case interpretation') 'by showing that [their] existence could have been inferred – either deductively or with a high probability – by applying certain laws of universal or of statistical form to specified antecedent circumstances' (Hempel, 1965, pp. 299–303). Those who consider this the only way of interpreting cases scientifically hold that the theoretical bases of case interpretations should always be made explicit, and that *ad hoc* additions to a framework of case interpretation should always be made as if they were general laws, not unique factors operating only in the case in point. The bases of case interpretation, in other words, should be established theories or, lacking them, provisional ones, and such interpretations can be sound only to the extent that their bases are in fact valid as general laws. Case studies so constructed are 'disciplined-configurative studies'. The terminology is Verba's, who recommends such studies to us. [...]

Disciplined-configurative studies need not just passively apply general laws or statements of probability to particular cases. A case can impugn established theories if the theories ought to fit it but do not. It may also point up a need for new theory in neglected areas. Thus, the application of theories to cases can have feedback effects on theorizing, as Hempel recognizes. In addition, it is unlikely that all aspects of a case can be nomologically explained. As in the field of engineering, where general theories are applied to achieve conscious ends in particular circumstances, there are nearly always elements of prudence, common sense or 'feel' in case interpretations. Theory building, however, aims at the constant reduction of those elements, by stating notions that fit particular cases as general theoretical rules and subjecting them to proper theoretical tests.

In essence, the chain of inquiry in disciplined-configurative studies runs from comparatively tested theory to case interpretation, and thence, perhaps, via *ad hoc* additions, newly discovered puzzles and systematized prudence, to new candidate-theories. Case study thus is tied into theoretical inquiry – but only partially, where theories apply or can be envisioned; passively, in the main, as a receptacle for putting theories to work; and fortuitously, as a catalytic element in the unfolding of theoretical knowledge. This is, of course, still close to the clinician's conception of his role, and configurative studies that are disciplined in intent are not always easy to distinguish from unadulterated idiography. The two types of often intermixed and easily blend together.

2. The essential basis of Verba's argument about the relations between general theory and particular case interpretation is surely correct. If the interpretations of a case are general laws correctly applied to the case,

the interpretations may be valid or invalid, depending on whether the laws are valid; otherwise, their validity simply cannot be known at all. Moreover, if cases are complex, the number of possible alternative interpretations, equally plausible because not at variance with the facts of the case, is usually vast, so that undisciplined case interpretation in much-studied cases usually yields large inventories of quite different propositions, none of which is clearly superior to any other. Preferences among them depend on personal tastes or general intellectual fads. [...]

It remains to add a point insufficiently stressed in writings on disciplined-configurative studies. The application of theories in case interpretation, although rarely discussed, is not at all a simple process, even leaving aside the question of how valid theory is to be developed. Such applications only yield valid interpretations if the theories permit strict deductions to be made and the interpretations of the case are shown to be logically compelled by the theories. In the case of revolutions, for instance, it is not enough to know that a regularity exists and that a case somehow 'fits' it (that is, does not manifestly contradict it). One should also be able to demonstrate, by correct reasoning, that, given the regularity and the characteristics of the case, revolution must have occurred, or at least had a high probability of occurring. Not all theories permit this to be done, or at least equally well. For example, a theory attributing revolution to aggressions engendered by social frustrations will hardly fail to fit any case of revolution, nor tell us exactly why any case of it occurred. Unless it specifies precisely how much and what sort of frustration engenders revolution, on whose part, and under what complex of other conditions (Gurr, 1970), the frustration-aggression theory of revolution, applied, say, to the French Revolution, can yield about as many plausible case interpretations as can configurative-idiographic study (there having existed many sources of frustration in the *ancien régime*, as in all regimes).

This point brings out a major utility of attempting disciplined case interpretation. Aiming at the disciplined application of theories to cases forces one to state theories more rigorously than might otherwise be done – provided that the application is truly 'disciplined', that is, designed to show that valid theory compels a particular case interpretation and rules out others. As already stated, this, unfortunately, is rare (if it occurs at all) in political study. One reason is the lack of compelling theories. But there is another, which is of the utmost importance: political scientists reject, or do not even consider, the possibility that valid theories might indeed *compel* particular case interpretations. The import of that possibility, assuming it to exist, lies in the corollary that a case might invalidate a theory, if an interpretation of the case compelled by the theory does not fit it.

But this goes too far ahead, toward a crucial argument that will require much discussion below. The point for the present is merely that exponents of disciplined-configurative study have insufficiently considered both the difficulties and promises of the relations between general theories and particular case interpretations.[4]

Heuristic case studies

1. Disciplined-configurative study assumes that 'general laws' are available. It is not thought of as a part of the process of theory building as such, except in that the interpretation of cases may lead to *ad hoc*, serendipitous additions to existing theories in order to cover puzzling aspects of a case. However, the feedback effect in Verba's recommended sequence of inquiry can be isolated from the rest of the sequence and case study deliberately used to stimulate the imagination towards discerning important general problems and possible theoretical solutions. That is the essence of heuristic case studies (heuristic means 'serving to find out'). Such studies, unlike configurative-idiographic ones, tie directly into theory building and therefore are less concerned with overall concrete configurations than with potentially generalizable relations between aspects of them; they also tie into theory building less passively and fortuitously than does disciplined-configurative study, because the potentially generalizable relations do not just turn up but are deliberately sought out.

Heuristic case studies do not necessarily stop with one case, but can be conducted seriatim, by the so-called 'building-block technique' (Becker, 1968) [in other words, analytic induction – *Editors' Note*], in order to construct increasingly plausible and less fortuitous regularity statements. This technique is quite simple in principle. One studies a case in order to arrive at a preliminary theoretical construct. That construct, based on a single case, is unlikely to constitute more than a slim clue to a valid general model. One therefore confronts it with another case that may suggest ways of amending and improving the construct and achieve better case interpretation; and this process is continued until the construct seems sufficiently refined to require no further major amendment or at least to warrant testing by large-scale comparative study. Each step beyond the first can be considered a kind of disciplined-configurative study, but is better regarded as heuristic case study proceeding with increasingly refined questions and toward increasingly more specific ends. It is important not to confuse the whole process with comparative study. The latter seeks regularities through the simultaneous inspection of numerous cases, not the gradual unfolding of increasingly better theoretical constructs through the study of individuals. Of course, comparative studies can also employ the building-block technique by successively refined theories through a series of multi-case studies. [...]

2.   The justification for heuristic case studies runs as follows: (a) Theories do not come from a vacuum, or fully and directly from data. In the final analysis they come from the theorist's imagination, logical ability and ability to discern general problems and patterns in particular observations. (b) There are ineffable differences in such imaginative and other abilities, but various aids can be used to stimulate them: among them, the printouts from data banks or other comparative studies (which, however, never obviate the use of theoretical imagination, for example, for interpreting the print-outs into proper regularity statements and for determining what data banks should contain or how comparative studies should be designed in the first place). (c) The track record of case studies as stimulants of the theoretical imagination is good. (d) One reason it is good is precisely that, unlike wide-ranging comparative studies, case studies permit intensive analysis that does not commit the researcher to a highly limited set of variables, and thus increases the probability that critical variables and relations will be found. The possibility of less superficiality in research, of course, also plays a role here.

3.   Arguments in favour of heuristic case studies surely have merit. Whatever logic might dictate, the indubitable fact is that some case study writers in macropolitics have come up with interpretations notably incisive for their cases and notably plausible when taken as generalizations for sets of them, with or without the benefit of special frameworks or approaches. See, for example, the works of such men as Tocqueville, Bagehot, Halévy, Bryce and Bodley, or, in another field, anthropologists too numerous to mention.

Nevertheless, one may argue that too much is made of heuristic case studies, for two related reasons. One is that those who defend them sometimes seem to do so simply because they can see no more ambitious function to be served by case study. The other is that, not wishing to make other claims but to defend case studies, they claim too much for such studies as heuristic tools, especially in comparison to 'N = many' studies. Scenting a valid claim, they exaggerate it – and miss the possibility that a more persuasive brief might be based on a greater sense of limitation at the heuristic stage of theory building and a lesser one at others.

The point that case studies are good for more than getting clues will concern us later. But the anticipation of that point in the previous section can be supplemented here by a further suggestive argument. Case studies intended to serve a heuristic function can proceed much in the manner of 'clinical' study, that is, with a minimum of design or rigour, and tackle any case that comes to hand. In that event, however, nothing distinguishes the study from configurative-idiographic study, except the researcher's hopes and intentions, and results can only turn up by good fortune – which the bright will seize and the dull miss, but which the researcher can do nothing to induce. The alternatives are to use at least a modicum of design and rigour in research and not to choose just any case on any grounds but a special sort of case: one considered likely to be revealing, on some basis or other. The suggestive point in this for later argument is not that case study may often depart markedly from the archetype of clinical study (although that is noteworthy), but that *certain kinds of cases may be regarded as more instructive for theory building than others*. Actual heuristic case studies seem in fact generally, even if often just implicitly, to make that claim for the cases selected. The grounds are often obscure, and the claim often seems *post hoc* and intended to disarm charges of idiography. The point nevertheless remains that the brief for heuristic case study is strong only to the extent that cases especially instructive for theory, and subject to rigorous inquiry, can be identified. And if that possibility exists, then the further possibility arises that some cases might be especially instructive also at other stages of the theory-building process.

If the prevalent emphasis on heuristic functions is too modest, in what senses does it also exaggerate? First of all, the fact that case study writers have often spawned ideas notable as generalizations proves nothing. The Tocquevilles or Bagehots might have been successful in spawning plausible theories without writing case studies, since their imagination and incisiveness clearly matter more than the vehicles chosen for putting them to work. If they had used comparative studies they might have been even more successful, and more successful still if they had had available modern technology for accumulating, coding, storing and processing data – not to mention the fact that they do always make implicit, sometimes explicit, use of comparisons in their case studies (for example, Bagehot's contrasts between Britain and America, Tocqueville's between America and France), even if only to demonstrate that factors used to interpret their cases do in fact differ in different cases. Moreover, for every case study that has notably succeeded in spawning theory, there are scores that have notably failed – and this does not refer to idiography alone. Case study certainly furnishes no guarantee that theoretical abilities will be awakened or sharpened. And comparativists have been at least as successful in spawning theories as configurativists; for every Tocqueville or Bagehot we can produce an offsetting Aristotle, Machiavelli, Mosca, Pareto or Weber.

Second, the benefit of being able to take into consideration more variables in case study incurs the cost of highly circumscribed breadth of inference. And it is probable that the number of hypotheses suggested, hence also the number of invalid ones to be pursued, will be proportional to the number of variables considered. Heuristic case studies have a demonstrable tendency, as in the case of studies of the French Revolution, to spawn a crushing and chaotic number and variety of candidate generalizations, or hypercomplex multivariate theories, especially when these studies are made by imaginative people. And, unlike comparative studies, they cannot even yield initial clues about the generalizability of relations selected from all those that constitute the case – unless, to repeat, the case is considered, on some good basis, especially revealing for sets of phenomena, that is, one for which breadth-of-inference problems may be claimed to be slight.

These problems have led some to identify 'grounded theory' (theory that is initially derived from observations, not spawned wholly out of logic and imagination) with comparative inquiry rather than case study (Glaser and Strauss, 1967). The reasons for doing so are rather convincing. But the more sensible position surely is that, if we are really only concerned with the initial formulation of candidate-theories as a phase of theoretical inquiry (and not theory leaping full-blown out of data), case study is useful but by no means indispensable, as also is comparative study or any other exercise of the theoretical imagination. It is manifestly more useful for some people than others. It also would be generally more useful than it has been if more case studies were deliberately undertaken as exploratory means for arriving at candidate-theories, rather than simply allowing these to occur fortuitously, and if special characteristics of heuristically instructive cases could be specified and something like a heuristic 'method' could be developed.

If nothing more were to be said for case studies than that they may be helpful in initially formulating candidate regularity statements, we could only conclude that there is not special reason for either making or not making such studies. It follows that if there is a strong justification for case studies as tools in developing theories, it must be found in the special utility of such studies at some later stage of the sequence of inquiry by which theories are established, or, at a minimum, their availability as reasonable alternatives to comparative studies during the later, no less than earlier, stages of the theory-building process.

Plausibility probes

1.   After hypotheses are formulated, one does not necessarily proceed immediately to test them. A stage of inquiry preliminary to testing sometimes intervenes and ought to do so far more often than it actually does in political study (or in other social sciences). It involves probing the 'plausibility' of candidate-theories. Plausibility here means something more than a belief in potential validity plain and simple, for hypotheses are unlikely ever to be formulated unless considered potentially valid; it also means something less than actual validity, for which rigorous testing is required. In essence, plausibility probes involve attempts to determine whether potential validity may reasonably be

considered great enough to warrant the pains and costs of testing, which are almost always considerable, but especially so if broad, painstaking comparative studies are undertaken.

Such probes are common in cases where costly risks have to be run. These probes are roughly analogous to the trials to which one subjects a racehorse before incurring the costs of entering and preparing it for a major race: success cannot be guaranteed, but some kind of odds (ratios between certain coasts and probable benefits) can be established. The simple principle at work is that large investments in less likely outcomes are worse propositions than large investments in more likely outcomes. Here the analogy between theorizing and horse racing becomes a little specious, for in probing the plausibility of a theory we can hardly expect to know much, or anything, about previous performance or to have exact estimates of probability like those given by a stopwatch. But we do not lack means for at least getting a reasoned, not merely intuitive, 'feel' for the odds against a theory.

At a minimum, a plausibility probe into theory may simply attempt to establish that a theoretical construct is worth considering at all, that is, that an apparent empirical instance of it can be found. I take that (together with heuristic objectives) to be the purpose of Dahl's (1961) influential study of power in New Haven. Dahl, as I read him (contrary to some other interpreters of his work), wants to establish that power in democracy may be 'pluralistic', or may not be 'monolithic', not that it must be the former and cannot be the latter. The study certainly succeeds in that regard, although it would succeed even more if New Haven had been selected for study because it is typical of a specified class of cases.

Some ways of surmising the plausibility of a theory beyond that minimal point are non-empirical, and since they entail only the cost of thought, these should generally be used before, or instead of, empirical probes. We may have confidence in a theory because it is derived logically from premises that have previously yielded valid theory in a field or because it is derived from premises contrary to those that have led to major failures. We may also have confidence in a theory if it is able to account for both strengths and weaknesses in existing relevant hypotheses or otherwise seems to organize considerable volumes and varieties of unexplained data. An example of both these methods of estimating plausibility is furnished by those passages of my monograph on stable democracy that show the grounding of its main proposed regularity statement in (as I then thought) validated psychological theories and those that try to show how the strengths and weaknesses of three alternative hypotheses, all rather powerful yet flawed in certain ways, can be explained by the main proposed regularity statement (Eckstein, 1966). Demonstrating logically that proposed regularity statements can potentially explain data not yet explained, and/or provide a common foundation for previously validated but quite discrete and unconnected hypotheses, and/or extend assumptions found powerful in some areas to other areas, all create presumptions in favour of testing the statements independently, even by costly means.

Plausibility probes can also be directly empirical, that is, in the nature of preliminary, rather loose and inconclusive, but suggestive tests, before more rigorous tests are conducted. Such probes confront theories with lesser challenges that they must certainly withstand if they are not to be toppled by greater ones. If, for example, it were posited that democratic power structures are normally monolithic (which is in fact often done in political theories) and one had strong reason to believe that New Haven was unlikely to be a deviant case (which is also arguable), then Dahl's study of its power structure would establish much more than that the counter-idea of pluralism in democratic power is not completely vacuous (Dahl, 1961). It would cast serious doubt on the posited regularity. Such empirical probes are especially important where non-empirical probes yield very uncertain results, and there is also reason to use them, as additions to others, as cheap means of hedging against expensive wild-goose chases, when the costs of testing are likely to be very great.

2.   There is no reason why empirical plausibility probes should not take the form of modest or rather diffusely designed comparative studies, as preludes to more ambitious and tighter ones. Indeed, most systematic comparative studies in macropolitics make more sense as plausibility probes (or as 'heuristic comparative studies') than as what they are generally claimed or regarded to be: that is, works presenting definitive results. Almond and Verba's *The Civic Culture* (1963) is surely a case in point. The sample of cases covered by the study is hardly large and dubiously representative; the regularity statements about 'democratic stability' emerging in its final chapter could certainly be made more exact, are mainly afterthoughts imputed to the evidence, and are hardly conclusively compelled by that evidence. But they seem sufficiently rooted in data and reasoning to warrant their statement in more precise form and their thorough testing, preferably by logically deduced predictions about findings in a project specifically designed not to get interesting data but to get those crucial to establishing the validity of the work's central propositions. (One may consider it reprehensible that so many comparativists are willing to stop where only that much, or little more, has been accomplished, and then go on to other, still merely plausible, ideas on different subject matter. We have no right to bewail the fact that others do not take up our ideas if we ourselves drop them far short of the point to which they could be taken.)

The essential point for us is that, as empirical plausibility probes, case studies are often as serviceable as, or more so than, comparative ones – and nearly always a great deal cheaper – a prime consideration in probing plausibility. The economic case for them is strongest where required information is not readily available in aggregate data or good secondary sources and is intrinsically hard to get. Case studies can certainly serve the purpose well if well selected, that is, if they are such that a result, for or against a theory, cannot readily be shrugged off. It is true that case studies have been little used in political studies as plausibility probes, but this is largely due to the fact that the idea of any sort of plausibility probe is foreign to the field, plus the fact that comparative studies to amass data from which finished theories supposedly emerge have been its dominant contemporary genre. (Comparative studies as plausibility probes are equally uncommon, except only in the sense that some of them appear better tailored for that purpose than the purposes they pretend to serve.) [...]

3.   And here again we come to a critical possibility. If studies of well-selected cases, no less than comparative studies, can serve the purposes of plausibility probes (the idea of which is, after all, to form estimates of probable validity), could they not also serve, painstakingly selected and rigorously carried out, as tests of validity itself, with similar economies in the work required? The possibility should at least be entertained and the case for it argued, since the potential practical gains could be enormous. It arises, at bottom, from the obvious fact that cases are not all equal in their import, even for the modest purposes of heuristic exploration. The question is whether their inequality extends to the point where certain types of cases, and modes of case study, can serve to test theories for validity – the step most demanding on rigour and in which breadth-of-inference problems seem most damaging to case studies.

To explore this question further, we shall have to look more closely at a suggestion made in the discussion on disciplined-configurative study: that if theory can compel particular case interpretations, then particular cases could invalidate or confirm theories.

Crucial case studies

1.   The position that case studies are weak or useless for testing theories rests, at bottom, on the mistaken application of a correct principle – a principle that applies more, but still imperfectly, to the discovery of theories in data than to their testing.

We can think of theory formulation as a process that leads one to postulate a curve or line to which observations of reality are expected to correspond; and we can think of theories as valid if the curves or lines that best fit relevant observations in fact match the theoretical expectation, or, put in a different manner, if the points yielded by measurements of relevant observations fall on or very near the postulated curve at logically specified locations. The principle that seems to rule out case study for the purpose of finding valid theory is the elementary one holding that any single instance of a relationship yields only one observed point, and that through any single point an infinite number of curves or lines can be drawn. (A less abstract variant of this principle is the argument above that any number of different explanations, not contrary to fact and thus at least minimally plausible, can be offered for any political event.)

The principle is, as stated, incontestable. But we are not constrained to conclude from it that comparative studies are indispensable to the development of valid theories and case studies useless for the purpose, unless we inject between the premise and conclusion a major fallacy that apparently dies hard: the inductive fallacy. The essence of that fallacy is the belief that theories, being contained in phenomena, can be fully derived from observations by simple inspection or, at any rate, sophisticated data processing. This is fallacious in several senses that should be disentangled, although the fallacies are all of a piece and usually all committed at once.

(a) One aspect of the fallacy involves confusion between the discovery of candidate-theories and their testing: in deriving theory from observations ('grounded theory') one may be tempted to think that curves suggested by comparative data are themselves valid theories. This hazard is not logically inherent in comparative study, but contemporary political science, among other fields, suggests that it is extreme in practice, most of all where the behavioural sciences' model of experimental study is closely followed. Such study, regardless of how punctiliously carried out, cannot, in and of itself, reveal general laws guaranteed to be valid. It only provides more or less powerful clues as to what they are, that is, helps to discover them. In some cases these clues may be so powerful that testing may seem superfluous or not worth the cost, but this is highly exceptional.[5]

Strictly speaking, generalizations directly inferred from data only hold (probabilistically) for the phenomena observed under the conditions prevailing during observation. If the observations are voluminous and accurate, and if the conditions of observation are highly various or controlled, then one may have very high confidence that the curve that best fits the observation in fact manifests, in graphic form, a valid theory. Nevertheless, the element of surmise in going from data to theory always is considerable, and the 'epistemic gap' between them, as Northrop calls it, ineluctable. And such great limitations usually exist, in practice, on the volume, accuracy and variety or control of observations (including, of course, the obvious limitation that we cannot observe the future) that the risk in identifying an empirical generalization with a theoretical rule usually cannot be defended unless special testing of the presumed rule is carried out.

(b) A second aspect of the fallacy concerns the discovery of candidate-theories in the first place. It is the principles that give rise to empirically discovered curves that constitute theories, not the curves as such: these only represent the principles, that is, show them at work. When an empirically grounded curve has been drawn, therefore, the principles it expresses must still be elucidated. Often this is not much of a problem, and statistical techniques (like causal path analysis) can help solve it. Nevertheless, curves can deceive as well as instruct, regardless of such techniques; and they most resist the discerning of *simple* regularities governing phenomena because the data from which they are constructed usually express all the complex interactions of factors in the concrete world, or sometimes even the laboratory. Nature, as Bacon knew, is a tough adversary capable of innumerable disguises. More than routine method is often required to strip off these disguises.

It seems, in fact, unlikely that the more powerful laws of physical science could have been discovered (their testing aside) by the mechanical processing of observations, however 'sophisticated'. Certainly one is struck by the small role played by systematic comparative observation in both their formulation and critical testing – in effect, by the thorough lack of correspondence between the psychologist's and physicist's conception of 'experimentation'. As illustration, take that touchstone of ancient, modern and contemporary physics: conceptions of gravity and the closely associated law of the velocity of freely falling objects.

The Galilean challenge to the Aristotelian conception of free fall (the heavier the object, the faster it falls), accepted as gospel for nearly two millennia, did not grow out of observation at all but out of a simple 'thought-experiment' (simple in retrospect, but apparently not at all obvious until performed). In gist (and with apologies for a layman's bowdlerization): if Aristotle is correct, then two bricks of the same weight, dropped at the same instant from the same height, must strike the ground at the same instant. If the two bricks are dropped side by side, as if cemented, the rate of fall of each must be the same as if dropped separately; but if cemented, they would be twice as heavy as a single brick and must therefore drop much faster; hence, since both conclusions cannot be right, the theory must be wrong. And the only way to square the two conditions logically is to make the weight of the falling objects irrelevant to acceleration in free fall, with the relevant variables being only the gravitational forces that account for falling and, possibly, the duration of the fall.

There is no observation here at all (and much doubt even about whether Galileo ever climbed the Tower of Pisa to check out, by a single 'probe', the plausibility of his conclusion). Had systematic comparative measurements been used, anomalies in the Aristotelian conception would certainly have turned up, at least in the fall of objects 'heavy' above a certain threshold. But if a well-chosen sample of objects had been dropped from a well-selected sample of heights under a well-selected sample of wind and other conditions, the likely conclusions would surely have been something like this: that the whole process of falling, like macropolitical phenomena, is 'immensely complicated and cannot be accounted for by one or two simple causes' (Verba, 1967, p. 114), that weight is a factor (as it is at certain heights and other conditions); and that weight, size, shape and density of object, and wind conditions account for such and such a (no doubt high) percentage of the variance in rates of fall, singly or in various combinations. A radical, deductively fertile simplification of the whole complex process might, but almost certainly would not, have emerged.

The Galilean notion was widely disputed until a crucial experiment could be conducted to check it out. Objects of different weights did demonstrably fall at different, sometimes vastly different, rates. So the Galileans' extraneous factors, having no place in the law, remained other people's favoured explanatory variables. Only with the invention of the air pump, about 1650, was a definitive experiment possible: dropping a heavy object (coin) and a light one (feather) in an evacuated tube. Again, no systematic comparative measurement was used, only a single experimental observation that foreclosed weaseling out by *ad hocery* to Galileans and Aristotelians alike. [...]

Comparative observations may be significant in fleshing out basic conceptions of regularities (for example, determining that the velocity of freely falling objects is described by $s = gt^2$, or measuring any specific value g). But they are far from necessary, and quite likely to deceive, when these basic conceptions – critical variables and their basic relationship – are to be formulated.

(c) The inductive fallacy has a third facet, pertaining exclusively to testing. It might be conceded that discovering and testing theories are different processes, but not that testing requires data different from those that help in discovery. The analysis of data may be so convincing that one might not consider it worthwhile to test rules derived from them but, despite this, the experiences in light of which theories are constructed cannot be used again as tests of them. Testing involves efforts to falsify, and anything giving rise to a theory will certainly not falsify it; nor will any body of replicated observations do so, if replication indeed is faithful. (Replication pertains to reliability, not validity.) The object of testing is to find observations that must fit a theory but have a good chance of not doing so. Nothing that suggests a theory, therefore, can also test it.

2.   Having established a need for the independent testing of theoretical curves (on the grounds that the discovery and testing of theories

are intrinsically different activities, that no method of discovery can guarantee validity, that even painstakingly gathered and analysed data can deceive, and that data which suggest regularities cannot also validate them), we come to the crux: the argument of the fifth option that, *in principle, comparative and case studies are alternative means to the end of testing theories, choices between which must be largely governed by arbitrary or practical, rather than logical, considerations.*

Comparative studies can certainly be used to test theories. If we use them for this purpose, our object, as stated, is to demonstrate that a curve that fits their results well in fact closely coincides with a curve postulated by theory, however that may have been worked out. In the case of a law like that of the velocity of falling objects, for example, one might try to demonstrate that the curve yielded by a set of observations sustains the expectation that the postulated law is an increasingly better predictor as one increasingly approximates the conditions under which the law is considered to hold absolutely.

However, there is available (not necessarily in all cases, but in many) an alternative to that rather cumbersome procedure, and it involves a kind of case study. One can use a well-constructed experiment, conducted to simulate as closely as possible the specified conditions under which a law must hold, and compare its result with that predicted by the law. In the history of science the decisive experiments have been mostly of that kind, a fact that makes one wonder how the comparative observation of unmanipulated cases could ever have come to be regarded as any sort of equivalent of experimental method in the physical sciences. (The main reasons are, by my reading, the influence of J.S. Mill's *Logic*, the intuitive decision reached by some influential contemporary social scientists that their regularity statements must unavoidably be 'probabilistic' in form, origin and testing, and the fact that much experimentation in the physical sciences is simply hopeful fishing for regularities in masses of data.) And if a well-constructed experiment can serve the purpose, then so may a well-chosen case – one that is somehow as crucial for a theory as are certain experiments, or indeed natural observations, in the physical sciences.

This argument is not at all impugned by the incontestable principle regarding the relations between points and curves with which we started. For there is another principle about those relations that is equally incontestable. This is that any given point can fall only on an infinitesimal fraction of all conceivable curves: it will not fall on any of the curves, the number of which is also infinity, that do not in fact pass through the point. (A less abstract variant of this principle is that for every plausible explanation of a political event, there is an infinite number that are not even minimally plausible.) The fact that a point falls, or does not fall, on a curve, therefore, is not at all insignificant. If the curve is not constructed to pass through the point but preconstructed to represent a theory, and if, given the nature of a case subsequently examined, we can predict, according to the theory, that it must fall on, or very near, the curve at a specified location, the fact that it does so is of the utmost significance, and its location far from the predicted point will impeach the theory no less than the tendency of several points to describe a divergent curve. At any rate, this is the case if the bases for predicting the location of an unknown point are really compelling – which is the object of crucial case study. In such case study, the compelling instance 'represents' a regularity as, in comparative study, a sample of individuals 'represents' a population.

3.   Crucial case study presupposes that crucial cases exist. Whether they do or not in macropolitics can hardly be settled abstractly. All one can say on the subject is the following: (i) If they do not, no reasonable alternative to testing theory by comparative study exists. (ii) The inability to identify cases crucial for theories may be the result not of their non-existence but of the loose way theories are stated, their relative lack of [...] 'rulefulness'. (iii) Any *a priori* assumption as to their non-existence manifestly is a self-fulfilling prophecy, and it is difficult to see with what compelling reasoning such an assumption might be justified. (iv) If that reasoning rests on the inability to use controlled laboratory experiments in macropolitics, it suffices to point out that crucial measures in the physical sciences can be of natural observations (as, for example, the confirmation of Einsteinian relativity). And, obviously most important, (v) both hypothetical and actual examples of (apparently) crucial observations in the social sciences, including observations of complex collective individuals, can be found – and would almost certainly be found more often if deliberately sought more often.

A more important question, therefore, is how a crucial case can be recognized. What guidelines can be used?

The essential abstract characteristic of a crucial case can be deduced from its function as a test of theory. It is a case that *must closely fit* a theory if one is to have confidence in the theory's validity, or, conversely, *must not fit* equally well any rule contrary to that proposed. The same point can be put thus: in a crucial case it must be extremely difficult, or clearly petulant, to dismiss any finding contrary to theory as simply 'deviant' (due to change, or the operation of unconsidered factors, or whatever 'deviance' might refer to other than the fact of deviation from theory *per se*) and equally difficult to hold that any finding confirming theory might just as well express quite different regularities. One says difficult and petulant because claims of deviance and the operation of other regularities can always be made. The question is therefore not whether they are made but how farfetched or perverse the reasons for them (if any) are. [...]

An alternative is to focus inquiry on 'most-likely' or 'least-likely' cases – cases that ought, or ought not, to invalidate or confirm theories, if any cases can be expected to do so. The best-known example in political study probably is Michels' inquiry into the ubiquitousness of oligarchy in organizations, based on the argument that certain organizations (those consciously dedicated to grass-roots democracy and associated ideologies, representing classes whose interest lies in such democracy, having highly elaborate and pure formal democratic procedures, and leaders from the same social strata as the membership) are least likely, or very unlikely, to be oligarchic if oligarchy were not universal. (One may argue with Michels' choice of social units, his methods, or his findings – see Willey, 1971 – but the principle of the idea is surely sound.) Another example is Malinowski's (1926) study of a highly primitive, communistic (in the anthropological sense) society, to determine whether automatic, spontaneous obedience to norms in fact prevailed in it, as was postulated by other anthropologists. The society selected was a 'most-likely' case – the very model of primitive, communistic society – and the finding was contrary to the postulate: obedience was found to result from 'psychological and social inducements'. A similar example is Whyte's (1943) study of Boston slum gangs, collective individuals that should, according to prevailing theory, have exhibited a high level of 'social disorganization', but in fact exhibited the very opposite.

The 'least-likely' case (as in Michels) seems especially tailored to confirmation, the 'most-likely' case (as in Whyte and Malinowski) to invalidation. [...]

4. To this point, the discussion has presented the case only for Option 5: that case and comparative studies are best conceived as equally useful, alternative means for testing theories. The utility of case study and the weaknesses of comparative studies have been stressed only because the reverse is far more common in [political science].

If logic does not intrinsically favour one method or another, the method to be used must be selected for other reasons, that is, out of practical, prudential considerations. One such reason may be the unavailability of clearly crucial cases. But assuming that not to be the case, probably costs and benefits become the pertinent calculus. On that calculus rests the case for the sixth option on case study, which pertains only to macropolitics. Inquiry into macropolitical units involves problems of scale and of sound comparison that point strongly toward crucial case study as the preferable method; the same considerations might also apply to stages of inquiry other than testing but are less telling there since rigour is at a lesser premium.

The most manifest practical advantage of case study is, of course, that it is economical for all resources: money, manpower, time, effort.

The economies are not strictly equal to $1/N$, where N is the number of cases studied comparatively, since some resources usually have to be devoted to the identification of crucial cases, and some work needed to prepare rigorous case study is similar to that required by rigorous comparative studies. But even so they are likely to be considerable. This economic advantage is especially important, of course, if studies are inherently costly, as they are if units are complex collective individuals. Sociologists of knowledge might note, in this connection, that the growth of comparative studies coincided with the influx of unprecedented research monies and other facilities (research institutions, crowds of postgraduate students) into political study, and that my revisionism coincides with a sudden shrinkage in these factors. If that shrinkage compels us to develop less costly means to the same ends, it will be a blessing in disguise.

A second practical advantage involves access to the subjects of study. Samples of macropolitical units are always likely to be poor and highly uncertain in result: small in number (the population being small) despite the likelihood of a sizeable range of variation. If, as is usually the case, they consist of contemporary cases, they are also bound to be a badly biased sample for all cases relevant to general laws. These problems in principle are compounded by practical problems of access resulting from the political exclusion of researchers (as in Burma), the inaccessibility of subjects in other cases, the lack of local research facilities (for example, survey research organizations), and language problems for foreign researchers, among many other factors. As a result, contemporary comparative studies in macropolitics predominantly have one or more of three characteristics: (1) small numbers of cases chosen by intuition or for convenience; (2) the use, in wide-ranging studies, of readily available, aggregate data that are often quite untrustworthy and dubious indicators of traits they supposedly represent; or (3) think-pieces based on discussions of cases by 'country-experts' in light of a common framework that are usually not at all well coordinated. Crucial case study may, of course, also suffer from problems of access. However, since crucial cases rarely appear singly, the likelihood of being unable to study properly even one of them seems considerably smaller than the likelihood of working with poor samples in comparative studies or that of having to tailor theoretical research to practical possibilities rather than the far more desirable vice versa.

A huge practical problem in comparative research involves special knowledge of the cultures being studied. The arguments made by the German exponents of the view that the *Naturwissenschaften* and *Kulturwissenschaften* are ineluctably different, and the arguments of the clinicians inspired by them are surely right insofar as they hold that 'social facts', personal or collective, are embedded in widely varying, even in each case unique, cultural systems of meaning and value, and that one can neglect these only at great peril. Their position may not imply that 'social laws' are therefore unattainable, but they do imply that the cultural sciences impose a requirement of special cultural 'understanding' that does not exist in natural science. Crucial cases can often be selected to satisfy this requirement for individual researchers, and it is always possible to acquire a great deal of cultural *Verstehen* in the course of in-depth study of a case if one does not already possess it. Even if we reject the notion of a special inherent requirement for cultural science, this point can still be made to rest convincingly on the question of special language skills and special historical and sociological knowledge of cases, for lack of which comparativists are often justly criticized.

At the very least, one can obviously, if other things are equal, go more deeply into a single case than a number of them and thus compensate for loss of range by gains in depth: to that extent, at least, the clinicians have a foolproof case. In crucial case study, the advantages of traditional scholarship, as displayed in configurative-idiographic studies, can thus be combined with those of modern technique and rigour. And it is also more possible to apply in crucial case study certain techniques developed in social science for overcoming the imperfections of single measures, especially the 'triangulation of imperfect measures' technique developed in social psychology and applied, impressively, by Greenstein and Tarrow (1971) in political socialization research. [...]

At this point it should be clear that the practical advantage of crucial case study does not lie merely in resources. Case studies yield methodological payoffs as well. This is in large part due to the fact that they help avoid difficulties that are hard to reduce or abolish in cross-cultural research. Not the least of these are two related difficulties not yet mentioned: the problem of the proper cross-cultural translation of research instruments, a subject rapidly becoming a methodological field in itself and one that absorbs ingenuity and thought better devoted to theory construction and testing themselves. In addition, if we conduct crucial case studies, we are far more likely to develop theories logically and imaginatively, rather than relying on mechanical processing to reveal them. More important still, we are more constrained to state them tightly and in proper form, suitable to testing: that is, in a manner that permits their deductive and predictive application to cases. Sloppiness in the forms of theory compatible with the criteria developed in the section on 'definitions' above is not inherent in comparative studies (certainly not in the 'disciplined' variety), but crucial case study involves far more compelling practical demands for the proper statement of theories, or else exposes far more manifestly when theories are not properly stated: that is, when nothing – or a great number of different things – can be deduced for any case from regularity statements about it.

More thought, more imagination, more logic, less busy work, less reliance on mechanical printouts, no questions about sampling, possibly firmer conclusions (including that extreme rarity in political study, the conclusively falsified hypothesis), fewer questions about empathy: these surely establish a heavy credit. It remains to see whether any debits may cancel it out.

Objections to the argument and replies to the objections

A number of arguments that might be, or have been, raised against my brief for crucial case studies should now be considered. None seem unanswerable, except in ways not very damaging to the argument. But others may see more merit in the objections than in the ways they are answered – and it is also possible that the really telling objections have been missed, or subconsciously avoided to restrict discussion to those that can be answered. The most telling objection of all, of course, would be that crucial cases simply are not available in macropolitics, but that has already been ruled out as unlikely for most, or many, theories. It is true that the literature of political science is not rich in crucial cases, but neither does it abound in efforts to find them; the most likely reason is that the very idea of crucial case study is alien to the field.

Objection I

Comparative studies have the advantage over case studies of allowing one to test for the null hypothesis that one's findings are due to chance. Case studies may turn up validating or invalidating results fortuitously, not because theories are actually valid or invalid, but because one cannot determine by single measures whether or not this is so.

Answers

(a) The possibility that a result is due to chance can never be ruled out in any sort of study; even in wide comparative study it is only more or less likely. Now, it is surely very unlikely that, out of all possible states of affairs (which normally are vastly more than the two faces of a coin and sometimes approach infinity), just that predicted by theory should fortuitously turn up in a case carefully chosen as crucial for the theory, and also improbable that in such a case the predicted result should, just by chance, be greatly out of line with actual observation. The real difference between crucial case study and comparative study, therefore, is that in the latter case, but not the former, we can assign by various conventions a specific number to the likelihood of chance results (for example, 'significant at the .05 level'). Thus, if a theorist posits that democratic stability varies directly with level of economic development and inversely with rate of economic growth, and finds a case of extreme instability with high E_d and low E_r, he cannot rule out plain bad luck, but the presumption that he has an invalid theory surely is vastly greater.

(b) Any appreciable likelihood of unlucky chance findings in a crucial case study arises from the fact that very short-run fluctuations generally occur in any measure of a variable. (Think of air temperature, or rainfall, or the climate of a marriage.) For example, a polity generally high in performance will probably experience some peaks and troughs in its level, and peaks and troughs will also occur in variables used to explain levels of performance. If we then measure a dependent variable at a peak and an independent variable at a trough, a deceptive result will certainly be obtained. But the remedy is obvious: observe over a reasonable period of time.[6]

(c) There is, of course, also a possibility of observer bias in the observation of a case (seeing only what one wishes to see), hence of misleading, if not literally fortuitous, measures. That problem exists also in comparative studies, but not so acutely because of the prophylaxis provided by statistical measures of significance. But again, simple remedies are available. The most obvious is to recognize that falsifying a theory is to be reckoned as success rather than failure, and thus to redefine what one generally wants; knowing what is valid tells one more than knowing what is not, but knowing something to be invalid does signify progress and often provides very powerful clues as to what is valid. It is true that the reward structure of the social sciences overvalues positive findings, especially in publication – which may be why methods that maximize the probability of some sort of positive result (for example, multiple regression) are so widely used. But such prizing of positive results, however tenuous, indicates scientific immaturity or insecurity and ought not to be perpetuated. It works like Gresham's law: bad theory crowds out good. (In fact, the question most frequently, and fearfully, asked about the preliminary version of this paper was: 'What do you do if a prediction about a crucial case fails?' Answer: You publish the result – if editors permit and the failure is informative, as it is almost bound to be – and you go on, trying to do better.) Apart from that fundamental point, the problem of observer bias arises more in configurative-idiographic studies than in the more rigorous varieties of case study – hence the stress on it in existing critiques of case study (Becker, 1968) – and can certainly be reduced in the study of collective individuals by the same methods used to reduce it in comparative studies, such as the correct sampling of the micro-units that constitute the case.

(d) In crucial case studies a powerful substitute for the null hypothesis can be put to work: testing for a theory's 'counter-theories', that is, likely alternative solutions if a theory is invalid, or a theory's 'antithesis', if one is available. (This can also be done in comparative research, but practical considerations make it more feasible in case study, especially if theory and counter-theories cannot be tested by exactly the same data.) The process of testing simultaneously for alternative hypotheses ('strong inference') has been held persuasively by John Platt as the correct way to put Baconian empiricism to work and, also persuasively, as the hallmark of the most rapidly developing hard sciences (high-energy physics and molecular biology). [...] A crucial case study can readily be designed not only to determine whether a case lies off a predicted point on one curve but also whether it lies on, or nearer, a predicted point on a crucial counter-curve. Since only one case is involved, the cost of doing both will not be much greater than that of performing one operation alone. Several advantages accrue. We may not merely establish that a theory is false but also why, at bottom, it is false, and what sort of theory would serve better. Furthermore, a finding near a predicted point on one curve but far off such a point on the counter-curve adds to one's case enormously. One may thus shed not only special light on one's theory, but also more general light on the more fundamental bases for further theory construction. And if both theories are confirmed, a false contradiction is exposed; if neither is, the same result is obtained, or sloppy deduction is unmasked. All this takes one far beyond the mere void of statistical nullness.

Objection 2

If preliminary comparative studies are required to identify crucial cases (for example, cases extreme on pertinent measures, or highly changeable on a measure, or having the characteristics of natural experiments), the practical advantages of case study are severely reduced. And if they are severely reduced, certain practical advantages of comparative studies, such as their ability to provide data for reanalysis or simply data from numerous contexts, tend to tip the scales in their favour.

Answers

(a) Independent comparative study is not always required to identify crucial cases, simply because in an ongoing discipline the evidence needed to identify a crucial case often is already available.

One may want to recheck that evidence or try to improve on it, but that is not tantamount to starting from scratch.

(b) Even if one starts from scratch, comparative studies specifically designed to uncover crucial cases can be very limited in scope, even confined to a single variable, and so much reduced in costs of all kinds. Common knowledge, no less than disciplinary knowledge, can also reduce problems of sampling in the search for such cases. For example, if the object were to discover a long stable polity, it would take more than ordinary ignorance to include, say, Germany in the search. Comparative studies to uncover crucial cases thus have little in common, in regard to required breadth of study or data requirements, with comparative studies as currently conducted.

(c) The fact that comparative studies provide 'extensive' data from many contexts can be offset by the usual claim for 'intensive' study: that it can provide more varieties of data (and is likely to do so not only if study is clinical but also if strong inference procedures are used). Such data, moreover, are as much subject to reanalysis as any others. They may not suit well the purposes of others, but then neither might those produced by comparative study; and virtually any body of data has import for a variety of purposes.

Objection 3

Several crucial case studies are always better than one. Some degree of additional safety is always provided by additional numbers. If, therefore, the intent is to be conclusive, crucial case study ends as comparative study anyway.

Answers

(a) The basic problem here again is the equation of success with confirmation. A single crucial case may certainly score a clean knock-out over a theory (as Galileo's thought-experiment would have, had it been a real experiment, and as the falling feather and coin in the evacuated tube later did). The problem arises only if confirmation occurs. Because distrust is a required element of the scientific culture, confirmation only eggs us on to allay our own always remaining doubts and disarm those of carping adversaries; and thus we may want to know whether a theory that fits crucial case X also fits cases Y and Z, assuming these are also crucial, and whether, despite precautions and great unlikelihood, chance has tricked us after all. But the further examination of other cases can be restricted much more than in comparative studies that rest their case on sampling, and in such studies 'added confirmation' may also be deemed advisable – in fact, is necessary if the studies merely establish curves rather than matching them.

(b) Conceivably, the most powerful study of all for theory building is neither the presently common from of comparative study (of cases studied randomly, or intuitively selected, or simply studied because they seem readily available or accessible) nor the study of single crucial cases, but, so to speak, 'comparative crucial case studies'. The case for such studies, however, is strong only to the extent that the most crucial cases available are not very crucial, so that high confidence in the results they yield needs the increment of other crucial case findings. Thus, the feather and coin falling in a vacuum leave virtually no doubt to the sceptic or the inquirer devoted to the tested theory, while a case of change in governmental performance highly unlikely to be due merely to the disappearance of performance-depressing factors, as against the factor posited to be required for high performance, probably leaves enough doubt to both to make desirable a further study or two of equal import. The study of such a more tenuous case might also, in some instances, be considered an especially powerful 'plausibility probe', warranting the (costly) comparative testing of a probabilistic hypothesis like that logically implied in the congruence theory of governmental performance that 'in all cases, the correlation between performance and congruence will be high' (Eckstein, 1966, p. 282). The comparativist may treat any and all crucial case studies as plausibility probes, warranting the costs of using his favoured method. The notion of the crucial case study was, after all, devised largely from that of the plausibility probe. The point is that he need not do so, unless the crucial case falls far short of the ideal.

Objection 4

Crucial case studies turn out to be comparative studies in disguise. For instance, when dropping a coin and feather through an evacuated tube we take two simultaneous measures and compare them; or, when studying the correlates of a change from low to high governmental performance we again take two measures at different points in time and compare them. The distinction between comparative studies and case studies thus vanishes, along with that between the clinical and experimental modes of inquiry.

Answers

(a) Not all crucial measures are like that. Observing the deflection of light near the rim of the sun compares nothing with anything (unless it is claimed that it compares deflection with non-deflection). The same holds true if only high governmental performance, not change towards it, is the critical observation.

(b) It is by no means sophistic to maintain that the supposedly dual measures above are single measures, that is, measures of the amount of change in performance between an earlier and a later period or the amount of difference in the rate of fall of two objects. Such changes and differences can be used as points on a curve no less than measurements of static conditions at a particular point in time, and thus satisfy the exacting technical definition of case study.

(c) Measures of 'more than', 'less than' and 'equal to' do presuppose two anchoring measures (see also Objection 5, Answer (d) below), but are not to be confused with comparative measures of samples, and $N = 2$ always suffices to establish them. Thus the distinction between case studies and comparative studies is watered down little, even if points (a) and (b) are disregarded.

Objection 5

Social science, especially on the macro level, does not have available measures precise and discriminating enough to make the sort of predictions needed for crucial case study.

Answers

(a) If this is true, the fact must bedevil comparative studies as much as any others, unless there is some magic by which many poor measures are equal to one that is good. Numerous poor measures can, of course, cancel one another out, or increase confidence in any one of them. But they can also make for increased distortion, that is, reinforce one another, and will certainly do so if a measuring instrument contains a consistent bias.

(b) What gospel ordains that social measures must be highly inexact and undiscriminating? That of experience? Perhaps; but perhaps only because of the prevalent assumption that nothing precise can be done in social study – surely a self-fulfilling prophecy if ever there was one. And while there is research there is hope: most of the natural sciences had to live long, and managed quite well, with rather imprecise measures too, and ours have been improving.

(c) Highly discriminating measures are *not* required to put crucial case study to work. If the measure to be predicted is, let us say, the level of democratic stability in postwar Germany, it is not necessary to be able to say that the level is at 112.56 [...] with reasonable assurance that it is not then at 112.57. It may quite suffice to say that the measure must come out somewhere between 8 and 10 on a ten-point scale, either because theory permits or because of recognized possible error in a measuring technique. The possibility of disconfirmation then still exists, and is, after all, about four times as likely as confirmation. There must, of course, be a limit on imprecision. The minimum requirement is that measures must not be so inexact that any measure considered to validate (or invalidate) a theory could also, because of inherently possible measurement error, be taken to imply the opposite. If we cannot do much better than that in the social sciences, we might as well not measure at all, in any kind of study. Therefore, arguments about imprecision impugn quantitative social science, not crucial case study only.

(d) If no more than a single point is measured, however, crucial case study does presuppose interval measures (even if measurement techniques do not allow discrimination between minute intervals). If only ordinal measures are available, then (and only then) one must have two measurements to confirm, or invalidate, the prediction that a variable will have a higher, or lower, value at one time than another, or under one condition than under another. Ordinal measures only state 'more than', 'less than' or 'equal to', and that always requires two points of reference, as stated above. And, as also already stated, this still concedes next to nothing to comparative study, and perhaps nothing at all if the predicted measure is interpreted as the measure of a difference of some discernible magnitude.

Objection 6

Crucial case studies cannot confirm multivariate theories, in which one deals with one dependent and several independent variables. The social sciences (especially on the macro level, where crucial case study is most advantageous) deal with multivariate phenomena: phenomena in which a variety of determinants converge upon observed experience.

Answers

(a) Again one wants to know: What gospel ordains that social pheno-mena must be multivariate, or decisively more so than any others? One might answer, the phenomena themselves: look, for instance, at all the factors associated with revolution, or authoritarian political behaviour, or political instability, or non-voting. True – but not decisive, and quite probably pernicious. In the natural sciences, too, 'causes' converge in phenomenal experience, but notable successes have been achieved in cutting through the phenomenal complexities to simple theoretical constructs that are powerful tools in explaining particular occurrences or, by engineering, for bringing them about. (For example, the law of velocity of freely falling objects consists of one dependent variable, velocity, and one independent variable, time, gravitational force being a constant; but actual 'falling' depends on many more factors, although some operate only with infinitesimal effects.) The problem of multivariate complexity largely dissolves if theory is thought of as a tool of explanation of the behaviour of concrete individuals rather than as total explanation. And the probable perniciousness of the assumption that theories must be multivariate if phenomena are resides precisely in the fact that then they will be, thus missing beautiful and powerful simplicities, even if they might be found.

(b) Multivariate theories do *not* necessarily rule out crucial case study in testing, provided that one does not simply list independent variables that affect a dependent variable (*x* has some relationship to *a*, *b*, *c*, ... *n*) but specifies precisely the relationship of each to the dependent variable and their effects on one another. Newton's theory of gravity, for example, is multivariate: the dependent variable, gravitational force, is determined by two independent variables, mass and distance. But it specifies a direct relationship to one and an inverse relationship to the square of the other. Given the constant necessary to turn these ideas into an equation, predictions can be made for any case that may conclusively confirm or invalidate. The problem then lies more in the way multivariate theories are stated than in multivariation as such. The job of avoiding that problem is immensely difficult (most of us probably need not apply) but it ought to be tackled, even though here again the prevalent reward structure of the social sciences discourages the attempt to do the better work that is more likely to fail, or to be perceived as failure.

(c) A real problem is that a case finding may be the result of complex 'interaction effects'. The careful choice of a case may allow one to discount that as a probability, but never altogether, and the fact that the problem might also queer comparative findings (more factors are nearly always interacting than a research design takes into account or allows one to separate) does not abolish the difficulty. The only sensible response is to treat the possibility as reason for continued doubt of some magnitude or other, and thus for further research. If the findings confirm a theory, that simply implies that one might want additional assurance in another pertinent instance. The point here is exactly the same as that regarding the possibility of 'chance' results. If the findings disconfirm, and one has strong prior reasons to consider a hypothesis valid (for example, because of various sorts of estimates of plausibility), the sensible course is simply not to give in all at once but to try another crucial test. In neither case is comparative study the required solution. The responses simply involve added confirmation, or added disconfirmation, by further crucial case study. And studies of additional cases for added assurance are not, strictly speaking, 'comparative' studies.

Objection 7

Crucial case studies cannot test probabilistically stated theories.

Answers

(a) Agreed.

(b) Theories need not be probabilistic, and the more powerful are not, even if the occurrence of phenomena is. Here, once again, the difficulty lies in confusion between theory as a tool of explanation and theory as the full explanation of concrete events. (That confusion is especially reprehensible in this case because probability statements, inherently, are not total explanations either.) The position rests also on two further fallacies: that if something is true probabilistically of a numerous set of cases, then the probability of its being true is equal for each individual in the set (which is true only in rare cases, like tossing fair coins); and that no mere probability can be deduced from a 'law' (it can, to the extent that the conditions under which a law is supposed to hold absolutely do not in fact exist, or to the extent that a law treats variables as constants).

(c) Probability statements are used more often than they need be in political study because of the uncompelled belief that they must be, which works, like other methodological assumptions, as self-fulfilling prophecy.

Objection 8

Even if all these objections are answerable, it is highly suspicious that so many should arise. Case study seems more susceptible to challenge than comparative study, in regard to which most of these problems are not even raised.

Answer

The essential difference here is not the volume of issues, but that the issues differ because the methods differ. Moreover, comparativists have only recently begun to raise important difficulties inherent in their method, especially on the macro level. But, in a relatively short time, an impressive number of difficulties in the method have turned up. After all that has recently been written about difficulties in comparative cross-national study, or even in micro-level studies – problems concerning the selection and proper number of cases, the feasibility and trustworthiness of research instruments (like survey research schedules), the comparability of data, or the utility of various data-processing techniques and modes of inferring regularities from numerous data (for example, various types of significance tests, attributions of causal paths to correlations, attributing longitudinal characteristics to synchronous data) – it is impossible to take seriously the position that case study is suspect because problem-prone and comparative study deserving of benefit of doubt because problem-free.

Conclusion

Case study in macropolitics begins in idiography and is rooted in the traditional conception of clinical study. In recent years the position that case study cannot be 'nomothetic' has been increasingly attacked in psychology, the very field that made the distinction between idiographic and nomothetic study sharpest and most insuperable. But the notion of nomothetic case study has not been taken far. If not conceived as the application of established theory to case interpretation, it has merely been represented as case study in which rigorous methods, similar to those of 'experimental' study, are used and/or in which individual experience is used to help find clues to general theories. If more has been claimed, as by Chassan, it has turned out that the term case study ('$N = 1$' study) is indefensibly applied, by confusing a case with a concrete person rather than a measure (see Davidson and Costello, 1969).

My object has been to take the argument for nomothetic case study far beyond this point, following up clues provided by examination of more modest arguments in favour of it. The point has been to relate '$N = 1$' studies to all phases of theory building and particularly to stress the utility of case study where rigour is most required and case studies have been considered least useful. Comparative studies have not been attacked, except on practical grounds in limited fields of inquiry; nor is it claimed that appropriate case studies are always available for all theoretical purposes, and absolutely not that any kind of case study will serve all purposes. The types of case study are numerous, and that recommended for going beyond formulating candidate-theories is extremely rare in [political science] or related disciplines.

The argument thus is mainly abstract. There is no track record worth mentioning. But if the horse is run, the results just might be astounding – or, possibly, abysmal. The point is that trials seem in order, not in place of but alongside comparative researches.

It should be evident that case study can be nomothetic only if cases are not selected for the theoretically trivial reasons that nowadays predominate in their selection: because one knows the language, finds a culture congenial to live and work in, can get money for study in it through an affluent area programme, considers the case important for foreign policy or otherwise publicly marketable, finds it exotic, and the like. Considerations of congeniality or publicity are well and good if other things are equal, not otherwise. And not the least advantage of crucial case studies is that they may permit one to study intensively attractive or convenient cases without sacrifice of disciplinary conscience.

Notes

1 The power of theories can also be assessed by another criterion, not included in the text because it strikes me as something for which theorists generally hope, rather than something at which they consciously aim. This is 'deductive fertility': not just unexpected knowledge but knowledge in unexpected areas, that is, reliable and valid accounts of observations outside the original fields of interest. That criterion can, of course, be consciously pursued when one asks whether a single regularity statement can account for observations that several separate ones cover, or whether the separate regularities can be deduced from a higher-order rule.

2 The foreknowledge criterion also seems pivotal for economic theorists. Thus, Friedman writes: 'The belief that a theory can be tested by the realism of its assumptions independently of the accuracy of its predictions is widespread and the source of much of the perennial criticism of economic theory.' It seems pivotal as well in contemporary philosophy of science, for the emphases on the deductive elaboration of propositions and parsimony are mainly attributable to the stress on non-intuitive foreknowledge (that is, foreknowledge that is not prophecy or clairvoyance, but rigorously deduced from 'rules') as the crucial test of theories. I agree with these positions, except for holding that the ends sought do not manifestly require a unique form of theory. For a somewhat different 'hard', but not over-demanding, view of theory – also based on natural science models but making central 'generality' (that is, range of applicability) and parsimony (that is, the number of factors needed for complete explanation of a class of events) – see Przeworski and Teune (1970).

3 For bibliography, see Holt (1962, p. 402).

4 If the essence of disciplined-configurative study is its application to cases of pre-established theories or to tools for building theories, we can distinguish four subspecies of this type of case study. They are quite different and need to be differentiated. (1) *Nomological case studies*, as they might be called, are studies of the sort Verba has in mind: studies that interpret cases on the basis of theories considered generally valid. (2) *Paradigmatic case studies* involve the application to a case of a pre-established framework, or checklist, for analysis, such as Almond's functional framework or the decision-making framework used in some studies of foreign policies. In (3) *methodical case study* rigorous methods associated with experimental study are applied to the study of individual cases, as in the studies reprinted in Davidson and Costello (1969). In (4) *therapeutic case study* validated theories and rigorous methods are used to diagnose problems and difficulties

and to arrive at likely ways of eliminating or reducing them. (The labels used here are mine and arbitrary; they seem apt for the types.) The first subspecies is uncommon in all the social sciences, except economics, for reasons mentioned in the text. The third is common in psychology, the fourth more common in psychiatry than in other human sciences. In political science, the second subspecies predominates, exceeded in frequency only by configurative-idiographic studies.

5 These statements do not imply that *acting* on clues provided by empirically drawn curves is foolish. Usually it is wise – for example, not smoking if one wants to keep one's health – and often nothing better is available for making prudent decisions. The pre-eminent function of statistical analyses, as Wallis and Roberts emphasize, is in fact to help one to make wise decisions in the face of uncertainty. Hence such analyses are best used to help cope with problems of action (for example, traffic control problems, public health problems, problems of increasing agricultural yields, and the like) in which valid theories provide no better guide than plain statistics and in regard to which common sense is inadequate. As the field of statistics has become more and more powerful for this purpose, statistical findings have become increasingly confused with theories, but the distinction remains.

6 What constitutes a reasonable period of time for observations cannot be specified even in general terms. It depends on what one is studying, and it can generally be determined only by a combination of reasoning and reflection on findings. 'Reasonable' time spans make it unlikely that findings will be distorted by fortuitous short-term events. For example, I have argued, upon reasoning, that valid measures of performance require observations of polities over about a ten-year period at the least. Gurr and McClelland in *Political Performance* (1971), an empirical follow-up study, suggest, upon evidence, that a shorter time span might be serviceable for certain measures of performance.

References

Almond, G. and Verba, S. (1963) *The Civic Culture: Political Attitudes and Democracy in Five Nations.* Princeton, NJ: Princeton University Press.

Becker, H.S. (1968) 'Social observation and case studies', in D.L. Sills (ed.), *International Encyclopedia of the Social Sciences* (Vol. 11). New York: Macmillan and Free Press. Reprinted in H.S. Becker (1971) *Sociological Work.* Chicago: Aldine.

Buchanan, J.M. and Tullock, G. (1967) *The Calculus of Consent.* Ann Arbor: University of Michigan Press.

Curry, R.L. Jr and Wade, L.L. (1968) *A Theory of Political Exchange.* Englewood Cliffs, NJ: Prentice-Hall.

Dahl, R.A. (1961) *Who Governs?* New Haven: Yale University Press.

Davidson, P.O. and Costello, C.C. (eds) (1969) *N = 1: Experimental Studies of Single Cases.* New York: Van Nostrand Reinhold.

Downs, A. (1965) *An Economic Theory of Democracy.* New York: Harper & Row.

Eckstein, H. (1964) 'Introduction', in H. Eckstein (ed.), *Internal War.* New York: Free Press.

Eckstein, H. (1966) *Division and Cohesion in Democracy: A Study of Norway.* Princeton, NJ: Princeton University Press.

Glaser, B.G. and Strauss, A.L. (1967) *The Discovery of Grounded Theory: Strategies for Qualitative Research.* Chicago: Aldine.

Greenstein, F.I. and Tarrow, S. (1971) *Political Orientations of Children: Semi-projective Responses from Three Nations* (Professional Papers in Comparative Politics). Beverly Hills, CA: Sage.

Gurr, T.R. (1970) *Why Men Rebel*. Princeton, NJ: Princeton University Press.

Gurr, T.R. and McClelland, M. (1971) *Political Performance: A Twelve-Nations Study* (Professional Papers in Comparative Politics). Beverly Hills, CA: Sage.

Hempel, C.G. (1965) *Aspects of Scientific Explanation*. New York: Free Press.

Holt, R.R. (1962) 'Individuality and generalization in the psychology of personality', *Journal of Personality*, 30: 377–404.

Holt, R.R. and Richardson, J.M. (1968) *The State of Theory in Comparative Politics*. Minneapolis: Center for Comparative Studies in Technological Development and Social Change, University of Minnesota.

Kaufmann, H. (1958) 'The next step in case-studies', *Public Administration Review*, 18: 52–9.

Kemeny, J.G. (1959) *A Philosopher Looks at Science*. Princeton, NJ: Van Nostrand Reinhold.

Lowi, T.H. (1964) 'American business, public policy, case-studies and political theory'. *World politics*, 16: 677–715.

Malinowski, B. (1926) *Crime and Custom in Savage Society*. New York: Harcourt, Brace & World.

Merton, R.K. (1962) *Social Theory and Social Structure*. Glencoe, IL: Free Press.

Osgood, C.E. and Luria, Z. (1954) 'A blind analysis of a case of multiple personality using the semantic differential', *Journal of Abnormal and Social Psychology*, 49: 579–91.

Platt, J.R. (1966) *The Step to Man*. New York: Wiley.

Popper, K.R. (1959) *The Logic of Scientific Discovery*. London: Hutchinson.

Przeworski, A. and Teune, H. (1970) *The Logic of Comparative Social Inquiry*. New York: Wiley.

Riker, W.H. (1962) *The Theory of Political Coalitions*. New Haven: Yale University Press.

Riley, W.H. (1963) *Sociological Research: A Case Approach*. New York: Harcourt, Brace & World.

Verba, S. (1967) 'Some dilemmas in comparative research', *World Politics*, 20: 111–27.

Whyte, W.F. (1943) *Street Corner Society: The Social Structure of an Italian Slum* Chicago: University of Chicago Press.

Willey, J.R. (1971) *Democracy in the West German Trade Unions: A Reappraisal of the 'Iron Law'* (Professional Papers in Comparative Politics). Beverley Hills, CA: Sage.

Windelband, W. ([1982]/1998) 'History and natural science', *Theory & Psychology*, 8 (1): 5–22.

CHAPTER 7

CASE AND SITUATION ANALYSIS

J. Clyde Mitchell

Clearly one good case can illuminate the working of a social system in a way that a series of morphological statements cannot achieve. (Gluckman, 1961, p. 9)

The current division between those sociologists who prefer to rely on survey techniques and quantitative analysis in the prosecution of their art as against those who prefer to rely on observation and verbal types of analysis has had a long history. Just over fifty years ago – in the late 1930s in fact – the division manifested itself in a lively debate in some of the journals about the validity of statistical methods of inquiry on the one hand as against what were called 'case studies'.[1]

Textbooks on sociological methods of research published before, say, 1955, such as Young (1939: 226–54) or Goode and Hatt (1952: 313–40) invariably included a chapter on case studies, but since then the topic seems to have lost its appeal, for while non-quantitative procedures such as participant observation receive extensive treatment the issue of the role of case studies as such seems to have disappeared. The change in emphasis is dramatically reflected in the general index of the *American Journal of Sociology*, which had its origin in Chicago, from which the most important case studies first emerged and which carried the account of the debate in its pages. The Cumulative Index at 1950 contained sixteen references to case studies and case histories.[2] The most recent reference is to Oscar Lewis' discussion of the detailed studies of families in 1950. After that the entry for case studies disappears from the index! A paper on case studies appeared in *Social Forces* at about the same time (Foreman, 1948). Since then it appears to have faded from sociological discussion, but it has survived in education research (see Simons, 1980).

This eclipse of interest in case studies as a method of sociological analysis is partly due to the vast expansion of quantitative techniques stimulated by the wide availability of computers, which has broken the back of formerly extremely time-consuming processing of large sets of survey data. Hand in hand with the steady strides in the sophistication of statistical techniques, a theory of sampling soundly based on probability mathematics has grown up so that the survey analyst has available

Originally published in (1983) *Sociological Review*, 31 (2): 187–211.

an extensive armamentarium of procedures and techniques all resting on firm epistemological grounds.

The foundation of statistical inference from samples representative of a wider population has now become commonplace knowledge, and most first-year students in the social sciences are made familiar with such notions as 'a representative sample', 'sampling error', 'biased and unbiased estimates' and similar ideas developed to express the logic of making inferences about a larger population from a considerably smaller sample.

In the course of this development the epistemology of the case study seems to have been neglected, with a corresponding confusion about the degree to which those who either by force of circumstances or by deliberate choice find themselves engaged in case studies. The consequence is that we find criticism of their findings to the effect that these findings are invalid because they are based on only one case.[3] This confusion of procedures of statistical inference with those appropriate to case studies is indexed particularly by the challenge frequently addressed to those who have chosen to pursue the deviant path of case studies: 'How do you know that the case you have chosen is typical?'

I shall argue that this question betrays a confusion between the procedures appropriate to making inferences from statistical data and those appropriate to the study of an idiosyncratic combination of elements or events which constitute a 'case'. It is my purpose to establish what these differences are, and thereby one hopes to provide guidelines for the use of case studies in social investigation and theory building.[4]

The case study in social anthropology

The method of case studies is, of course, general and has been extensively used, for example, in political science and in sociology. But more than in other social sciences, perhaps, each fieldworker who presents a study of some 'people' or another in a social anthropological monograph is in fact doing a case study. Possibly because quantitative techniques do not play so central a role in social anthropology as in sociology there has been more discussion of the method of case study in anthropology. One of the earliest general statements about the role of case studies by Barnes in 1958 drew a contrast between the formal method of institutional analysis and the complexity of the 'Russian novel' approach through case studies (Barnes, 1958). In 1960 he described the case-history approach as a 'distinctive feature' of present-day social anthropology (Barnes, 1960, p. 201).

Each people an anthropologist studies may be looked upon as displaying a unique combination of cultural characteristics. But the anthropologist sets out to interpret some aspect of the way of life of this people by using an approach which an anthropologist studying some quite different people may also employ. In short nearly the whole of the respectable body of anthropological theory has been built up over the years from a large number of separate case studies from which the anthropologists have been prepared to draw inferences and to formulate propositions about the nature of social and cultural phenomena in general. What appears not to be so widely discussed in anthropology, however, is the epistemological basis upon which these generalizations have been made, and it is to this question that I wish to turn, with its implication for the role of case studies in the development of theories in general, whether in social anthropology or not.

A more focused statement appeared in 1961 when Max Gluckman discussed the history and use of case material in anthropological analysis (Gluckman, 1961). In it he drew the important distinctions among what he called 'apt illustrations', 'social situations' and 'extended case studies', the implications of which I return to later (see pp. 170–1 below). The basic problem with the use of case material in theoretical analysis, however, is that of the extent to which the analyst is justified in generalizing from a single instance of an event which may be – and probably is – unique. This problem is normally presented as that of the 'typicality' of the case which is used to support some theoretical analysis. A typical case implies that the particular set of events selected for report is similar in *relevant* characteristics to other cases of the same type.

Gluckman (1967) was well aware of this since he raises the question in the following terms:

> I can touch only briefly on the problem of typicality for a society of the area of social life selected for analysis in this way. In the first place the use of the extended case does not do away with the need for the outline of social morphology, on which Malinowski insisted, and this may have to be illustrated by apt examples. But here the increasing use of statistics, in more refined form, by anthropologists provides an important safeguard. (p. 14)

He argues in effect that a specification of the general wider context in which the events of the case are located must be based on other analytical techniques. Typicality, therefore, in his argument pertains to the social morphology rather than to the case, which may only be an apt illustration of it. Similarly the use of statistical analysis as a countermeasure to the untypicality of the case material also implies the use of methods other than the case study as a basis to assure typicality. Gluckman does not develop these points, which remain peripheral issues to his argument as a whole, so that the crucial issue of the basis upon which the case analyst may extrapolate from his material is left unanswered.

In another important discussion of case analysis, van Velsen (1967) once again addressed the problem of the typicality of the case chosen for analysis. His essay is concerned with a variant of case analysis, that is, with situational analysis, and his main purpose is to redress the imbalance he saw in the over-emphasis on structuralist types of analysis in anthropology at that time. He argues instead for a greater emphasis on the optative approach in which the choice taking of actors is given due weight as against the concentration on the institutional framework within which the actors were operating. Analysis of this kind requires a very detailed and intimate familiarity by the observer of the behaviour and cognitive orientations of the actors in the events being described. The restriction on the coverage such detailed investigation requires necessarily imposes limitations on the extent to which the observer is able to describe the whole 'culture' or whole 'society' of the people being studied. These restrictions, van Velsen (1967) argues, raise 'the question of the typicality of the anthropologist's analysis' (p. 145). Van Velsen resolves this question by arguing that the object of the analysis is not in fact 'culture' or 'society', of which the events studied might be considered samples, but rather social processes, which may be abstracted from the course of events analysed.

At this point, I feel, van Velsen stops short of making the essential point about the basis of making inferences from case material: that the extrapolation is in fact based on the validity of the analysis rather than the representativeness of the events. This is a point to which we will need to return, but before doing so it is necessary to specify more exactly the sort of material implied by the terms 'social situation' or 'case'.

Specification of the case study

The term 'case study' may refer to several very different epistemological entities, and it is necessary at the outset to specify the particular meaning I am attributing to it here.

In its most basic form a case study may refer to the fundamental descriptive material an observer has assembled by whatever means available about some particular phenomenon or set of events. The case material here is simply the content of the observer's field notes prior to any deliberate analysis or selection for presentation in some analysis. Similar in character are the case records developed by practitioners in some field of action – physicians, clinical psychologists, psychiatrists, social workers, probation officers, and the like. Normally these practitioners are trained in the art of systematically recording information which may be germane for their practical action.

Both of these types of 'case study' may become the basis of the rather more specific means I shall be attributing to the terms here, that is, as material from which some theoretical principles are to be inferred.

Some writers, like Madge (1953, p. 100), are mainly concerned with material of this kind, so that the problem then becomes the procedure upon which data may be extracted from material of this kind for theoretical purposes.

But throughout what follows I shall be assuming that the 'case study' refers to an observer's data: that is, the documentation of some particular phenomenon or set of events which has been assembled with the explicit end in view of drawing theoretical conclusions from it.[5] The focus of the case study may be a single individual, as in the life-history approach, or it may be a set of actors engaged in a sequence of activities either over a restricted or over an extended period of time. What is important is not the content of the case study as such but the use to which the data are put to support theoretical conclusions.

In what way, then, does a case study differ from any other way of assembling systematic information about social phenomena for research purposes? Goode and Hatt (1952), the authors of one of the few textbooks on sociological methods which discusses case studies, describe the case study as a 'a way or organizing social data so as to preserve the *unitary character of the social object being studied'*. They go on:

> Expressed somewhat differently, it is an approach which views any social unit as a whole. Almost always this means of approach includes the development of that unit, which may be a person, a family or other social group, a set of relationships or processes (such as a family crisis, adjustment to disease, friendship formation, ethnic invasion of a neighborhood, etc.) or even an entire culture. (p. 331; original italics)

They contrast this with the 'survey' type of analysis in which the person is replaced by the trait as the unit of analysis. The wholeness 'characterizing' the case study, they point out, is determined by the extent to which the analyst has assembled enough information about the object of study to provide sufficient specification of the research purpose in mind.[6] As they point out, 'The case study attempting to organize the data around the unit of growth, or group structure, or individual life pattern, does force the researcher to think in these terms rather than fall back on trait analysis alone' (p. 339).

But Goode and Hatt, in this early – and relatively rare – discussion of the use of case studies in sociological research, overlook two crucial features of the case study which bear directly on the main topic of this paper, that is, the basis of extrapolation or of inference from case studies. In the first instance, Goode and Hatt assume without demur that the *only* way of extrapolating from data is on the basis of a statistically representative sample, and they spend a good deal of space pointing to the problems of securing representative cases for subsequent statistical analysis. The second point is that, while they emphasize the 'wholeness' of the case, they appear to be unaware that each individual case is influenced by circumstances which the researcher may wish to control for in the analysis. All cases, as van Velsen (1967, p. 146) and Garbett (1970, p. 217) point out so clearly, are located within some wider context which in turn imposes constraints on the actions of the protagonists in the case study. These contexts constitute a panoply of *ceteris paribus* conditions which the analyst will need to allow for in some way.

With this background in mind, we may now turn to a specification of what we imply by the term 'case' or the cognate term 'social situation'. As a working definition, we may characterize a case study as a detailed examination of an event (or series of related events) which the analyst believes exhibits (or exhibit) the operation of some identified general theoretical principle.

The important point here is the phrase 'the operation of some general theoretical principle' since a narrative account of some event or a series of related events does not in itself constitute a case study in the sense in which I am using the notion here. A case study is essentially heuristic; it reflects in the events portrayed features which may be construed as a manifestation of some general, abstract theoretical principle.

Material derived from cases or from social situations, however, may be used analytically in different ways, and it is to this question that we now turn.

Types of case study

It was one of the merits of Gluckman's early (1961) essay in which he discussed case studies that it drew a sharp distinction between 'apt illustrations', 'social situations' and 'case studies', and how they may be used in theoretical analysis. These types of case phenomena may be viewed as falling along a continuum of increasing complexity.

1.   Near one limit – the simple end – would fall what Gluckman (1967, p. 7) called 'the apt illustration'. The apt illustration is normally a description of some fairly simple event or occurrence in which the operation of some general principle is clearly illustrated. An anthropologist may, for example, describe how he had noticed a man step off a path to conceal himself as his mother-in-law approached, and use this account to illustrate the operation in daily life of mother-in-law/son-in-law avoidance. The particular event is sequestrated either from all other ongoing events connected with the behaviour among other in-laws or from other events going on at the same time in the vicinity. The use of case material in this way is, as Gluckman's terminology indicates, merely illustrative. A *sine qua non* is that the observer must be convinced of its typicality to be able to use it as an illustration.

2.   Considerably more complex is the analysis of a social situation. A social situation is a collocation of events which the analyst is able

to construe as connected with one another and which take place in a relatively restricted time span.[7] The classic example of a social situation used as an analytical tool is Gluckman's (1958) description and analysis of the offical opening of a newly built bridge in Zululand in 1935. In the analysis of a social situation some restricted and limited (bounded) set of events is analysed so as to reveal the way in which general principles of social organization manifest themselves in some particular specified context. The official opening of the bridge brings together representatives of different sectors of the population in Zululand, Blacks and Whites, Christians and pagans, officials and citizens, Zulu nobles and commoners, and Gluckman shows how their behaviour leading up to, during and following the opening of the bridge reflects the structure of South African society, with all its alliances and cleavages, at the time when the study was done. The analysis of social situations has become a significant example of case analysis and has been discussed particularly by van Velsen (1967) and Garbett (1970).

3.   At the complex end of the continuum is the extended case study. This is a further elaboration of the basic study of case material for it deals with a sequence of events, sometimes over quite a long period, where the same actors are involved in a series of situations in which their structural positions must continually be re-specified and the flow of actors through different social positions specified. The particular significance of the extended case study is that since it traces the events in which the same set of main actors in the case study are involved over a relatively long period, the processual aspect is given emphasis. The extended case study enables the analyst to trace how events chain on to one another, and therefore how events are necessarily linked to one another through time. I used this procedure in a study of the social sturcture of a people in Malawi (Mitchell, 1956, pp. 86ff.). In the first four chapters of the book I set out the general features of morphology of social life of the people. In this section, in order to locate the operation of the general features of morphology, as, for example, the struggle for status among village headmen, I use case material as apt illustrations.

Subsequently I move to an analysis of the process whereby the villages grow and break up. For this purpose I make use of several case studies, including one which is in fact an extended case. The events described started some eight years before I was in the field and continued while I was in the field – and no doubt continued after I left it. The circumstances revolve around the daily incidents, the squabbles and altercations, the births and deaths, all of which the protagonists relate to their position in the general matrilineal kinship structure of the village, in which witchcraft accusations, marriage arrangements, village moots and even physical assaults are involved. These events in juxtaposition with one another provide us with an analytical prism through which the basic principles of matrilineal kinship located in the context of local politics may be refracted into relatively clear-cut terms.

The extended case is similar to, but broader than, the 'social dramas' which Turner (1957) used in his analysis of Ndembu social life. Social dramas are accounts of a series of crises in the daily life of the people, during which, as Turner expresses it:

> The social drama is a limited area of transparency on the otherwise opaque surface of regular, uneventful social life. Through it we are enabled to observe the crucial principles of social structure in their operation and their relative dominance at successive points in time. (p. 93)

The rationale upon which the distinctions among 'apt illustration', 'social situations' and 'extended cases' are differentiated is not immediately explicit in Gluckman's presentation. While the three types of case material are all used to support theoretical statements, as against the distinction between 'clinical' and 'theoretical' case studies referred to earlier, the distinction between 'apt illustration' and 'social situations' is clearly one of the degree of complexity of the events described; the distinction between 'social situations' and 'extended cases' is partly one of even more complexity, but it is also one of the duration of time spanning the events described. Complexity and duration are obviously linked since events covering a longer time period are likely to reflect changes and adjustments as well as simple patterns of relationships.

For this reason the classification of case studies suggested by Eckstein (1975, pp. 94–123) is perhaps more instructive. Eckstein distinguishes five categories of case study which highlight the way in which they may be used as a contribution to theoretical thinking.

These five ways of using case material are as follows:

1.   *Configurative-idiographic studies* in which the material is largely descriptive and reflects the particular concatenation of circumstances surrounding the events in a way which, while they may provide insights into the relationships among the component elements in the case, do not easily lead to direct general theoretical interpretations.

2.   *Disciplined-configurative studies*, as their name implies, are still configurations or patterns of elements but the observer does not look upon these as unique or 'idiographic'. Instead the analyst seeks to interpret the patterns in terms of general theoretical postulates. Eckstein writes:

> In essence, the chain of inquiry in disciplined-configurative studies runs from comparatively tested theory to case interpretation, and thence, perhaps, via *ad hoc* additions, newly discovered puzzles and systematized prudence, to new candidate-theories. Case study thus is tied into theoretical inquiry – but only partially, where theories apply or can be envisioned; passively, in the main, as a receptacle for putting theories to work; and

fortuitously, as a catalytic element in the unfolding of theoretical knowledge. (Eckstein, 1975: 100; see p. 135 above)

However, Eckstein goes on to point out that

> The application of theories in case interpretation, although rarely discussed, is not at all a simple process, even leaving aside the question of how valid theory is to be developed. Such applications only yield valid interpretations if the theories permit strict deductions to be made and the interpretations of the case are shown to be logically compelled by the theories. (Eckstein, 1975, p. 103; see p. 136 above)

He argues that the major utility of attempted disciplined case interpretation is that it 'forces one to state theories more rigorously than might otherwise be done – provided that the application is truly "disciplined", that is, designed to show that valid theory compels a particular case interpretation and rules out others' (Eckstein, 1975, p. 103; see p. 136 above).

3. *Heuristic case studies* are distinguished from configurative-idiographic and disciplined-configurative studies in that they are deliberately chosen in order to develop theory. As Eckstein phrases it, the heuristic case study is

> deliberately used to stimulate the imagination towards discerning important general problems and possible theoretical solutions. ... Such studies, unlike configurative-idiographic ones, tie directly into theory building and therefore are less concerned with overall concrete configurations than with potentially generalizable relations between aspects of them; they also tie into theory building less passively and fortuitously than does disciplined-configurative study, because the potentially generalizable relations do not just turn up but are deliberately sought out. (Eckstein, 1975, p. 104; see p. 137 above)

4. *Plausibility probes* are case studies used specifically to test interpretive paradigms which have been established either by previous case studies or by other procedures. Eckstein writes:

> In essence, plausibility probes involve attempts to determine whether potential validity may reasonably be considered great enough to warrant the pains and costs of testing, which are almost always considerable, but especially so if broad, painstaking comparative studies are undertaken. (Eckstein, 1975, p. 108; see pp. 140–1 above)

Plausibility probes may be undertaken after heuristic case studies have been successfully concluded. They may constitute part of a series of case studies devoted to the expansion and development of an interpretive schema or theoretical formulation relative to phenomena represented by the case. As Eckstein points out, 'The essential point for us is that, as empirical plausibility probes, case studies are often as serviceable as, or more so than, comparative ones – and nearly always a great deal cheaper' (Eckstein, 1975, p. 110; see pp. 142–3). Plausibility probes are used, then, as a preliminary test of theoretical formulations previously established by some other procedures, before a rigorous test by formal procedures.

5.   *Crucial case studies* are, as the name suggests, similar to the crucial experiment in the natural sciences, and offer the circumstances which enable the analyst to reject some theoretical proposition or, which amounts to the same thing, to support it when the circumstances appear to be loaded against it. The selection of the case is clearly difficult: the assumption is that enough will be known about the phenomenon *a priori* to enable the analyst to recognize its particular significance for the way in which the proposition has been formulated. A detailed study of the case will then enable the analyst to relate events to the theoretical proposition.

Throughout this discussion the role of theory and of theorizing in the use of case material is of paramount importance, and it is this feature which provides the means through which the fundamental problem in case studies may be approached: the basis upon which general inferences may be drawn from them.

Inference and extrapolation from case studies[8]

However clearly the basic principles are reflected in some particular case material, the crucial question upon which there is much misgiving is that of the extent to which the analyst is justified in making generalizations from that particular case to all instances of that type. In ordinary English usage there is a strong connotation that the word 'case' implies a chance or haphazard occurrence.[9] This connotation is carried over into more technical and sociological language in the form of implying that a case history or case material refers to one 'case' and is therefore unique or is a particularity. If this is true, then how can unique material form the basis of inference about some process in general?

That case material may so be used is apparent since, as previously mentioned, most social anthropological and a good deal of sociological theorizing has been founded upon case studies. The difficulty arises, I conjecture, out of the common assumption that the only valid basis of inference is that which has been developed in relation to statistical analysis. In the procedure considerable care is taken to select a sample from some parent population in such a way that no bias is introduced to the sample. The implication of the notion of 'no bias' is that the examples in the sample are not selected in a way which would reflect inaccurately the characteristics of the parent population. The procedures for achieving this are varied, the most straightforward of which is the simple random sample. The assumption behind this procedure is that if the instances for inclusion in the sample are selected in a way which excludes any possibility of biased selection, then the characteristics of the sample will reflect those of the parent population within some range of certainty which may be estimated using the assumptions of probability theory. By this procedure the sample is typical of the parent population, or, in more common terminology, it is a 'representative sample'.

The logic in this procedure is that the incidence and in fact the coincidence of charateristics in the sample reflect within the range of sampling error the incidence or coincidence of the characteristics of the parent population. Inferences are made about the parent population from the characteristics in the sample population so that dependence on a 'representative' sample is, of course, vital.

Insofar as the descriptive features of the sample (and therefore of the parent population) are concerned, the validity of the inference is probably sound. The distribution of age of a representative sample drawn from a parent population probably reflects reasonably accurately – given sampling errors – the distribution of ages within that population. A difficulty arises, however, when the relationship *between* characteristics is considered. In the sample analysed, a relationship – a correlation – in fact may be noted between, say, age and the probability of being married. In terms of the canons of statistical inference the analyst may assume that the same relationship exists between the same characteristics in the parent population. Note, however, that the inference from the sample in relation to the parent population is simply about the concomitant variation of two characteristics. The analyst must go beyond the sample and resort to theoretical thinking to link those characteristics together – in terms, for example, of an appreciation of normal life-cycle processes in the instance of age and marriage. The relationship between the characteristics may be validated by other types of observation and encapsulated in the values of the people concerned. The inference about the *logical* relationship between the two characteristics is based not upon the representativeness of the sample and therefore upon its typicality, but rather upon the plausibility or upon the logicality of the nexus between the two characteristics.

The point is well illustrated in another context by Lykken (1970), who, for purposes other than those I have in mind, quotes a finding reported by Sapolsky, who records the responses to Rorschach ink-blots of respondents with or without dietetic disorders. Sapolsky found that among sixty-two respondents some identified the ink-blots as a frog and some did not but that there was an appreciable tendency for those with dietetic disorders to react to the blot in terms of a 'frog' response and for those without these disorders not to do so. In fact some 61 per cent of those with dietetic disorders reacted with the 'frog' response to the ink-blots whereas only 16 per cent of those without dietetic disorders responded with a 'frog' response. If we are able to assume that the sample of respondents is in fact representative of the population at large, we would estimate from the chi-square statistic that a sample with a departure of this extent from the state where the frog response is distributed equally among those with and those without dietetic disorders would arise by chance sampling errors in less than one occasion in 1,000 samples.

We may be reasonably confident, therefore, that the relationship between a respondent's interpreting the ink-blot as a frog and also having a dietetic disorder seems unlikely to have arisen purely by chance, and we rely on statistical inference to assert this. But the explanation that Sapolsky advanced for this association was, according to Lykken, 'an unconscious belief in the cloacal theory of birth', which involves notions of oral impregnation and anal parturition. The excretary and reproductive canals of the frog are – they constitute the cloacal – common and this biological fact presumably provides the rationale for the belief. 'Since patients should be inclined to manifest eating disorders: compulsive eating in the case of those who wish to get pregnant and anorexia in those who do not ... such patients should also be inclined to see cloacal animals such as frogs on the Rorschach' (Lykken, 1970, p. 267). Lykken then asked twenty of his colleagues, many of them clinicians, about the hypothesis. As Lykken reports it, their reaction before they were given the experimental results was 'I don't believe it', and after they were given the experimental results it was 'I still don't believe it' (p. 268).

The issue raised here is essentially that of the relationship between the theory linking the interpretation of the Rorschach ink-blots with dietary disorders. While the clinical psychologists may well have accepted that more people with dietary disorders saw the blots as frogs than those without, they could not accept the *explanation* of the relationship between the two characteristics the original author chose to link to one another.

The distinction is that of the commonly accepted distinction between what has been called statistical inference, on the one hand, or scientific or causal inference, on the other (see Henkel and Morrison, 1970, *passim*). Statistical inference is the process by which the analyst draws conclusions about the existence of two or more characteristics in some wider population from some sample of that population to which the observer has access. Scientific or causal – or, perhaps more appropriately, logical – inference is the process by which the analyst draws conclusions about the essential linkage between two or more characteristics in terms of some systematic explanatory schema – some set of theoretical propositions. In analytical thinking based on quantitative procedures *both* types of inference proceed *pari passu*, but there has been some tendency to elide logical inferences with the logic of statistical inference: that the postulated *logical* connection among features in a sample may be assumed to exist in some parent population simply because the features may be inferred to *coexist* in that population. This is the point that Lykken was making about Sapolsky's study of the frog response among people with dietary disorders. By contrast I argue that the process of inference from case studies is only logical or causal and cannot be statistical, and that extrapolability from any one case study to like situations in general is based only on logical inference. We infer that the features present in the case study will be related in a wider population not because the case is representative but because our analysis is unassailable. The emphasis on case studies is used to relate theoretically relevant characteristics reflected in the case to one another in a logically coherent way. Analytically sound studies using statistical procedures are of course doing the same thing, but two very different inferential processes are involved in them: logical inference is epistemologically quite independent of statistical inference.

Enumerative and analytic induction

This distinction between logical and statistical inference is related to the notions of enumerative and analytic induction introduced to sociology by Znaniecki as long ago as 1934. Znaniecki, a vehement opponent of the vogue for quantitative studies which were becoming popular at the time of his writing, contrasts the two modes of inference. Enumerative induction, in his view, exists in the form either of simple enumeration, in which the characteristics of a class of phenomena are established simply by listing them, or in the more elaborate form of statistical induction, in which probability theory is involved. In the simple form, he argues, enumerative induction has 'continued to be used with very little changes, in ethical and political works from antiquity, down to present times, whenever an author not satisfied with deducing rules of conduct from principles accepted *a priori* attempts to base this view on experience and observation' (Znaniecki, 1934, p. 221). He describes its general principles as

> an attempt to discover some final truths about a certain class of empirical data, circumscribed in advance, by studying a number of cases belonging to this class. Originally and fundamentally, the truths sought for are to be characters common to all data of the given class and only to these. (p. 222)

This implies identification of a class of phenomena by some identifiable but not necessarily essential characteristics and then examining a set of instances of this class to identify those features of the instances that define that class. By contrast,

> in analytic induction certain particular objects are determined by intensive study, and the problem is to define the logical classes which they represent. No definition of the class precedes in analytic induction the selection of data to be studied as representatives of this class. The analysis of data is all done before any general formulations; and if well done, there is nothing more of

importance to be learned about the class which these data represent by any subsequent investigation of more data of the same class. (p. 249)

Znaniecki goes on to say:

> It may be said that analytic induction ends where enumerative induction begins; and if well conducted, leaves no real and soluble problems for the latter. With such a radical difference in logical problematization, the logical procedure should naturally differ widely. While both forms of induction tend to reach general and abstract truths concerning particular and concrete data, enumerative induction abstracts by generalization, whereas analytic induction generalizes by abstracting. The former looks in many cases for characters that are similar and abstracts them conceptually because of their generality, presuming that they must be essential to each particular case; the latter abstracts from the given concrete case characters that are essential to it and generalizes them, presuming that insofar as essential, they must be similar in many cases. (pp. 250–1)

The process of analytic induction proceeds, according to Znaniecki, not by developing a self-sufficient theory from one instance well analysed, for he criticizes Durkheim's analysis of religion based on Australian totemism (p. 237), but rather by examining cases so selected as to illuminate formerly obscure aspects of the general theory.

Znaniecki's discussion of the significance of exceptions and how they may be made to 'prove the rule' (pp. 305–6) appears to contradict his austere statement quoted earlier to the effect that 'if well done there is nothing more of importance to be learned about the class which these data represent by any subsequent investigation of more data of the same class'. But we should distinguish here between the *principles* of analytic induction and its *practice*. The intention behind analytic induction is to specify the necessary connections among a set of theoretically significant elements manifested in some body of empirical data. But in practice any one set of data is likely to manifest only some of the elements whose explication would contribute to a cogent theoretical interpretation of the processes involved. An indeterminate number of strategically selected sets of events would need to be examined, therefore, before the state of complete knowledge that Znaniecki refers to can be approached:

This issue was specifically recognized by Znaniecki, for after developing the point about the establishment of complete knowledge from only one instance he goes on to say:

> Of course the inductive scientist continuously goes on investigating objects or processes already defined and classified even though he does not doubt the validity of his former definition, for there is always something to learn about individual data: concrete reality, as we have said, is an inexhaustible source of new knowledge. (p. 250)

But he goes on to specify that the new knowledge he refers to is not a mere supplement to pre-existing knowledge but rather an extension of *theoretical* knowledge.

Robinson (1951, 1952) subsequently, in a criticism of Znaniecki's ideas, distinguished between analytic induction as a research procedure, as a method of causal analysis, and as a method of proof [see also Chapter 8 – *Editors' Note*]. Any of these epistemologically disjunct implications might be conveyed by the term. The main burden of Robinson's argument, however, is that there is no essential contradiction between analytic induction and enumerative induction on the grounds that by its procedures analytic induction isolates the *necessary* circumstances for the manifestation of some phenomenon but does not in itself establish *sufficient* conditions. Analytic induction, Robinson argues, enables the analyst to establish the conditions without which the phenomenon would not appear (Robinson, 1951), whereas enumerative induction, as exemplified by statistical procedures, establishes sufficient conditions for the phenomenon to occur. His argument is based on the premise that analytic induction as exemplified by case studies examines only instances in which the phenomenon under investigation in fact occurs, whereas statistical procedures ideally would also take into account those occasions when the phenomenon does not occur. This, he argues, allows the analyst to establish sufficient conditions as distinct from necessary conditions for the phenomenon to occur. He goes on to argue that as a practical as against a logical procedure there is little difference between enumerative and analytic induction, since practitioners of the art of analytic induction indirectly study cases in which the phenomenon in which they are interested does not occur. Radcliffe-Brown, it is said, was interested in totemism. In order to understand it more fully, therefore, he elected to study the Andamanese islanders amongst whom there was no totemism. The point is that if an analyst is working with some conception of the general role of totemism in a social system, then an examination of the operation of the social system in which totemism does not occur ought to enable the analyst to [come to] some assessment of the *absence* of totemism. The essential point is the one which Robinson makes: 'The success of analytic induction in producing complete explanation is due to its procedure, to its systematization of the method of the working hypothesis, and not to its logical structure' (1951: 816; see below p. 192).

In reality no case study can be presented in isolation from the corpus of empirical information and theoretical postulates against which it has significance. The point is well made by Kaplan, who quotes Hartmann in relation to clinical observation pyschiatry: 'Every single clinical "case" represents, for research, hundreds of data of *observed regularities* and in hundreds of respects' (Kaplan, 1964, p. 117; original italics). The single case becomes significant only when set against the accumulated experience and knowledge that the analyst brings to it. In other words the extent to which generalization may be made from case studies depends upon the adequacy of the underlying theory and the whole corpus of related knowledge of which the case is analysed rather than on the particular instance itself.

The significance of the atypical case

This consideration justifies the selection of the case for study (or for exposition) in terms of its explanatory power rather than for its typicality. Formally any set of events deemed to reflect the abstract characteristics that the observer wishes to use in analysis may be used. Since the analyst's purpose is to demonstrate how general explanatory principles manifest themselves in the course of some ongoing set of events, the particular set of events is in itself a subsidiary consideration.

There is absolutely no advantage in going to a great deal of trouble to find a 'typical' case: concern with this issue reflects a confusion of enumerative and analytic modes of induction. For general purposes any set of events will serve the purpose of the analyst if the theoretical base is sufficiently well developed to enable the analyst to identify within these events the operation of the general principles incorporated in the theory.

There is, however, a strategic advantage in choosing particular sets of events for study or for exposition. It frequently occurs that the way in which general explanatory principles may be used in practice is most clearly demonstrated in those instances where the concatenation of events is so idiosyncratic as to throw into sharp relief the principles underlying them.[10] The point is analogous to the crucial role that untoward events have played in the elucidation of unexpected connection in the natural sciences. A dramatic example is provided by the veterinary scientist W.I.B. Beveridge, who describes how in 1889 a laboratory assistant chanced to notice that flies had congregated around the urine of a dog from which the pancreas had been removed. A test showed sugar in the urine, thus leading to the establishment of the connection between the pancreas and diabetes (Beveridge, 1950, p. 28).[11] So in the social sciences an illuminating case may make theoretical connections apparent which were formerly obscure.

It is of course obvious that the significant case is only so because the analyst is able to perceive the illuminating contradictions in the material. But the contradictions only become significant because of the observer's familiarity with current theoretical formulations in terms of which the contradictions are articulated. This highlights the point made earlier that the presentation of a case study is significant only in terms of some body of analytical theory. Pasteur's aphorism is highly apposite: 'Where observation is concerned, chance favours only the prepared mind' (*Oxford Dictionary of Quotations*, 1979, p. 369).

The case in its context

The characteristic uniqueness of each case is largely due to the fact that the particular events described in the case are usually presented in the first instance at a fairly low level of abstraction. The observer provides a detailed account of who the *dramatis personae* were, what they did and how they reacted to the events (and their social relationships) in which they were involved. The particularities of the context, of the situation and of the actors, then, are important features of case studies.

It is this particularity of case studies which has been the basis of what I consider to be ill-founded criticism of the use of case studies as a basis for generalization. But of course in interpreting the events in any particular case theoretically the analyst must suppress some of the complexity in the events and state the logical connexions among some of the features which are germane to the interpretation. This process of abstraction and the suppression of contextually irrelevant features has led Ralph Turner to a critique of the process of analytic induction. Turner sees analytic induction primarily as a procedure for establishing the necessary and essential features that characterize the phenomenon or class of events under consideration, that is, as a definitional procedure. These necessary and essential features, however, are usually part and parcel of some coherent and cogent theoretical explanatory system, so that analytic induction necessarily involves what Turner calls 'causal closure', that is, that the procedure must produce causally self-contained systems. This implies that an explanation of events based on analytic induction relates typically to a limited set of events restricted in the sense that the events must of necessity be explicable in terms of the explanatory rubric that informed the analysis. In these circumstances, Turner argues, the 'causal prime mover' must be outside the set of events being considered, or, in his words, the system 'is not capable of activation from within, but only by factors coming from outside the system' (1953, p. 609) [see Chapter 9 – *Editors' Note*]. It is for this reason that predictions from an analysis based on case study techniques tend to be *theoretical* rather than *empirical*. External factors, or *intrusive* factors as Turner calls them, always influence the events in a case study but can only be included in the theoretical explanation by their incorporation into the case as one of the essential and necessary characteristics.

But it is not essential that events located, from the analyst's point of view, outside the events with which the case is concerned, and which need to be taken account of in the explication of the case material, need be treated in the same detail as the events in the case itself. The problem of isolating events intellectually from seamless reality in order to facilitate their analysis in terms of some explanatory system was discussed at some length by Gluckman and his colleagues (Gluckman, 1964). One of the points Gluckman makes is that it is perfectly justifiable for the analyst to operate with a simplified account of the context within which the case is located provided that the impact of the features of that context on the events being considered in the analysis is incorporated rigorously into the analysis.

All cases are necessarily contextualized and generalizations made from case studies must therefore be qualified with a *ceteris paribus* condition. It is incumbent on the observer to provide readers with a minimal account of the context to enable them to judge for themselves the validity of treating other things as equal in that instance.

The very particularity of the case study, located as it is in some setting, however, can be turned to good advantage; it can provide the opportunity to demonstrate the positive role of exceptions to generalization as a means of deepening our understanding of social processes. It is only under specified conditions that a clear and simple formulation of the operative principles underlying a social process can be stated. But the very circumstances of the case study make a strict imposition of a *ceteris paribus* condition impracticable. The analyst may therefore take account of the unique circumstances surrounding the event in the case being analysed in order to show how these circumstances obscure the simple and direct way in which the general principles should be operating. Because of the intimate knowledge of the relationships in the particular circumstances which connect the events in the case, the analyst might be able to show how the general principles being examined manifest themselves in changed form.

The contextual features surrounding the case are in effect held constant by a process of logical analysis. It is in this sense that Znaniecki (1934) remarks:

> Wherever, thus, an exception can be explained, that is, can be proved only apparent, not real, we gain not only a confirmation of our previous knowledge but also new knowledge: we discover the limits within which our causal processes occur or find some other causal process and thus determine the range of validity of our law or validate some other law.... it is not the exception that matters, but our attitude towards it: if we refuse to submit to it, but go on analyzing our data, it is a factor of scientific discovery, whereas if we passively accept it, it is a check on further progress. (p. 306)

The case study, because of the observer's intimate knowledge of the connections linking the complex set of circumstances surrounding the events in the case and because of the observer's knowledge of the linkages among the events in the case, provides the optimum conditions in which the general principles may be shown to manifest themselves even when obscured by confounding side-effects.

Conclusion

The argument that has been advanced here, then, is that case studies of whatever form are a reliable and respectable procedure of social analysis, and that much criticism of their reliability and validity has been based on a misconception of the basis upon which the analyst may justifiably extrapolate from an individual case study to the social process in general. A good deal of the confusion has arisen because of a failure to appreciate that the rationale of extrapolation from a statistical sample to a parent universe involves two very different and even unconnected inferential processes – that of statistical inference, which makes a statement about the confidence we may have that the surface relationships observed in our sample will in fact occur in the parent population, and that of logical or scientific inference, which makes a statement about the confidence we may have that the theoretically necessary or logical connection among the features observed in the sample pertain also to the parent population.

In case studies, statistical inference is not invoked at all. Instead, the inferential process turns exclusively on the theoretically necessary linkages among the features in the case study. The validity of the extrapolation depends not on the typicality or representativeness of the case but upon the cogency of the theoretical reasoning.

In terms of this argument, case studies may be used analytically – as against ethnographically – only if they are embedded in an appropriate theoretical framework. The rich detail which emerges from the intimate knowledge the analyst must acquire in a case study if it is well conducted provides the optimum conditions for the acquisition of those illuminating insights which make formerly opaque connections suddenly pellucid.

Notes

This paper has been in draft form for some time. I am grateful to the following who have provided me with bibliographical references or valuable comments: David Boswell, Robert Burgess, Jean Edwards, Barry Glassner, Les Green, Sheldon Himmelfarb, Elinor Kelly, Chris Pickvance, Dave Reason, Ralph Ruddock, Sue Smith, Rory Williams; seminar groups at Adelaide, Durham and Oxford and two anonymous referees. Unfortunately I have not been able to take all of their suggestions into account.

1 Prior to the development of the social survey in the 1930s case studies seemed to feature regularly in sociological research (see bibliography in Young, 1939, pp. 569–72) and there were several useful discussions of the method for example Cooley (1930).

Znaniecki, writing in 1934 (pp. 246–8), reflects this division very clearly and lists a number of contemporary works that have used the case approach. Znaniecki points out that at that time the model for sociological case studies was the clinical methods in psychiatry, particularly since the spread of psychoanalysis, but also social work. He lists several sociological studies which had used case studies analytically, most of them part of the 'ethnographic' wing of the Chicago School such as works by Thomas, Cooley, Shaw, Park and Burgess. He also, however, drew attention to the division of opinion between those using case methods and those using survey methods. Articles bearing on the debate are Burgess (1927, 1945), Eldridge (1935), Hotelling and Sorokin (1943), Jocher (1928), Jonassen (1949), Lewis (1950), Queen (1928) Sarbin (1943), Shaw (1927) and Waller (1935).

2 The references to case studies were Burgess (1945), Eldridge (1935), Hotelling and Sorokin (1943), Komarovsky and Waller (1945), Lewis (1950), Sarbin (1943) and Waller (1935).

3 As, for example, in Ashton's (1980) review of Blackburn and Mann's *The Working Class in the Labour Market*. Ashton's point, however – that Blackburn and Mann fail effectively to establish the *ceteris paribus* conditions of their generalization – is valid.

4 Recently Hamilton (1980), working in the field of educational studies, has yet again drawn the contrast between case studies and survey analysis and concludes that 'the assumptions of case study research and survey analysis stand in mutual opposition' (p. 90). My own argument, however, is that in the end the oppositions are more apparent than real.

5 c.f. '[The case study] attempts to arrive at a comprehensive understanding of the group under study. At the same time the case study also attempts to develop more general theoretical statements about the regularities in social structure and process' (Becker, 1968, p. 233).

6 Goode and Hatt go on to discuss other features that distinguish case studies from other research procedures such as the breadth of data, the levels of data, the identification of types and profiles, and the signifiance of the developmental aspects of the case.

7 Garbett (1970, p. 215) defines a social situation as a temporally and spatially bounded series of events abstracted by the observer from the ongoing flow of social life.

8 Stake (1980) provides one of the few discussions of the nature of generalizations from case studies and from survey findings but his emphasis is on the quality of the generalizations rather than on the basis upon which they are achieved. [See also Chapter 1 – Editors' Note.]

9 Captured by the *Shorter Oxford English Dictionary* phrase 'an event or occurrence, hap or chance'. The word 'hap' is defined in the same dictionary as 'a chance accident or occurrence'.

10 Lindesmith (1952), in his comments on Robinson's paper, phrases the same point in terms of discovering the case that *disproves* the rule. He writes: 'There is no point to the random selection of cases when this is obviously not the most efficient manner of seeking evidence' (p. 492).

11 Beveridge's chapter, in which he discusses the role of chance in making important theroretical connections in physiology, is headed with a quote from Charles Nicolle: 'Chance favours only those who know how to court her.'

References

Ashton, D. (1980) [Review of R.M. Blackburn and M. Mann, *The Working Class* in the labour Market], *Sociological Review*, 28: 433–4.

Barnes, J.A. (1958) 'Social anthropology: theory and practice'. Inaugural lecture at Sydney University, in *Arts: the Proceedings of the Sydney University Arts Association*, 1: 47–67.

Barnes, J.A. (1960) 'Intensive studies of small communities', *Meanjin: A Quarterly of Literature Art Discussion*, 19: 201–3.

Becker, H.S. (1968) 'Social observation and case studies', in D.L. Sills (ed.), *International Encyclopedia of the Social Sciences* (Vol. 11). New York: Macmillan and Free Press. Reprinted in H.S. Becker (1971) *Sociological Work*. Chicago: Aldine.

Beveridge, W.I.B. (1950) *The Art of Scientific Investigation*. London: Heinemann.

Burgess, E.W. (1927) 'Statistics and case studies as methods of sociological research', *Sociology and Social Research*, 12: 103–20.

Burgess, E.W. (1945) 'Sociological research methods', *American Journal of Sociology*, 50: 474–82.

Chassan, J.B. (1960) 'Statistical inference and the single case in clinical design', *Psychiatry*, 23: 173–84.

Cooley, C.H. (1930) 'The case study of small institutions as a method of research', in *Sociological Theory and Social Research*. New York: Henry Holt & Co.

Eldridge, S. (1935) 'Textbooks, teachers and students', *American Journal of Sociology*, 40: 637–45.

Foreman, P. (1948) 'The theory of case studies', *Social Forces*, 26: 408–19.

Garbett, G.K. (1970) 'The analysis of social situations', *Man*, 5: 214–27.

Gluckman, M. (1958) *The Analysis of a Social Situation in Modern Zululand* (Rhodes–Livingstone Paper no. 28). Manchester: Manchester University Press for the Rhodes–Livingstone Institute.

Gluckman, M. (1961) 'Ethnographic data in British social anthropology', *Sociological Review*, 9: 5–17.

Gluckman, M. (ed.) (1964) *Closed Systems and Open Minds: The Limits of Naïvety in Social Anthropology*. London: Oliver & Boyd.

Gluckman, M. (1967) 'Introduction', in A.W. Epstein (ed.), *The Craft of Social Anthropology*. London: Tavistock.

Goode, W.J. and Hatt, P.K. (1952) *Methods in Social Research*. New York: McGraw-Hill.

Hamilton, D. (1980) 'Some contrasting assumptions about case study research and survey analysis', in H. Simons (ed.), *Towards a Science of the Singular: Essays about Case Study in Educational Research and Evaluation* (CARE Occasional Publications no. 10). Norwich: Centre for Applied Research in Education, University of East Anglia.

Henkel, R.E. and Morrison, D.E. (eds) (1970) *The Significance Test Controversy*. London: Butterworth.

Hotelling, H. and Sorokin, P. (1943) 'The prediction of personal adjustment: a symposium', *American Journal of Sociology*, 48: 61–86.

Jocher, K. (1928) 'The case study method in social research', *Social Forces*, 7: 512–15.

Jonassen, C.T. (1949) 'A re-evaluation and critique of the logic and some methods of Shaw and McKay', *American Sociological Review*, 14: 608–14.

Kaplan, A. (1964) *The Conduct of Inquiry: Methodology for Behavioral Science*. San Francisco: Chandler.

Komarovsky, M. and Waller, W. (1945) 'Studies of the family', *American Journal of Sociology*, 50: 443–51.

Lewis, O. (1950) 'An anthropological approach to family studies', *American Journal of Sociology*, 55: 468–75.

Lindesmith, A.R. (1952) 'Comments on W.S. Robinson's "The logical structure of analytic induction"', *American Sociological Review*, 17: 492–3.

Lykken, D. (1970) 'Statistical significance in psychological research', in R.E. Henkel and D.E. Morrison (eds), *The Significance Test Controversy*. London: Butterworth.

Madge (1953) *The Tools of Social Science*. London: Longman, Green & Co.

Mitchell, J.C. (1956) *The Yao Village*. Manchester: Manchester University Press for the Rhodes–Livingstone Institute.

Oxford Dictionary of Quotations (1939) (3rd edn). Oxford: Oxford University Press.

Queen, S. (1928) 'Round table on the case study in sociological research', *Publications of the American Sociological Society:* 22.

Robinson, W.S. (1952) 'Rejoinder to comments on "The logical structure of analytical induction"', *American Sociological Review*, 17: 494.

Sarbin, T.R. (1943) 'A contribution to the study of actuarial and individual methods of prediction', *American Journal of Sociology*, 48: 593–602.

Shaw, C.R. (1927) 'Case study method', *Publications of the American Sociological Society*, 21: 149–57.

Simons, H. (ed.) (1980) *Towards a Science of the Singular Essays about Case Study in Educational Research and Evaluation* (CARE Occasional Publications no. 10). Norwich: Centre for Applied Research in Education, University of East Anglia.

Turner, V.W. (1957) *Schism and Continuity in an African Society*. Manchester: Manchester University Press for the Rhodes–Livingstone Institute.

van Velsen, J. (1967) 'The extended case method and situational analysis', in A.L. Epstein (ed.), *The Craft of Social Anthropology*. London: Tavistock.

Waller, W. (1935) 'Insight and scientific method', *American Journal of Sociology*, XL (3): 285–97.

Weinberg, S.K. (1952) 'Comment on W.S. Robinson's "The logical structure of analytic induction"', *American Sociological Review*, 17: 493–4.

Young, P. (1939) *Scientific Social Surveys and Research*. New York: Prentice-Hall.

Znaniecki, F. (1934) *The Method of Sociology*. New York: Farrar & Rinehart.

CHAPTER 8

THE LOGICAL STRUCTURE OF ANALYTIC INDUCTION

W.S. Robinson

Since Znaniecki stated it in 1934, the method of analytic induction has come into important use. Angell used it in his *The Family Encounters the Depression* (1936, pp. 296–7). Sutherland (1939, pp. 66–7) refined the method and recommended it for general use in studying the causes of crime. Lindesmith (1947) used it in his well-known study of opiate addiction. Cressey (1950)[1] has used it most recently in his study of the causes of embezzlement, and the method is probably in current use by others also.

Znaniecki (1934, pp. 236–7) holds that analytic induction is the true method of the physical and biological sciences, and that it ought to be the method of the social sciences too. He contrasts analytic induction with what he calls enumerative induction, which is the ordinary statistical way of studying relationships with correlations. He holds that analytic induction gives us universal statements, of the form 'All *S* are *P*', instead of mere correlations to which there are always exceptions (pp. 232–3). He holds that analytic induction gives us exhaustive knowledge of the situation under study, so that further study will not and cannot reveal anything new (p. 249). Finally, he holds that analytic induction leads us to genuinely causal laws. (pp. 305–6)

There is, however, some confusion as to the real nature and function of analytic induction. The purpose of this paper is to clarify this confusion by exploring the logical structure of analytic induction. It will be convenient to take up the problem in three steps: to discuss analytic induction first as a research procedure directing activity in the field, second as a method of causal analysis, and third as a method of proof.

Analytic induction as research procedure

Cressey (1950) has given the most explicit and systematic statement of analytic induction as a research procedure, as follows:

(1) A rough definition of the phenomenon to be explained is formulated.
(2) An hypothetical explanation of that phenomenon is formulated. (3) One

Originally published in (1951) *American Sociological Review*, 16 (6): 812–18.

case is studied in the light of the hypothesis with the object of determining whether the hypothesis fits the facts in that case. (4) If the hypothesis does not fit the facts, either the hypothesis is reformulated or the phenomenon to be explained is re-defined, so that the case is excluded. (5) Practical certainty may be attained after a small number of cases has been examined, but the discovery by the investigator or any other investigator of a single negative case disproves the explanation and requires a re-formulation. (6) This procedure of examining cases, re-defining the phenomenon and re-formulating the hypothesis is continued until a universal relationship is established, each negative case calling for a re-definition or a re-formulation. (p. 31)[2]

Lindesmith (1947) provides an illustration of the procedure in describing how he successively revised his hypothesis:

> The first tentative, and obviously inadequate hypothesis formulated was that individuals who do not know what drug they are receiving do not become addicted and, on the positive side, that they become addicted when they know what they are getting and have taken it long enough to experience withdrawal distress when they stop. This hypothesis was destroyed almost at once by negative evidence … In the light of [additional cases], the second hypothesis of the investigation was that persons become addicts when they recognize or perceive the significance of withdrawal distress which they are experiencing, and that if they do not recognize withdrawal distress they do not become addicts regardless of any other considerations.
>
> This formulation proved to be much more significant and useful than the first one, but like the first one it did not stand the test of evidence and had to be revised when cases were found in which individuals who had experienced and understood withdrawal distress, though not in its severest form, did not use the drug to alleviate the distress and never became addicts. The final revision of the hypothesis involved a shift in emphasis from the recognition of withdrawal distress, to the use of the drug after this insight has occurred for the purpose of alleviating the distress. (pp. 7–8)

In terms of procedure, then, the method of analytic induction begins with an explanatory hypothesis and a provisional definition of something to be explained. The hypothesis is then compared with facts, and modifications are made in two ways: (1) the hypothesis itself is modified so that the new facts will fall under it, and/or (2) the phenomenon to be explained is redefined to exclude the cases which defy explanation by the hypothesis. Let us consider these two modifications in turn.

The first, that of altering the hypothesis, is well known as the method of the working hypothesis (cf. Dubs, 1930, p. 128). Scientists have long known that even a false hypothesis may be useful, for it does direct our observation, and in checking it against facts we usually get ideas as to how to bring it better into accordance with the facts.

> The logical procedure of verification or disproof is intimately bound up with the procedure of discovery, and the character of the observations that bring

about the disproof of one hypothesis often suggests the sort of modification that ought to be made to create a better hypothesis. (Dubs, 1930, p. 128)

The fact that the method of analytic induction formalizes and systematizes the method of the working hypothesis is probably one reason why it has been so fruitful in applications such as Angell's, Lindesmith's and Cressey's. The method performs an important service in emphasizing the need for study of deviant cases in a situation in which the explanation is not complete.

However, this insistence upon analysis of deviant cases is not logically different from the similar insistence of the sophisticated practitioner of enumerative induction. The practitioner of enumerative induction phrases it differently. He says that he looks for a new variable correlated with his residuals, so as to include it in a new multivariate analysis; but it amounts to the same thing. The point is that he keeps modifying his hypothesis to account for the failures of his original relation to predict infallibly. The fact that few statistically oriented investigators actually do this is regrettable, but the fact that they *might* do it indicates no basic difference between analytic and enumerative induction on this count. It is a particular excellence of the method of analytic induction, however, that it insists upon this knowledge-building, self-corrective procedure of the analysis of deviant cases.

The second modification which may come about in applying the method of analytic induction is that of redefining the phenomenon so as to exclude cases which contradict the hypothesis. This is what Dubs (1930, p. 260) calls 'limiting the universal', limiting the range of applicability of the explanatory hypothesis.

An exception, even though it is a real and not an apparent exception, may not overthrow a hypothesis, but may merely indicate that the hypothesis in question is a limited universal. ... If, then, a universal is only true within limits, it is important to know what are those limits and to consider the limits as well as the universal. (Dubs, 1930, pp. 260, 282)

This limitation of the universal in analytic induction is to ensure causal homogeneity in the cases to be explained, to ensure that the same process functions in all the cases to be examined. Thus Lindesmith (1947) found it necessary to distinguish between true addiction and habituation, 'in which the physiological factors occur in isolation, without arousing the self-conscious desire for the drug which characterizes the addict and around which he organizes his life' (p. 45). Similarly, Cressey (1950, pp. 33–40) found it necessary to restrict himself to a study of persons who had violated a financial trust undertaken in good faith, for the process involved was very different from that involved when a person accepted a trust for the express purpose of violating it.

Such limitation of universals has occurred not infrequently in the history of science, and is now a matter of common acceptance. The relation between Newtonian physics and the relativity theory is a case in point (cf. Dubs, 1930, pp. 278–80). The failure of Newton's laws to account for the observed motion of Mercury and the failure of the Michelson–Morley experiment reduced Newtonian physics to a limited universal, restricted its application to cases in which velocities did not approach the velocity of light. The usual history of limited universals in the physical sciences is that they are eventually shown to be special cases of more general universals. The relativity theory includes all of Newtonian physics as a special case, and considerably more besides. This might well be the case with the limitation of universals by the method of analytic induction. It would be the case, for example, were Cressey to develop a more general explanation which would include trust violations in both good faith and bad faith as special cases.

Analytic induction as method of causal analysis

It is easy to show that the method of analytic induction *as described* gives only the necessary and not the sufficient conditions for the phenomenon to be explained. The method calls for studying only those cases in which the phenomenon occurs (Cressey, 1950, p. 31, quoted *supra*), and not cases in which it does not occur. To study cases in which the phenomenon does not occur would involve us in enumerative induction, the comparative method, for which Znaniecki (1934, pp. 225–7) would substitute the method of analytic induction.

What analytic induction does *as described* can be shown most easily with the accompanying fourfold table (Table 8.1), in which P stands for instances in which the phenomenon occurs, and $\bar{P}$ for instances in which it does not occur. Thus all instances in which the phenomenon occurs fall in the left column, and all instances in which it does not occur fall in the right column.

The method of analytic induction consists in taking a number of instances in which the phenomenon occurs, a number of instances in the left column, and finding a set of conditions which always accompany

Table 8.1

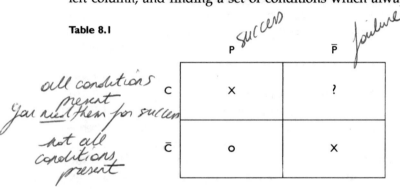

	P *success*	$\bar{P}$ *failure*
C	X	?
$\bar{C}$	O	X

all conditions present
You need them for success

not all conditions present

that phenomenon and without which it does not occur. Let C in Table 8.1 stand for instances in which these conditions are present, and $\bar{C}$ for instances in which not all of them are present. Thus the first row of the table contains instances in which the conditions C are present, and the second row contains instances in which not all of them are present.

As the method is described, it consists in studying cases in the left column of Table 8.1 and then so defining C, the conditions, as to make all these cases fall in the upper cell of the column, as indicated by an X in the upper cell and the zero in the lower cell. We may go further, moreover, and point out that all of the cases in the lower row must fall in the right column. There are certainly instances at large in which the conditions C are not all present, and since we know that these do not occur in the P-column, they must occur in the $\bar{P}$-column, as indicated in the table by an X in the lower right cell.

The relation between analytic and enumerative or statistical induction is now clear. A statistician would study cases in all four cells of the table. He would hope, but not insist, that there would be zeros in the lower left and upper right cells – and there he would stop. A person practising analytic induction, however, would study cases only in the left column of the table, and would insist that he get a zero in the lower cell of that column. By an additional argument he could then show, if he wanted to, that all cases in the lower row fell in the right column. But he could not determine whether or not there were cases in the upper right cell, as indicated by the ? in that cell.

This argument shows why the method of analytic induction as described by Sutherland and Cressey cannot enable us to predict. It cannot because it gives us only the necessary and not the sufficient conditions for the phenomenon to be explained. Only if we know that the phenomenon never fails to occur in the presence of the conditions C, only if we know that the upper right cell in the table contains a zero, can we predict the occurrence of the phenomenon from C.

This argument also shows that the explanation provided by the method of analytic induction is only a partial explanation. It is now well established that prediction and explanation have identically the same logical form:

> It may be said … that an explanation is not fully adequate unless … [it] … if taken account of in time, could have served as a basis for predicting the phenomenon under consideration. The logical similarity of explanation and prediction, and the fact that one is directed towards past occurrences, the other towards future ones, is well expressed in the terms 'postdictability' and 'predictability' used by Reichenbach. (Hempel and Oppenheim, 1948, p. 138)

We have an adequate explanation, in other words, only when we have both the necessary and the sufficient conditions for the phenomenon to be explained, that is, only when we have zeros in both the lower left and the upper right cells of Table 8.1.

Both Lindesmith and Cressey have sensed this inadequacy of analytic induction as stated, and neither has applied it in the form in which it is stated. Lindesmith (1947, p. 14) made a systematic study of non-addicts to determine whether addiction ever failed to occur when his conditions were present. Cressey did not study persons who had not violated a financial trust at the time he interviewed them, but he has pointed out that he actually did study non-violators as well, because each of his subjects was a non-violator before his defection. Cressey therefore systematically studied the history of each subject to determine whether the conditions had been present in the past without a violation. Cressey, that is, assumed that before their defection his violators were representative of all non-violators, that is, of all the cases in the right column of Table 8.1. His assumption is open to question and should be tested, but his intention to include non-violators as well as violators in unmistakable.

Thus in practising the method of analytic induction both Lindesmith and Cressey found it necessary for adequacy to study the cases in the right column of Table 8.1, that is, to determine that the ? was actually a zero. This leads to the interesting conclusion that the method of analytic induction *in practice* leads directly to the use of the comparative method, the method of enumerative induction, which it is designed to supplant.

The only evident difference between enumerative induction and analytic induction in practice is that analytic induction insists upon zeros in two cells of Table 8.1, and provides a procedure for trying to get them there, while enumerative induction is satisfied with relatively small frequencies. Choose a sophisticated approach to enumerative induction, one that realizes that a perfect explanation is the ultimate goal, and there is no difference between an analytic and an enumerative induction except that the latter is incomplete. Or imagine that someone practising analytic induction has failed to achieve perfection and publishes his results as a progress report; he has made an enumerative induction. The success of analytic induction in producing complete explanations is due to its procedure, to its systematization of the method of the working hypothesis, and not to its logical structure. The qualitative contrast which Znaniecki sets up between analytic and enumerative induction as methods of causal analysis is thus only a quantitative contrast and is not basic. The difference is in how far you push your study before you publish your results.

Analytic induction as method of proof

Analytic induction is regarded by Znaniecki as a special and *certain* way of proving that the generalizations to which it leads will apply to all instances of the phenomenon under study, whether they have yet been examined or not:

> The analysis of data is all done before any general formulations: and if well done, there is nothing more of importance to be learned about the class which these data represent by any subsequent investigation of more data of the same class (Znaniecki, 1934, p. 249)

Sutherland (1939, p. 67) follows in this line also, though with characteristic canniness he remarks that *practical* certainty may be attained after the examination of a few instances. This anti-probabilistic insistence is found in Angell (1936, p. 7) too. No sampling considerations are involved, and no merely probable generalizations are admitted; the method leads to certainty.

Lindesmith and Cressey do not follow here in word, for each points out that future instances may necessitate revision of his hypothesis. But they do follow in deed, for neither shows particular concern for the coverage of his sample, and both seem to rely implicitly upon Znaniecki's claim to extend their generalizations to as yet unenumerated instances. It will be instructive, therefore, to examine Znaniecki's claim for analytic induction as a method of proof, and then to consider the possibility of integrating analytic induction with the probabilistic approach of modern science.

Znaniecki argues that analytic induction leads to certainty without benefit of representative cases because it isolates the 'essential' characters which determine the phenomenon under study. The method leads to certainty because the characters C in Table 8.1 are 'essential' to the phenomenon P.

> [A]nalytic induction ends where enumerative induction begins; and if well conducted, leaves no real and soluble problems for the latter. ... [Analytic induction] abstracts from the given concrete case characters that are essential to it and generalizes them, presuming that insofar as essential, they must be similar in many cases. This is why the method of analytic induction has been also called the *type* method. ... Thus, when a particular concrete case is being analyzed as typical or eidetic, we assume that those traits which are essential to it, which determine what it is, are common to and distinctive of all the cases of a class. (Znaniecki, 1934, pp. 250, 251-2)

Znaniecki's belief that there are 'essential' characters which determine phenomena is reminiscent of Aristotelian ontology, in which 'the membership of an object in a given class was of critical importance, because for Aristotle the class defined the essence or essential nature of the object and thus determined its behavior in both positive and negative respects' (Lewin, 1935, p. 4). But Znaniecki (1934, p. 231) denies that his belief in 'essential' characters has any ontological implications. We therefore still have the problem of trying to assess the claims of analytic induction as a method of proof, operating through its isolation of the 'essential' characters which determine phenomena.

We can attack this problem by considering what analytic induction actually does. Znaniecki clearly holds (though not in these terms) that analytic induction is an operational definition of essentiality, that the method is a way of isolating the essential characters which determine a phenomenon. But we have already seen that the method as stated leads merely to the necessary conditions for the phenomenon, to conditions which must be in existence before the phenomenon occurs but which are not shown to be sufficient to produce the phenomenon, and we should hardly consider these conditions essential in the sense of determining what the phenomenon is.

We have also seen that the method leads in practice to the isolation of the necessary and sufficient conditions for the phenomenon. It leads to the isolation of characters of such a nature that when the characters are all present the phenomenon occurs, and when the characters are not all present the phenomenon does not occur. However, the method does not lead us to the conclusion that these characters are 'essential' apart from the fact that they are necessary and sufficient as operationally defined.

We are, in fact, in a situation which has a well-known philosophical analogue. When Hume looked at instances of causal relations he was never able to discover any 'necessary connection'. All he could conclude was that one event invariably followed the other (Hume, 1945, p. 64). Considering analytic induction as an operational definition of essentiality, then, leads us to the conclusion that those characters which are essential to a phenomenon are those whose appearance is followed by the phenomenon and whose non-appearance is not followed by the phenomenon. This is perhaps as good a definition of essentiality as any – except that it makes the essentiality superfluous. It does not provide a basis for saying that when we have located the 'essential' characters for a phenomenon *we may be sure* that those characters will appear in any future instance of the phenomenon.

There is no real reason, however, why analytic induction cannot be integrated with the probabilistic approach characteristic of other research procedures in modern science. In fact the integration has already been made, though implicitly, by Lindesmith and Cressey. We know how to set fiducial limits to an observed zero frequency of exceptions, and we know that the lower of these limits will be zero and that the upper will be some small fraction.

Frankly to espouse the probabilistic viewpoint would enhance the already valuable contribution of analytic induction to scientific procedure. It would point up the necessity for representative sampling. Practitioners of analytic induction would then no longer have to cling with anxiety to the ontologically based essentiality argument, but could openly state the confidence limits for the proportion of exceptions which might occur in the future. It is almost superfluous to add that the occurrence of future exceptions would then be a focal point for a new attack by the method; for as Znaniecki (1934) has so usefully pointed out, and as his method itself manifests, 'The exception is ... an essential instrument of scientific progress' (p. 233).

Notes

I am indebted for assistance in preparing this paper to Donald R. Cressey, Gloria F. Roman, Wendell Bell and the members of my seminar in the logic of social inquiry, all of whom helped me shape some rather vague initial ideas into this present form.

1 The findings of Cressey's dissertation are reported in his article with the same title in the *American Sociological Review*, 15, 1950: 738–43. References to Cressey will be to the first-named source.

2 Cressey's statement, however, differs little from Sutherland's.

References

Angell, R.C. (1936) *The Family Encounters the Depression*. New York: Scribner's Sons.

Cressey, D.R. (1950) 'Criminal violation of financial trust'. Dissertation, Indiana University.

Dubs, H.H. (1930) *Rational Induction*. Chicago: University of Chicago Press.

Hempel, C.G. and Oppenheim, P. (1948) 'Studies in the logic of explanation', *Philosophy of Science*, 15: 135–75.

Hume, D. (1945) *An Enquiry Concerning Human Understanding*. La Salle, IL.

Lewin, K. (1935) 'The conflict between Aristotelian and Galilean modes of thought in contemporary psychology', in *A Dynamic Theory of Personality*. New York: McGraw Hill.

Lindesmith, A.R. (1947) *Opiate Addiction*. Bloomington, IN: Principia Press.

Sutherland, E.H. (1939) *Principles of Criminology* (3rd edn). Chicago: J.B. Lippincott Co.

Znaniecki, F. (1934) *The Method of Sociology*. New York: Farrar & Rinehart.

CHAPTER 9

THE QUEST FOR UNIVERSALS IN SOCIOLOGICAL RESEARCH

Ralph H. Turner

In a book which has maintained attention and perhaps increased in influence over two decades, Florian Znaniecki (1934) describes the method he names 'analytic induction', and designates it as *the* method which should be adopted in all sociological research. Analytic induction is merely a special name for one formulation of a basic philosophy that research must be directed toward generalizations of *universal* rather than *frequent* applicability.[1] But Znaniecki's statement is unusually unequivocal and is specifically oriented toward sociological research. Hence it makes an excellent point of departure for a study of contrasting methodologies.

Znaniecki's position has recently been challenged by W.S. Robinson [see Chapter 8 – *Editors' Note*], who depicts analytic induction as an imperfect form of the method Znaniecki calls enumerative induction.[2] Robinson's contentions are further discussed by Alfred Lindesmith (1952) and S. Kirson Weinberg (1952) in replies to his paper. The three discussions extend our understanding of the method, but leave some questions unanswered.

Methodological advance requires more than the mere tolerance of alternative methods. Any *particular* methodology must be examined and assessed in the light of the total process of research and theory formulation.[3] Accordingly, the objective of the present paper is to offer a definition of the place of the search for universals in the total methodology for dealing with non-experimental data. The procedure will be to examine specific examples of empirical research employing the analytic induction (or similar) method, to note what they do and do not accomplish, to establish logically the reasons for their distinctive accomplishments and limitations, and on these grounds to designate the specific utility of the method in relation to probability methods.

Originally published in (1953) *American Sociological Review*, 18 (6): 604–11.

Empirical prediction

Robinson's contention that actual studies employing the method of universals do not afford a basis for empirical prediction appears sound. However, it is only when the method is made to stand by itself that this limitation necessarily applies. Furthermore, the reason for the limitation is more intimately linked to the intrinsic logic of the method than the incidental fact that investigators using the method have tended to neglect the right-hand side of the four-fold table (Robinson, 1951).[4] These statements may be substantiated and elaborated by an examination of selected studies.

Lindesmith's well-known study of opiate addiction will serve as a useful first case. The causal complex which is essential to the process of addiction involves several elements. The individual must use the drug, he must experience withdrawal distress, he must identify these symptoms or recognize what they are, he must recognize that more of the drug will relieve the symptoms, and he must take the drug and experience relief (Lindesmith, 1947, pp. 67–89, *et passim*).

From the standpoint of predicting whether any given individual will become an addict or not, the formulation has certain limitations. First, it does not tell who will take the drug in the first place, nor give any indication of the relative likelihood of different persons taking the drug.[5] Second, the thesis itself affords no clue to variability in intensity of withdrawal symptoms, nor any guide to instances in which the symptoms will be mild enough not to result in addiction. Third, the theory does not provide a basis for anticipating who will recognize the symptoms and the means of securing relief. Fourth, personal and social factors involved in taking or not taking the drug to relieve the identified distress are not indicated. We cannot predict in an empirical instance unless there is some way of anticipating which people, given exposure to the drug, will recognize the nature of the withdrawal symptoms, will identify the means of relief, and will take that means of relief.[6] Finally, Lindesmith's theory does not indicate to us what will be the pattern of the addict's behaviour, since this is determined by the cultural definition and treatment of the drug and its addicts. In sum, Lindesmith provides us with a causal complex which is empirically verified *in retrospect*, but which does not in itself permit prediction that a specific person will become an addict nor that a specific situation will produce addiction.

Donald R. Cressey's (1953) statement regarding the violation of financial trust likewise is posited as a system of universal generalizations and is similar to Lindesmith's in format.[7] Three elements are essential to trust-violation. The person who will violate a financial trust has, first, a 'non-shareable financial problem', a difficulty which he feels he cannot communicate to others. Second, he recognizes embezzlement as a way of meeting this problem. And third, he rationalizes the prospective embezzlement, justifying it to himself in some way.

First, the points at which Lindesmith's and Cressey's statement are parallel and points at which they are not parallel may be noted. The withdrawal symptoms and the non-shareable problem can be equated as the conditions which require some relief which cannot be secured through conventional channels. There is also a parallel between recognition that the drug will relieve the distress and recognition of embezzlement as a possible solution to the non-shareable problem. On the other hand, because drug addiction ensues from but one type of problem, withdrawal distress, Lindesmith can specify the taking of an opiate as essential. Cressey can specify no specific 'first step' because of the variety of problems which may come to be non-shareable. The rationalization stage is absent from Lindesmith's formulation though he discusses it as a *frequent* phenomenon.

It is difficult to find a logical reason why rationalization should be *essential* in the one instance and merely *frequent* in the other. Perhaps the explanation lies not in the logic of the phenomena themselves, but in the conditions necessary for a sense of closure on the part of the investigators. Since Lindesmith is explaining the existence of a continuing psychological state, it is sufficient for his purposes that the prospective addict be carried from a particular state of recognition (the symptoms and role of the drug) to an overt act with specific psychological consequences (relief by taking the drug). Cressey, however, is explaining a single action and so he seeks to fill the gap more fully between the particular state of recognition (that embezzlement will solve a non-shareable problem) and the act of embezzling, which he does with the rationalization.[8]

In light of the parallels between the two schemes, it is not surprising that the same limitations with regard to empirical prediction apply to Cressey's statement as did to Lindesmith's. The theory does not indicate who will have non-shareable problems, what specific conditions will make a problem non-shareable, and in what circumstances a problem may cease to be non-shareable. Nor do we have a guide to the circumstances surrounding recognition of embezzlement as a solution to the problem. And, finally, there are no systematic indicators of who will be able to rationalize and who will not.

There are perhaps two general reasons why the Lindesmith and Cressey studies do not produce empirical prediction, reasons which are applicable because of the very specifications of their method itself. One of these reasons has already been extensively illustrated, namely that there is no basis for determining beforehand whether the conditions specified as necessary will exist in a particular instance.

The second general reason for lack of empirical prediction is that the alleged *preconditions* or essential causes of the phenomenon under examination cannot be fully specified apart from observation of the condition they are supposed to produce. In any situation in which variable *A* is said to cause variable *B*, *A* is of no value as a predictor of *B* unless we establish the existence of *A* apart from the observation of *B*. This limitation is in particular applicable to Cressey's study. Is it possible, for example, to assert that a problem is non-shareable *until* a person embezzles to get around it? If a man has not revealed his problem to others today, can we say that he will not share it tomorrow? The *operational* definition of a non-shareable problem is one that has not been shared up to the time of the embezzlement. Similarly, Cressey must be referring to some *quality* in the recognition of embezzlement as a solution which may not be identifiable apart from the fact that under appropriate conditions it eventuates in embezzlement. With embezzlement techniques and tales of successful embezzlement a standard part of the folklore of banks, offices handling public and private payrolls, and the like, mere recognition of embezzlement as a solution to problems is probably a near-universal characteristic of persons in a position to be able to embezzle. Similarly, rationalizations of embezzlement are part of the folklore and their use is standard joking behaviour among persons in such positions. Consequently both recognition of embezzlement as a potential solution and ability to rationalize the act only become discriminating conditions when some sort of qualitative or quantitative limitation is imposed upon them. But under the present formulation it is only possible to identify what is a sufficient recognition or a sufficient ability to rationalize by the fact that they eventuate in embezzlement.

Lindesmith's theory, though less subject to this limitation, reveals the same vulnerability. Since withdrawal distress varies in degree according to size of dose and the number of shots taken, and since several shots may precede the existence of addiction as Lindesmith defines it, definition of the point at which the individual is taking the drug *to relieve withdrawal distress*, as distinct from the point at which he is simply taking another shot, must be arbitrary in some cases. But the distinction is crucial to Lindesmith's theory, since before this point the individual is not addicted and presumably may interrupt the process, while after this point he is addicted and the process is complete. Hence, the identification of what constitutes an effective recognition of the relief the drug will bring can only ultimately be determined by the fact that addiction follows such recognition.[9]

As a final case, we shall refer to a study which is in important respects rather different, but which is couched in terms of a parallel logic. In Robert C. Angell's well-known study of fifty families that suffered a serious reduction in income during the Depression, he attempted to work out a set of categories which could be applied to a family before the Depression which would predict how it would respond to the drop in family income. On the basis of assessments of 'integration' and 'adaptability', Angell (1936) 'predicts' the response to financial crisis in terms of a 'vulnerability–invulnerability' continuum and a 'firm–readjustive–yielding' continuum. Through his designation of a presumably comprehensive pair of concepts for describing those characteristics of the family which are essential in predicting his post-crisis variables, Angell follows an analytic induction model, though his variables are not simple attributes as are those of Lindesmith and Cressey.

On the surface, Angell's formulation looks a good deal more like a device for empirical prediction since he provides categories which can be assessed before the process of responding to the Depression gets under way and without reference to the consequences. A careful examination of the nature and manner of assessment of the two essential variables will indicate whether the impression is justified.

The idea of integration seems to refer to the degree to which a family is a unit, which is a fact not observable in the same direct sense as the fact of taking a drug, for example. Integration conveys a meaning or feeling which is recognized by a number of symptoms, such as affection, common interests and sense of economic interdependence. Integration in practice, then, is identified by an impressionistic assessment of several observable variables.[10] Of these variables there is no single one by which alone integration can be identified, nor is there any single 'symptom' which may not be lacking in families classified as highly integrated.

The prediction which is provided by this scheme is *theoretical* prediction according to an analytic induction model. But the theoretical prediction cannot be converted into empirical prediction unless integration can be assessed beforehand. The assessment is made by an implicitly statistical operation, a mental weighting of several items of observation. In order, then, to gain *empirical* prediction the investigator shifts over to an 'enumerative induction' procedure.

The concept of adaptability is both more important and more complex, combining two elements as Angell uses the term (Hill, 1971, p. 132, citing Cavan, n.d.). First, if a family has been flexible in the face of minor crises or problems that have occurred in the past, it is said to be adaptable and the prediction is consequently made that it will maintain its unity in the face of a larger crisis. This, of course, is merely an application of the principle that there is a constancy in the response of a given system to situations of the same sort, and has no causal significance. The other aspect of adaptability consists of a number of criteria, such as commitment to material standards, concerning which the same comments apply as in the case of integration.

Thus in the three cases cited empirical prediction is not provided by statements of universally valid relationships taken alone. What, then, do such efforts accomplish?

Analytic induction as definition

What the method of universals most fundamentally does is to provide definitions. Not all definitions are of equal value for deriving scientific generalizations, and the definitions produced by the analytic induction procedure are intended to be characterized by causal homogeneity.

The effort at causal homogeneity is evident in the refinements of definition that accompany the method. In the process of attempting to generalize about addiction, Lindesmith had to distinguish between those drugs that produce withdrawal distress and those that do not. Early in his work he concluded that it would be futile to seek a single theory to explain both types. Cressey points out that he could not study everyone who is legally defined as an embezzler. Unless he restricted his subjects, for example, to those who entered the situation in good faith, he could not form valid generalizations having universal applicability. Angell also rules out certain types of families. He recognized that some of his families were units merely in a formal sense, and that he could not observe uniform principles which would be applicable to [these].

Saying that the principal accomplishment of the search for universals is to make definitions depends upon showing that the generalizations which it produces are deducible from the definitions. This is clearest in the case of Lindesmith's theory. In Lindesmith's presentation he has outlined the essential stages in becoming addicted by the time that he has arrived at his full definition of the phenomenon. The essential stages are implicit in the concept of addiction as he presents it.[11]

In place of the empirical attributes viewed essential by Lindesmith, Angell constructs two theoretical categories to which he ascribes the character of essentiality. But Angell is really getting the definition of his causal variables from the dependent or effect variables which he sets up. Adaptability seems to correspond to the firm–yielding dimension and integration to the vulnerability dimension. Adaptability and integration are the logically deducible counterparts to the dependent variables.

Cressey's formulation is less completely amenable to this interpretation. The recognition of embezzlement as a solution is a logically deducible component, since one cannot perform a purposive self-conscious act unless its possibility is recognized. By definition the subjects of Cressey's study possessed longstanding conceptions of themselves as law-abiding individuals, and were socially recognized as such at the time of the offence. While perhaps not from the definition alone, at least from the body of established theory which is implicit in the definition, it follows that the individuals must at the time of the crime in some way reconcile their behaviour with their law abiding self-conception. Indeed, we cannot help wondering whether failure to report rationalization could be entirely independent from the criteria by which an investigator would exclude some subjects from his study on grounds of doubting the honesty of their initial intentions.

The non-shareable problem, however, is probably only partially deducible. Given the fact that all people have problems that might be solved by stealing, given the fact that these subjects were mature individuals, and recognizing that they must, by definition, have resisted situations in the past which could have been improved by stealing, then it would seem to follow that a very distinctive type of problem would be required for people to deviate from their established life-patterns. The non-shareability of the problem might be deducible as a *frequent* characteristic, but probably not as a universal characteristic.

Thus, with the exception of non-shareability, the theories that have been examined serve chiefly to delimit a causally homogeneous category of phenomena, the so-called essential causes of the phenomenon being deducible from the definition.

It is, of course, not accidental but the crux of the method that these generalizations should be deducible. It is through the causal examination of the phenomenon that its delimitation is effected. The operation in practice is one which alternates back and forth between tentative cause and tentative definition, each modifying the other, so that in a sense closure is achieved when a complete and integral relation between the two is established. Once the generalizations become self-evident from the definition of the phenomenon being explained, the task is complete.

The intrusive factor

The next step in our argument must be to ask why the search for universals does not carry us beyond formulating a definition and indicating its logical corollaries, and why it fails to provide empirical prediction. The answer may be that there are no universal, uniform relations to be found except those which constitute logical corollaries of conceptual definition. The positing of operationally independent causal variables, empirically assessable prior to the existence of the postulated effect, always seems to result in relationships of statistical probability rather than absolute determination.[12]

A minor reason for these limited findings is the fact of multiple determination, with which analytic induction is rather ill-equipped to cope. When such complex phenomena as family integration, rather than individual behaviour, are examined, the method very rapidly shifts into the ideal-type technique, which is no longer subject to the sort of straightforward empirical verification as analytic induction. As in Angell's study, the logic of the method is preserved but the empirical problems become quite different.

But as the central thesis of this paper we shall call attention to another explanation for the absence of universal, uniform relations which are not logical corollaries of definitions. The 'closed system', which is the core of Znaniecki's statement and whose isolation is the objective and accomplishment of the method, is a causally self-contained system. As such, it is not capable of activation from within, but only by factors coming from outside the system. While, by definition, uniform relations exist within closed causal systems, uniform relations do not exist *between* any causal system and the external factors which impinge on it. *External variables operating upon any closed system do not have a uniform effect because they have to be assimilated to the receiving system in order to become effective as causes.* The outside variable has to be translated, in a sense, into a cause relevant to the receiving system. Normally there will be alternate ways in which the same external variable may be translated depending upon the full context within which it is operative. The situation in which a man finds himself, for example, can only activate the closed system of the embezzlement process when it becomes translated into a non-shareable problem. Cressey finds no type of problem, phenomenologically speaking, which necessarily and uniformly becomes a non-shareable problem.

The external factor which activates a system may be referred to as an *intrusive* factor. This idea is taken from Frederick Teggart's discussion of what he calls an 'event'. 'We may then define an event as an intrusion from any wider circle into any circle or condition which may be the object of present interest' (Teggart, 1925, p. 149, quoted by Case, 1933, p. 513). There are always intrusive factors which are accordingly not predictable in terms of the causal system under examination, but which serve to activate certain aspects of the system. The same idea may be thought of as levels of phenomena. There are no uniform relations between levels of phenomena, only within levels.

Empirical prediction always concerns the way in which one closed system is activated by various intrusive factors. Hence empirical prediction always requires some statistical or probability statements, because there is some uncertainty or lack of uniformity in the *way* in which the intrusive factors will activate the causal system and even in *whether* they will activate the system.

Universals and statistical method

The utility of defining universals within closed systems lies in the translation of *variables* into *concepts*. A variable is any category which can be measured or identified and correlated with something else. A concept is a variable which is part of a theoretical system, implying causal relations. That correlations among variables, of themselves, do not provide a basis for theory, or even for anticipating future correlations, is well known. Analytic induction fails to carry us beyond identifying a number of closed systems, and enumerative induction fails to go beyond the measurement of associations. The functions of the two methods are not only distinct; they are complementary. When the two methods are used together *in the right combination*,[13] they produce the type of findings which satisfies the canons of scientific method.

What the identification of closed systems does is to provide a basis for organizing and interpreting observed statistical associations. For example, valid research would probably reveal some correlation between liking-to-run-around-with-women and embezzlement. Cressey's findings do not discredit such an observation but afford a basis for interpreting it. In the light of certain American mores such a behaviour pattern is likely, in some circumstances, to create a problem which would be difficult to discuss with others. The crucial aspect of this behaviour for the determination of embezzlement would be its creation of a non-shareable problem.

With the closed system described it is possible to take the various correlations and get order from them. Identification of the closed system also gives us guides to significant variables, correlations that would be worthy of test. At the present point it should be profitable to search for the kinds of situations which most often become non-shareable problems, the characteristics which are correlated with the ability to rationalize an activity which would normally be regarded as contrary to the mores of society, the personal and situational characteristics associated with taking opiates (other than by medical administration) sufficiently to experience withdrawal symptoms. A study of correlations between certain sex patterns and the acquisition of non-shareable problems would build cumulatively in a way that a study of correlation between the former and embezzlement would not do. Some quantitative measure of such correlation would in turn provide the basis for using the closed-system formulation for empirical prediction.[14]

One useful indication of the way in which a statement of universals can function in the total research operation is afforded by Edwin Sutherland's 'differential association' theory of criminality (Sutherland, 1939, pp. 4–9).[15] While this theory is not the product of a specific empirical research operation of the sort that Lindesmith or Cressey undertook, the form of Sutherland's proposition is that of the analytic induction model. He employs a felicitous term in stating his theory. Differential association, he says, is 'the specific causal process' in the genesis of systematic criminal behaviour. He does not say that differential association is *the* cause or the *only* one; poverty and the like may be in some sense causes. But differential association is the specific causal process through which these other factors, or more removed causes, must operate. Poverty and other correlated factors only facilitate criminal behaviour because they affect the person's likelihood of learning a pattern of criminality from a model of criminality which is presented to him. The differential association theory identifies a hypothesized closed system, in terms of which the many correlated variables gain their meaning.

There are many theories already extant which have this same character, but which have not always been viewed as logical counterparts to the analytic induction method. Edwin Lemert's proposition that 'The onset of insanity coincides with the awareness of one's behaviour as being invidiously different from that of all other people's' points to the same sort of *specific causal process* in the genesis of insanity, or 'secondary psychotic deviation' (Lemert, 1951, p. 428). And Sorokin's interpretation of Durkheim's theory of suicide follows the same form (Sorokin, 1947, pp. 8–13).

Statements of this sort are devices for placing in bold outline the meaningful components of the phenomenon under study. In order to achieve the form of a universally valid generalization the investigator either states his causes as inferential variables (Angell), or states empirically continuous variables as attributes (Lindesmith, Cressey). In the latter case, the dividing point between the two phases of the crucial attribute is identifiable only retrospectively on the basis that the specified sequence is or is not completed. But if the essential components of the causal complex are viewed as continuous variables, capable of measurement independently of completion of the hypothesized sequence, the *essential degree* of the components will vary from instance to instance. Hence, in the process of designating the essential causes in a manner susceptible to empirical identification prior to their expected effect, the investigator must recast his thesis in terms of probability rather than uniform and universal relations.

A danger of the search for universals lies in the inadequate utilization of much valuable data. Cressey has information on the types of backgrounds his subjects came from, but because these are not universals the information has been filed away, or handled impressionistically. Lindesmith likewise secured abundant information which he uses only to demonstrate that absolute uniformity does not exist. Angell describes the frequent characteristics of the integrated and the adaptable family, but he does not systematize this material because such aspects of it are not universals. In these cases the imposition of particular methodological restrictions has limited what can be found out about the phenomenon under examination.

Analytic induction or some logical counterpart of the method is an essential aspect of research directed toward accumulating an ordered body of generalizations. But, for the reasons developed in this paper, Znaniecki's statement that 'analytic induction ends where enumerative induction begins; and if well conducted, leaves no real and soluble problems for the latter' represents an untenable position (Znaniecki, 1934,

p. 250). It is through conceiving the 'essential' conditions in a closed system as the avenues through which correlated factors can operate as causes that generalizations about closed systems can escape their self-containment, and probability associations may be organized into meaningful patterns.

Notes

This paper has benefited from discussion with W.S. Robinson's seminar in methodology and from a critical reading by Donald R. Cressey.

1 This point is brought out by Lindesmith (1952, p. 492).

2 Robinson's argument may not altogether escape a logical pitfall. He first makes a careful description of the analytic induction procedure, but does it by describing its elements within the framework of statistical method. Any such operation necessarily slights any aspects of the first framework which lack counterparts in the second. The conclusion that analytic induction is a special but imperfect form of statistical procedure would then be inherent in the operation itself rather than a legitimate finding.

3 Lindesmith's (1952) statement that 'Statistical questions call for statistical answers and causal questions call for answers within the framework of the logic of causal analysis' (p. 492) seems to be an evasion of the problems of *why* and *when* each type of question should be asked. 'Methodological parallelism' is of dubious fruitfulness.

4 The writer doubts that this limitation inheres logically in the conception of analytic induction as described by Znaniecki.

5 Some of Lindesmith's arguments with current theories of drug addiction (1947, pp. 141–64) rest upon a difference of purpose. Some of the theories he criticizes can be defended if reworded in terms of likelihood of first taking the drug in other than a medical treatment situation, rather than in terms of the likelihood of becoming addicted.

6 Lindesmith does not overlook these considerations in his descriptive treatment of the process. However, his treatment of them remains anecdotal and impressionistic rather than systematic and they are not integrated into the rigorous statement of his theory. The nearest he comes to a systematic statement concerning one of these variables is his observation that, 'as long as a patient believes he is using the drug solely to relieve pain, and regards it as a "medicine", he does not become an addict' (Lindesmith, 1947, p. 56). Weinberg (1952, p. 493) suggests the use of measurement in some of these connections.

7 A brief statement of the theory also appears as Cressey (1950).

8 Perhaps there is an object lesson indicated by this comparison. If the perspective of the investigator can determine what will be necessary for inclusion as the *essential* elements, there may be no theoretical limit to the number of such perspectives and consequently to the variations in what is considered essential. Such an observation would make it difficult to defend Znaniecki's dictum that the investigator can arrive at a point beyond which no new knowledge about a class can be added. (Cf. Znaniecki, 1934, p. 249).

9 Lindesmith admits some vagueness on the matter of what genuinely constitutes knowledge that an opiate will relieve withdrawal distress, but regards the vagueness as a present limitation of his knowledge rather than an intrinsic limitation of his method. (Cf. Lindesmith, 1947, p. 37).

10 Not only is the weighting of the various data of observation impressionistic but these criteria are themselves impressionistic. The implicitly statistical nature of Angell's operation has been noted before and his documents subjected to a restudy under Social

Science Research Council auspices. In the restudy, scales for the measurement of integration and adaptability were devised to objectify ratings and translate them into numerical values. See Cavan (n.d.).

11 Robinson (1952, p. 494) has suggested this.

12 These remarks and some of the subsequent observations must be qualified by noting that Cressey's 'non-shareable problem' is an apparent exception. If the statements in this paragraph are correct, we should expect further research to eventuate either in some modification of the concept 'violation of financial trust', or in the re-evaluation of the non-shareable problem as a *frequent* rather than essential characteristic.

13 In no sense can those research reports which devote a section to statistical findings and another section to case study findings be said to illustrate the thesis of this paper. In most cases such contrasting categories refer only to the method of data *collection*, the method of *analysis* being enumerative in both cases, but precise in the former and impressionistic in the latter.

14 Cressey proposes a study of such related conditions in much the same manner as is indicated here, but does not clarify whether this should be by a further extension of the method he has used or by the measurement of probabilities. (Cf. Cressey, 1950, Chap. V).

15 The third edition of Sutherland's work is cited here because he has modified the features of his theory most relevant to the argument of this paper in his fourth edition (1947).

References

Angell, R.C. (1936) *The Family Encounters the Depression*. New York: Scribner's Sons.

Case, C.M. (1933) 'Leadership and conjuncture: a sociological hypothesis', *Sociological and Social Research*, 17: 513.

Cavan, R. (n.d.) 'The restudy of the documents analysed by Angell in *The Family Encounters the Depression*'. Unpublished manuscript.

Cressey, D.R. (1950) *Other People's Money*. Glencoe, IL: Free Press.

Cressey, D.R. (1953) 'Criminal violation of financial trust', *American Sociological Review*, 15: 738–43.

Hill, R. (1971) *Families Under Stress*. Westport, CT: Greenwood Press.

Lemert, E.M. (1951) *Social Pathology*. New York: McGraw-Hill.

Lindesmith, A.R. (1947) *Opiate Addiction*. Bloomington, IN: Principia Press.

Lindesmith, A.R. (1952) 'Comment on W.S. Robinson's "The logical structure of analytic induction"', *American Sociological Review*, 17: 492–3.

Robinson, W.S. (1951) 'The logical structure of analytic induction', *American Sociological Review*, 16: 812–18.

Robinson, W.S. (1952) 'Rejoinder to comments on "The logical structure of analytic induction"', *American Sociological Review*, 17: 494.

Sorokin, P.M. (1947) *Society, Culture and Personality*. New York: Harper.

Sutherland, E.H. (1939) *Principles of Criminology* (3rd edn). Chicago: J.B. Lippincott Co.

Teggart, F.J. (1925) *Theory of History*. New Haven: Yale University Press.

Weinberg, S.K. (1952) 'Comment on W.S. Robinson's "The logical structure of analytic induction"', *American Sociological Review*, 17: 493–4.

Znaniecki, F. (1934) *The Method of Sociology*. New York: Farrar & Rinehart.

CHAPTER 10

SMALL N'S AND BIG CONCLUSIONS

An Examination of the
Reasoning in Comparative Studies
Based on a Small Number of Cases

Stanley Lieberson

This chapter evaluates an approach which is gaining in usage, especially for historical and comparative problems. Namely, we will consider the causal inferences drawn when little more than a handful of nations or organizations – sometimes even fewer – are compared with respect to the forces driving a societal outcome such as a political development or an organizational characteristic.[1] Application of this method to a small number of cases is not new to sociology, being in one form or another a variant of the method of analytic induction, described by Znaniecki (1934, p. 236) and analysed succinctly by Robinson (1951) and Turner (1953) [see Chapters 8 and 9 – respectively *Editors' Note*].[2] These conclusions rely on a formalized internal logic derived from Mill's method of agreement and his method of difference (see the discussion of Mill in Nichols, 1986, pp. 170ff.). The formal rigour of this type of analysis sets it off from other small-sample procedures which also imply causality, as, say, in *Street Corner Society* (Whyte, 1943) or in the development of the model of urban structure and growth of Burgess (1925). It is also different from case studies which seek to point out merely that a given phenomenon *exists* in some setting, as opposed to an analysis of its causes. The comments are, however, to some degree relevant for evaluating the Boolean method proposed by Ragin (1987) for dealing with somewhat larger samples used in comparative and historical research. Moreover, although the analysis is stimulated by recent developments in macrohistorical research, it is pertinent to a wide variety of other studies that use Mill's logic with a small number of cases.

One has no difficulty appreciating the goal of applying formal procedures to make causal inferences in a manner analogous to what is

From C.C. Ragin and H.S. Becker (eds) (1992) *What is a Case? Exploring the Foundations of Social Inquiry*. Cambridge: Cambridge University Press.

otherwise restricted to studies based on a much larger number of cases. If data were available with the appropriate depth and detail for a large number of cases, obviously the researcher would not be working with these few cases (assuming a minimal time-energy cost). Since the data are not available, or the time-energy cost is too great, one can only approach these efforts with considerable sympathy for their objective. We address three questions: (1) What are the assumptions underlying these studies? (2) Are these assumptions reasonable? (3) What can be done to improve such studies in those instances when they might be appropriate forms of inquiry?

Probabilistic and deterministic perspectives

Let us start by distinguishing between causal propositions that are *deterministic* as contrasted with those that are *probabilistic*. The former posits that a given factor, when present, will lead to a specified outcome. The latter is more modest in its causal claim, positing that a given factor, when present, will increase the likelihood of a specified outcome. When we say, 'If X_1 then Y', we are making a deterministic statement. When we say, 'the presence of X_1 increases the likelihood or frequency of Y', we are making a probabilistic statement. Obviously, if given the choice, deterministic statements are more appealing. They are cleaner, simpler and more easily disproved than probabilistic ones. One negative case, such that Y is absent in the presence of X_1, would quickly eliminate a deterministic statement.

Alas, a probabilistic approach is often necessary to evaluate the evidence for a given theoretical perspective, even if we think in deterministic terms. This occurs for a variety of reasons, not the least being measurement errors – a serious problem in the social sciences. The existence of a measurement error means that a given data set may deviate somewhat from a hypothesized pattern without the hypothesis being wrong. In addition to this technical matter, there is an additional problem: complex multivariate causal patterns operate in the social world, such that a given outcome can occur because of the presence of more than one independent variable and, moreover, may not occur at times because the influence of one independent variable is outweighed by other influences working in the opposite direction. Under such circumstances, the influence of X_1 is only approximate (even without measurement errors), unless one can consider all of the other independent variables, through controls or otherwise.

Furthermore, we often do not know or cannot measure all of the factors that we think will influence Y. As a consequence, we are again obliged to give up on a deterministic *measurement* of the influence of X_1 on Y, even if we are prepared to make a deterministic statement about its influence. There are yet other reasons for reverting to a probabilistic rather than a deterministic approach, namely the role of chance in affecting outcomes. Beyond consideration here is the question of whether *chance per se* exists or is simply a residual label referring to our ignorance about additional influences and/or inadequate measures for the variables under scrutiny. In either case, some form or another of indeterminacy is clearly useful to employ in the physical sciences, let alone in the social sciences (see examples in Lieberson, 1985, pp. 94–7). Any of these factors would lead to probabilistic statements rather than deterministic statements of outcome.

This distinction is more than merely an academic one. Rather, it is embedded in our daily thinking. Suppose we examine the influence of alcohol on automobile accidents. Even if we believe there is such an influence, we still will expect some sober drivers to have chargeable accidents and not all drunk drivers to experience accidents. If we find that some sober drivers did cause accidents and some drunk drivers did not, these deviations would not lead us to reject automatically the proposition that drunkenness causes automobile accidents.[3] Rather, we would look at a set of data and ask if the probability or frequency of accidents were greater for drunk than for sober drivers. Why is this so? Even if taking a deterministic view, we would expect several factors to influence the likelihood of an accident, alcohol being only one of them. Indeed, we would expect an interaction effect for drunkenness, such that one drunk driver might run a red light in a busy intersection and have an accident, whereas another driver might be fortunate to enter the intersection when the light was green. To be sure, we might want to take some of these additional factors into account, and we would then expect the influence of drinking to be more sharply displayed. But it is unlikely that we could isolate alcohol's influence from all of the additional conditions that either prevent drinking from causing an accident or lead a sober driver to have an accident. The net effect is that we will not totally reject our idea about alcoholism and driving if we compare a drunk driver with a sober one and find the latter has an accident and the former does not. Likewise, if we learn of one drunk driver who has an accident and a sober driver who does not, that will hardly be persuasive data that the pattern is indeed in the direction anticipated. The point is clear-cut: *a deterministic theory has deterministic outcomes, but often we can measure it only in probabilistic terms.*

Despite these facts, small-N studies operate in a deterministic manner, avoiding probabilistic thinking either in their theory or in their empirical applications. As one distinguished proponent of the small-N approach puts it,

> in contrast to the probabilistic techniques of statistical analysis – techniques that are used when there are very large numbers of cases and continuously quantified variables to analyse – comparative historical analyses proceed

through logical juxtapositions of aspects of small numbers of cases. They attempt to identify invariant causal configurations that necessarily (rather than probably) combine to account for outcomes of interest. (Skocpol, 1984, p. 378)

One good reason for this disposition is the following principle: *except for probabilistic situations which approach 1 or 0 (in other words are almost deterministic), studies based on a small number of cases have difficulty in evaluating probabilistic theories.*

Let us draw an analogy with flying a given airline. Suppose a rude employee is encountered, or luggage is lost, or the plane is delayed. One could, after such an experience, decide to use a different airline. However, one would know that although airlines may differ in their training programmes, employee relations, morale, luggage practices, airplane maintenance and other factors affecting their desirability, a very small number of experiences is insufficient to evaluate airlines with great confidence. If airlines differ, it is in the *frequency* of unpleasant experiences rather than that one airline has only polite employees, never loses luggage or avoids all mechanical problems. Based on a small number of experiences, one may decide to shun a certain airline, and the decision is not totally wrong, since the probability of such experiences in any given small number of events is indeed influenced by the underlying distribution of practices in different airlines. However, conclusions drawn on the basis of such practices are often wrong. We would know that passengers with small numbers of experiences will draw very different conclusions about the relative desirability of various airlines. This is because a small number of cases is a bad basis for generalizing about the process under study. Thus if we actually knew the underlying probabilities for each airline, it would be possible to calculate how often the wrong decision will occur based on a small number of experiences. The consumer errors are really of no great consequence, since making decisions on the basis of a small number of events enables the flyer to respond in some positive way to what can otherwise be a frustrating experience. Such thinking, however, is not innocuous for the research problems under consideration here; it will frequently lead to erroneous conclusions about the forces operating in society. Moreover, other samples based on a small number of different cases – when contradicting the first sample, and this is almost certain to occur – will create even more complicated sets of distortions as the researcher attempts to use deterministic models to account for all of the results. This, in my judgement, is not a step forward.

Briefly, in most social-research situations it is unlikely that the requirements of a deterministic theory will be met. When these conditions are not met, then the empirical consequences of deterministic and probabilistic theories are similar in the sense that both will have to accept deviations: the former because of errors in measurement and controls; the latter both because of those reasons and because the theory itself incorporates some degree of indeterminacy (due to inherent problems in either the measurement or knowledge of all variables or because of some inherent indeterminacy in the phenomenon).

The implications of this are seen all the time in social research. In practice, for example, it is very difficult to reject a major theory because it appears not to operate in some specific setting. One is wary of concluding that Max Weber was wrong because of a single deviation in some inadequately understood time or place. In the same fashion, we would view an accident caused by a sober driver as failing to disprove the notion that drinking causes automobile accidents.

Suppose, for example, there is a single deviation among a small number of cases or a modest number of deviations among a larger number of cases. What are the consequences for the deterministic theory under consideration?[4] If the deterministic theory is univariate, that is, either only one variable or one specific combination of variables (an interaction) causes a given outcome, the theory can be rejected with a single deviation if one is confident that there are no measurement errors (a non-trivial consideration for either statistical or 'qualitative' descriptions) and there are no other possible causes of the dependent variable.[5] As for a multivariate deterministic theory, where more than one variable or more than one combination of variables could account for the consequence, it can be rejected with a single deviation if there is confidence that there are no measurement errors – as before – *and* also that all other factors hypothesized to be affecting the outcome are known and fully taken into account.

The importance of all of this is that the formal procedures used in the small-N comparative, historical and organizational analyses under consideration here are all deterministic in their conception. Indeed, small-N studies cannot operate effectively under probabilistic assumptions, because then they would require much larger N's to have any meaningful results. This becomes clear when we watch the operation of their reasoning with the methods described by Mill.

Mill's method

As Skocpol (1986) observes, the key issue is the applicability of Mill's 'method of agreement' and 'method of difference' to such data. Nichols (1986) agrees, but then criticizes the application of this logic in an earlier study; for example, she shows that it assumes interaction effects but no additive influences. I will build on, and modify, this important critique here.

Let us start with the method of difference, which deals with situations in which the level of the dependent variable (outcome) is not the same for all of the cases. Here the researcher examines all possible independent variables that might influence this outcome, looking for a pattern where all but one of the independent variables do not systematically vary along with the dependent variable. Examples of this might be where X_1 is constant in all cases or varies between cases in a manner different from the dependent variable. This method is applied even with two cases, so long as only one of the independent variables differs, while the others are constant across the cases (Orloff and Skocpol, 1984). Table 10.1 illustrates this type of analysis. For simplicity, let us assume that all the independent variables as well as the explanandum are dichotomies with 'yes' and 'no' indicating the presence and absence of the attribute under consideration. To illustrate my points as clearly as possible, I have used an illustration based on automobile accidents. The logic is that followed in Mill's methods and is identical with that employed in these deterministic studies of macrophenomena.

Applying the method of difference to the hypothetical data in Table 10.1, we would conclude that the auto accident was caused by X_2, because in one case a car entered the intersection whereas in the other case no car did. We would also conclude that the accident was *not* caused by drunk driving or the running of a red light, because the variables (respectively X_1 and X_4) were the same for both drivers, yet only one had an accident. Such conclusions are reached only by making a very demanding assumption that is rarely examined. The method's logic assumes no interaction effects are operating (that is, that the influence of each independent variable on Y is unaffected by the level of some other independent variable). The procedure cannot deal with interaction effects; procedure cannot distinguish between the influence of inebriation or running a red light and the influence of another constant, such as the benign fact that both drivers were not exceeding the speed limit. Since X_1 and X_4 are constant, under this logic it would follow that neither inebriation nor running a red light had anything to do with the accident occurring. *The procedure does not empirically or logically eliminate interaction effects. Rather, it arbitrarily assumes that they do not operate and that therefore constants cannot influence the dependent variable.*[6] Unless interactions are automatically ruled out *a priori*, this means that the results in Table 10.1 (and all other small-N applications of the

Table 10.1 *Application of the method of difference*

Accident (Y)	Drunk driving (X₁)	Car entering from right-hand direction (X₂)	Driver speeding (X₃)	Runs a red light (X₄)
Yes	Yes	Yes	No	Yes
No	Yes	No	No	Yes

method) *fail* to provide any determination of the influence of variables X_1, X_3 and X_4 on the phenomenon under consideration.[7] Just to make the point very clear, consider another example of the same sort: ten people apply for a job; five are blacks and five are whites. One of the five blacks and all the five whites are hired. Applying the method of difference, one would conclude that race did not affect employment. Rather, it would have to be some variable that separates all of the employed persons from the four who did not get a job. Using a small N with the method of difference, it is not possible to examine inter-action effects or multiple causes. Their absence is assumed.

The reader should also note how this method has a certain limited generality unless one assumes, *a priori*, that only one variable causes the phenomenon under study. For variables that are constant, it is impossible to rule out their influence under different levels simply because there are no measurements. From Table 10.1, for example, we know that an accident occurs although X_3 is constant. Even ignoring the question of interaction effects, it is impossible to conclude that X_3 does not cause accidents unless one assumes there is only one cause of accidents. In this case, and this asymmetry is common in small-N stud-ies, we only know about situations where drivers are *not* speeding. Note again the results, it means that only a single causal variable is operating, otherwise, under the logic used in such studies, the influ-ences of constants are not really taken into account in the method of difference.[8] This has a great bearing on the generality of such small-N comparative studies.

In Table 10.2, we have a new situation in which two drivers both experience accidents. As before, the two drivers are drunk, both cars run red lights, and again in only one instance another car was appropriately entering the intersection, whereas in the other instance there was none. This time, however, the second person was driving at a high speed, whereas the first driver was not. Intuitively, it is not unreasonable that high-speed driving could affect the chances of an accident, say causing a skid, or the car could have failed to make a turn in the intersection. At any rate, since both drivers have accidents, the logic generated by Mill's method of agreement is applied here, where presumably the causal variable is isolated by being the only constant across the two instances, whereas all of the other attributes vary. However, notice what happens

Table 10.2 Application of the method of agreement

Accident (Y)	Drunk driving (X_1)	Car entering from right-hand direction (X_2)	Driver speeding (X_3)	Runs a red light (X_4)
Yes	Yes	Yes	No	Yes
Yes	Yes	No	Yes	Yes

under that logic here. The previous cause, X_2, is now eliminated since it varies between two drivers who both have accidents. Previously, X_1 and X_4 could not have caused an accident, but are now the only two contenders as a possible cause. Since only one driver is going at a high speed now and both drivers have accidents, it follows that the addition of this factor could not have caused an accident, an extraordinary conclusion too. What has gone wrong? This is an example of how Mill's method cannot work when more than one causal variable is a determinant and there are a small number of cases. Comparison between the two tables shows how volatile the conclusions are about whether variables cause or do not cause accidents. Every fact remains the same regarding the first driver in both cases, but the fact that the second driver was speeding and therefore has an accident completely alters our understanding of what caused the first driver to have an accident. Another shortcoming to such data analyses is that the conclusions are extremely volatile if it turns out that a multideterministic model is appropriate. Moreover, with a small-N study, although it is possible to obtain data which would lead one to reject the assumption of a single-variable deterministic model (assuming no measurement error), it is impossible for the data to provide reasonable assurance that a single-variable deterministic model is correct, even if the observed data fit such a model.

These comparisons suggest more than the inability of Mill's methods to use a small number of cases to deal with a multivariate set of causes. As Nichols (1986) points out, Mill had intended these methods as 'certain only where we are sure we have been able to correctly and exhaustively analyse all possible causal factors' (p. 172). Nichols goes on to observe that Mill rejects this method when causality is complex or when more than one cause is operating. Beyond these considerations, important as they clearly are, the foregoing analysis also shows how exceptionally vulnerable the procedure is to the exclusion of relevant variables. In Table 10.2, had we left out X_4, inebriation clearly would have been the causal factor, but it is not clear because X_4 is included. This is always a danger; large-N studies also face the potential danger that omission of variables will radically alter the observed relations, but the susceptibility to spurious findings is much greater here.

Suppose a researcher has a sufficient number of cases such that there are several drivers who have accidents and several who do not. Would the deterministic model based on a small number of cases now be facilitated? In my opinion, it is unlikely. If drinking increases the probability of an accident but does not always lead to one, and if sobriety does not necessarily enable a driver to avoid causing an accident, then it follows that some drunk drivers will not experience an accident, and some accidents will be experienced by sober drivers. Under the circumstances, there will be no agreement for these variables among all drivers experiencing an accident, and there will be no agreement among those not experiencing an accident. This means that neither of Mill's methods will work. A difference in the frequency of accidents linked to drinking will show up, but this of course is ruled out (and more or less has to be) in the deterministic practices involving small-N studies. Multicausal probabilistic statements are simply unmanageable with the procedures under consideration here.[9]

One way of thinking about this small-N methodology is to visualize a very small sample taken from a larger population. Let us say we have a small sample of nations or of political developments drawn randomly from the universe of nations or the universe of political developments.[10] What is the likelihood that the application of Mill's methods to this small sample will reproduce the patterns observed for the larger universe? Rarely, in my estimation, do we encounter big-N studies in which all of the relevant causal variables are determined and there are no measurement errors such that all cases are found so neatly as is assumed here with small-N studies. Yet in order to draw a conclusion, the small-N study assumes that if all cases were equally well known, the patterns observed with the small sample would be duplicated without exception. Is this reasonable? Also ask yourself how often in large-N studies would restrictions to a deterministic univariate theory make sense.

It is also impossible for this type of analysis to guard against the influence of chance associations. Indeed the assumption is that 'chance' cannot operate to generate the observed data. Because it is relatively easy to develop a theoretical fit for small-N data, researchers are unable to guard against a small-N version of the *ad hoc* curve fitting that can be employed in large-N studies (see the discussion of Taylor's theorem in Lieberson, 1985, p. 93). Ironically, small-N deterministic analyses actually have the same goal as some types of large-scale empirical research, namely explaining all of the variance. The former is just another version of this, subject to the same dangers (Lieberson, 1985; Chap. 5), along with special ones due to their very demanding assumptions necessary when using a small N.

Theoretical concerns

Two implications follow from this review; one is theoretical and the other deals with empirical procedures.

Dealing with the theoretical questions first, obviously the small-N applications of Mill's methods cannot be casually used with all macrosocietal data sets. The method requires very strong assumptions: a deterministic set of forces; the existence of only one cause; the absence of interaction effects; confidence that all possible causes are measured; the absence of measurement errors; and the assumption that the same 'clean' pattern would occur if data were obtained for all cases in the universe of relevant cases.

At the very least, users must recognize that these assumptions are mandatory in this procedure. The issue then becomes this: Under what conditions is it reasonable to make these assumptions ('reasonable' in the sense that they have a strong likelihood of being correct)? Keep in mind that the empirical data themselves cannot be used to test whether the assumptions are correct or not; for example, the empirical data gathered in the typical small-N study cannot tell us if a univariate deterministic cause is operating or if there are no interaction effects. Theories of large-scale organizations, 'qualitative' or not, must direct themselves to these questions before the data analyses begin. Moreover, the theories have to develop ways of thinking about these problems so the researcher can decide if they are reasonable. Admittedly, this is vague advice, and hopefully those dealing with this type of research will come up with solutions. Certainly, the Boolean method proposed by Ragin (1987) is a step in the right direction, although it does require a relatively larger N than the type of small-N studies under consideration here.[11]

The quality of qualitative data

It should be clear how critical it is that small-N studies take extraordinary care in the design and measurement of the variables, whether or not it is a so-called qualitative study. Care is always appropriate, but the impact of error or imprecision is even greater when the number of cases is small. Keep in mind that the deterministic model used in these studies requires error-free measurement. The choice of cases for study is itself critical, requiring great thought about the appropriate procedure for choosing them. Presumably, these are self-evident facts to practitioners of this approach, and the intense scrutiny of a small number of cases should mean exceptional care with the descriptions.

However, exceptionally rigorous practices are necessary to avoid some methodological pitfalls. If a small number of cases are selected using reasonably rigorous criteria, then it makes a great difference whether the outcomes are the same or not in each case. If the same, then the method of agreement is used such that a solution occurs only if one variable is constant in all cases; if different, then the only solution occurs when all but one of the variables are constant across all the cases. All of this is nothing more than a repetition of procedures dating back to Mill. Less obvious, at least as far as I can tell, are the implications this has for the delineation of each independent variable. If an independent variable consists of nominal categories, there should be little difficulty, since presumably trained observers would agree on the classification of each measure. The researcher uses the same checks as would be performed in any large-scale study (for example, content analysis). But if the independent variable is even ordinal, there is a certain arbitrariness in the way an ordered variable is dichotomized or otherwise divided (polytomized).

To simplify the point, just consider dichotomies. The method of agreement will work only if all the cases for one causal variable fall in the same category *and* if no other variable has such uniformity. This means that the cut-offs are critical. The same holds for the method of difference, but here the results must be such that the results are uniform for all but one variable, with the one critical exception being associated with differences in the dependent variable. Under the circumstances, the delineation of the dichotomies or polytomies is critical and has to be done as rigorously as possible since the boundaries will influence the results enormously. All of this means that rigour is mandatory when locating the variables if they are nominal, and even more so when they are ordinal, for example careful driver versus careless driver, and so on.

With the method of difference, where there is an inverse relationship between the number of cases and the difficulty of finding all but one variable constant across cases, researchers have to guard against using such broad categories as to make it relatively easy for cases to fall under the same rubric. With the method of agreement, where it is vital that all but one variable be different across the cases, the danger is in constructing narrow categories within each variable so that it will be relatively hard for cases to fall under the same rubric. In short, because of the subtle pressure to obtain only one variable that is homogeneous (in the case of agreement in the dependent variable) or only one variable that is heterogeneous (in the case of disagreement in the dependent variable), one must also guard against the bracketing of attributes in the former case, and decomposition in the latter. For this method to work at all, researchers must introduce formal criteria for these decisions which can be followed in advance of a given research project. To my knowledge, they do not exist at this time. (It would be an interesting study in both the sociology of knowledge and research methodology to see if the breadth of categories used in recent studies is related to whether the study involves cases calling for one or the other method.)

Because of the small N's and the reasoning this method requires, it is vital to include all possible causal variables. Yet this will tend to lead to inconclusive results if carried out in a serious way, since the method of agreement will probably turn up with more than one variable that is constant for all the cases and, likewise, the method of difference will have more than one independent variable that is associated with the difference in the dependent variable. Suppose, for example, we find that a drunk driver has no automobile accident, but the sober driver experiences one. In such a case, using the small-N methods practised in historical sociology, the investigator is in danger of concluding that sobriety causes automobile accidents, or at the very least is the cause in the observed situation. At best, and only if the correct causal factor is included, the study will conclude that either sobriety or some other factor causes automobile accidents. At worst, if the correct causal factor is excluded, sobriety will be the cause. So there is a kind of dilemma here; a 'clean' result will tend to occur only with a modest number of independent variables, but this very step is likely to increase the chances of an erroneous conclusion.

Also, the relationship between the independent variables and the dependent variable is distorted if the cases are selected so as to have agreement or disagreement with respect to the dependent variable (rather than simply sampling from all of the cases). It can be shown that sampling in order to obtain a certain distribution with respect to the dependent variable ends up distorting the explanandum's association with the independent variables (unless the ratio of odds is used). Obviously not all cases are equally good, since the quality of the data presumably varies between them, as does the researcher's access to and knowledge about the relevant information. However, this distortion is beyond that problem and makes it even harder to assume that one small sample and another small sample by a second researcher can be combined to generate a more accurate model of the forces under consideration.

Conclusions

A number of assumptions made in these small-N macrocomparative studies are not only very demanding, but to my knowledge they are normally not made explicit or seriously examined. Yet they are assumptions that are usually indefensible in social research. This leads to a certain curiosity. One possibility is that these assumptions occur because they are the only way of proceeding with such data sets, not because the investigators commonly believe they are correct. In that circumstance, the same assumptions will collapse when studies based on large N's are attempted. Another possibility is that such assumptions are appropriate for certain subject matters such as major institutions, nations, and the like. If that is the case, then a very important step is missing, since these assumptions are rarely justified with empirical data based on a larger number of cases. (That is, as a test, by sampling an extremely small number of cases from large macrosocietal data sets it should be possible to show that the same conclusions would occur with Mill's method as by studying the universe of cases.) At the moment, however, it appears that Mill's procedures cannot be applied to small-N studies. There are strong grounds for questioning the assumptions essential to causal analyses generated by such procedures.

As matters now stand it appears that the methodological needs are generating the theory, rather than vice versa. Put bluntly, application of Mill's methods to small-N situations does not allow for probabilistic theories, interaction effects, measurement errors or even the presence of more than one cause.[12] For example, in the application shown earlier, the method cannot consider the possibility that more than one factor causes automobile accidents or that there is an interaction effect between two variables.[13] Indeed, if two drivers are drunk, but one does not have an accident, the procedure will conclude that the state of inebriation could not have been a cause of the accident that did occur.

I have selected the automobile-accident example because it should be patently clear that the special deterministic logic does not operate in that instance. Perhaps one may counter that nations and major institutions are neither persons nor roulette wheels; surely their determination is less haphazard, and therefore deterministic thinking is appropriate for these cases. Hence, one might argue, the points made are true for automobile accidents but not for major social institutions or other macrosocietal phenomena. This sounds plausible, but is it true? It turns out that many deep and profound processes are somewhat haphazard too, not so easily relegated to a simple determinism. Elsewhere, I have cited a wide variety of important phenomena which appear to involve chance processes, or processes that are best viewed that way. These include race riots, disease, subatomic physics, molecules of gas, star systems, geology and biological evolution (Lieberson, 1985, pp. 94–9, 225–7). One must take a very cautious stance about whether the methods used in these small-N studies are appropriate for institutional and macrosocietal events. At the very least, advocates of such studies must learn how to estimate if the probabilistic level is sufficiently high that a quasi-deterministic model will not do too much damage.

Notes

I am indebted to William Alonso, Rogers Brubaker, John Campbell, William Kruskal and Peter V. Marsden for stimulating discussions or comments on this topic.

1 This is different from historical or comparative analyses based on larger numbers, as, for example, in Isaac and Griffin (1989).

2 A brief history of earlier applications of this reasoning is given by Znaniecki (1934, pp. 236–8).

3 Following Marini and Singer (1988), by 'cause' and 'causal' they distinguish 'causation from association, recognizing that causes are responsible for producing effects, whereas noncausal associations are not. Although causal terminology has been imprecise and has waxed and waned in popularity … the ideas of agency and productivity which it conveys have continued to be viewed as distinctive and important in social science' (p. 347).

4 It is not vital, for my purpose at this point, to define 'small', 'modest' or 'larger'.

5 Needless to say, determination of measurement error should not be made on the basis of whether deviations occur – all the more reason to expect rigorous procedures in both qualitative and quantitative analyses.

6 One cannot argue, by the way, that a new variable, combining being drunk and running a red light, could serve as a substitute for unmeasured interactions. This is because there would be no way of distinguishing such a combination from other combinations such as not speeding and running a red light, or for that matter a grand variable which includes all of the constants and the red-light variable.

7 Observe that were there to be a larger number of cases in Table 10.1, say 100, with 60 of them where Y is yes and 40 where Y is no, and where the presence or absence of X_2 is always in the form shown, whereas the other variables vary in a random way, there would be considerable confidence in the very same conclusion that is questionable with a small N.

8 In fairness, of course, the influence is tested if the constant is at a level where it is believed to affect the dependent variable.

9 To be sure, the method could still *possibly* work if all other conceivable causes of accidents were measured and recorded – a rather unlikely situation that requires exceptional good fortune in the recording of all possible causes and their precise measurement, for example the exact speed of each car entering the intersection, and the speed and timing of cars entering the intersection from other points, all of the qualities of drivers who enter from these other points who did not have accidents, and so on.

10 This ignores the added problem when the small sample is not a random one, but is a selective set of cases.

11 For the most part, I would say that his approach is, however, a deterministic one. Particularly relevant is his treatment of contradictions (pp. 113–18). The emphasis is primarily on finding additional variables which resolve the contradictions and/or changing the delineation of the dependent variable. However, he does consider a type of statistical solution as well.

12 The Boolean methods proposed by Ragin (1987) advance our ability to deal with some of these problems, although they require a larger number of cases than are often used in these attempts to apply Mill's methods.

13 As for the former, Turner observes that the method of analytical induction is 'ill-equipped to cope' with multiple causes (1953: 609).

References

Burgess, E.W. (1925) 'The growth of the city: an introduction to a research project', in R.E. Park, E.W. Burgess and R.D. McKenzie (eds), *The City*. Chicago: University of Chicago Press.

Isaac, L.W. and Griffin, L.J. (1989) 'Ahistorcism in time-series analyses of historical process: critique, redirection, and illustrations from U.S. labor history', *American Sociological Review*, 54: 873–90.

Lieberson, S. (1985) *Making It Count: The Improvement of Social Research and Theory*. Berkeley: University of California Press.

Marini, M.M. and Singer, S. (1988) 'Causality in the social sciences', in C.C. Clogg (ed.), *Sociological Methodology, 1988* (Vol. 18). Washington, DC: American Sociological Association.

Nichols, E. (1986) 'Skocpol and revolution: comparative analysis vs. historical conjuncture', *Comparative Social Research,* 9: 63–86.

Orloff, A.S. and Skocpol, T. (1984) 'Why not equal protection? Explaining the politics of public social spending in Britain, 1890–1911 and the United States, 1880s–1920', *American Sociological Review,* 49: 726–50.

Ragin, C.C. (1987) *The Comparative Method: Moving beyond Qualitative and Quantitative Strategies.* Berkeley: University of California Press.

Robinson, W.S. (1951) 'The logical structure of analytic induction', *American Sociological Review,* 16: 812–18.

Skocpol, T. (1984) 'Emerging agendas and recurrent strategies in historical sociology', in T. Skocpol (ed.), *Vision and Method in Historical Sociology.* Cambridge University Press.

Skocpol, T. (1986) 'Analyzing causal configurations in history: a rejoinder to Nichols', *Comparative Social Research,* 9: 87–94.

Turner, R.H. (1953) 'The quest for universals in sociological research', *American Sociological Review,* 18: 604–11.

Whyte, W.F. (1943) *Street Corner Society: The Social Structure of an Italian Slum.* Reprinted Chicago: University of Chicago Press, 1955.

Znaniecki, F. (1934) *The Method of Sociology.* New York: Farrar & Rinehart.

CASES, CAUSES, CONJUNCTURES, STORIES AND IMAGERY

Howard S. Becker

Cases

The problems associated with doing and understanding case studies involve, apparently necessarily, the question of explanation or description, which might be translated as the problem of what we can say about what we've found out in our research. Can we say that something we discovered causes or produces or influences or comes before or in some other way affects what happens to some other thing? We produce a lot of 'results' and then have to arrange them so as to 'say something'. What kinds of 'somethings' can we say? Where do they come from? What criteria do we use to judge them?

Causes

One way we approach this problem is to say that something 'causes' something else. The notion of cause is very tangled philosophically, at least (to my meagre knowledge) since Hume, and it is especially hard to separate from the simple fact of sequence, of one thing following another. Billiard ball *A* hits billiard ball *B*. Billiard ball *B* moves. Did *A*'s hitting it 'cause' it to move?

Leave these philosophical tangles aside. Sociologists have typically solved the problem of cause by embodying it in procedures which we agree will serve as the way we know that *A* caused *B*, philosophically sound or not. These procedures have the status of paradigmatic methods. They are parts of packages of ideas and procedures which some community of scientists has agreed to accept as plenty good enough for the purpose of establishing cause. For all the reasons Thomas Kuhn (1962) pointed out, these paradigmatic ideas are double-edged. Without them we can't get anything done. But they never really do what they say they do. They leave terrible anomalies in their wake. They have

From C.C. Ragin and H.S. Becker (eds) (1992) *What is a Case? Exploring the Foundations of Social Inquiry*. Cambridge: Cambridge University Press.

terrible flaws in their supporting logic. They are thus always vulnerable to attack, to being shown to be less and do less than they pretend.

Sociologists have agreed on paradigms for establishing causality many times, usually describing their procedures in the language of variables. The analyst identifies a 'dependent variable', some phenomenon which varies along some dimension, and then attempts to identify the 'independent variables' whose own variation 'causes' the variation in the dependent variable. The definition of cause is covariation. If the measure of dependent variable *A* changes in some regular way when the measure of the independent variables changes, cause has been demonstrated or, at least, researchers who accept this paradigm agree that evidence of causation has been produced.

Naturally, such procedures have many difficulties. Students learning correlation techniques traditionally also learn that correlation is not causation. A long list of standard troubles can derail the easy identification of covariation and causality. Nevertheless, sociologists routinely use this form of explanation, in a variety of forms, particularly in such paradigmatic applications as figuring out, say, what factors affect social mobility: to what degree do parental social position, education, occupation and similar variables covary with (and thus cause) someone's class mobility?

One standard procedure (or, better, family of procedures) has been a kind of quasi-experimental factoring out of the relative influence of the several causes we can imagine might explain or account for (a variety of terms have been used to describe this connection) the outcome we are interested in. Lieberson (1985) has criticized this family of statistical procedures profoundly, arguing that the notion of estimating the influence of a variable by holding other factors constant is untenable, because of the non-random distribution of the variables so introduced, the 'selection' problem. He has, in his chapter in this volume [Chapter 10 – *Editors' Note*], nevertheless tried to keep that logic going by cleaning up the occasions of its use.

The procedures used in studies based on this logic depend on comparing cells in a table (the cells containing cases which embody different combinations of the variables being studied), and the comparisons will not withstand standard criticisms unless they rest on large numbers of cases. The results of such studies consist of probabilistic statements about the relations between the variables, [...], statements whose subjects are not people or organizations doing things but rather variables having an effect or producing some measurable degree of variation in the dependent variable. The conclusions of such a study – that the cases studied have a particular probability of showing this or that result – are intended to apply to a universe of similar cases.

The logic of this approach, even in the cleaned-up version advocated by Lieberson, requires us to imagine that all the causes involved in the production of an effect operate more or less simultaneously and continuously, as in the well-known laws governing the relations among pressure, temperature and volume of gases. Even when we know better and know that *A* must precede *B*, the analytic procedures require us to treat them as though that were not true.

These procedures also require us to imagine that the variables proposed as causes operate independently. Each makes its own contribution to the variation in the dependent variable. To be sure, the analyst may have to contend with interaction effects, the effects on the dependent variable of the effects the independent variables have on each other. But these too are treated as though they are all operating simultaneously and continuously.

Lieberson's analysis of automobile accidents in his chapter in this volume exemplifies the point. Any automobile accident is a complex multi-step event: the drivers (there are two in the accident he analyses, although he is only interested in the one alleged to have been drinking) either drink or don't drink; they start their cars; they proceed to the intersection where they will meet; the traffic light at the intersection shows red in one direction, green in the other; one driver proceeds to enter the intersection legally, the other enters it illegally, each of these acts composed of a sequence of more detailed acts, such as looking for other cars and speeding up or slowing down on seeing another one in the intersection (one or more of these acts perhaps related to the drinking that may have occurred earlier); and so on. At each point, the drivers involved may proceed to the next step in the sequence leading to the accident, or they may take some other action that averts the accident. Lieberson's analytic tables, however, treat these events, which in fact are temporally dependent on one another, as though they occurred simultaneously and continuously.

To say that this family of techniques treats causes as operating in these ways does not imply that analysts using them are so stupid as not to recognize that variables have a temporal order, that they occur in recognizable and variable sequences, but rather that the techniques offer no simple way of dealing with this knowledge. The analysis proceeds 'as if' all the foregoing were the case. The logic of the techniques does not provide any special way of dealing with these problems. Such visual devices as path diagrams, which lay variables out in a diagram connected by arrows, purport to deal with temporal sequence, but time is only a visually represented metaphor in them. Later I deal with this failure further.

Conjunctures

Another approach recognizes that causal variables are typically not really independent, making their independent contributions to some vector which produces the overall outcome in a dependent variable. This approach, analysed by Ragin (1987), suggests instead that causes are effective when they operate in concert. Variable X_1 has an effect, but only if variables X_2 and X_3 and X_4 are also present. In their absence, X_1 might as well have stayed home.

This approach is often seen as necessary in studies which accumulate a great deal of information about a small number of cases, as is typical of detailed cross-national historical studies (in the instance Lieberson considers, studies of revolution or the development of state welfare policies in a few countries). Here, the analyst tries to deal with all the complexity of real historical cases, rather than the relations between variables in a universe of hypothetical cases. The conclusion is intended to make historical cases intelligible as instances of the way the posited variables operate in concert.

We do not have many rigorous numerical methods for the assessment of this kind of conjunctural influence of variables. Ragin's Boolean algorithm, which describes the likelihood of a particular outcome given the co-occurrence of specific values of the relevant independent variables, is one such device. He and his colleagues (Ragin et al., 1984) have, in a paradigmatic example, shown how probabilities of promotion in a federal bureaucracy vary for people with different combinations of values for such variables as race, gender, education and seniority. This differs from an approach which produces numbers said to describe, in general, the 'net relative effect' of those variables on promotion.

Stories

Another approach to this problem [...] is a focus on process, on the temporal dimension in which, as everyone recognizes, phenomena occur.

A process or narrative analysis has a story to tell. To continue using the language of variables (which, it should be obvious, becomes more and more inappropriate as we move away from simple causation models), this family of approaches treats the dependent variable, the thing to be explained, as something that comes about through a series of steps. It does not, as the cases and conjunctures approaches require themselves to assume, think of the result to be explained as having happened all at once. This shows up in several ways.

The analysis focuses first on discovering the sequence of steps involved in the process under study. The causal analysis takes the form of a tree diagram, showing how a case progresses from step to step in the story, each step understood as preceding in time the one that follows it. The tree-like character of the analysis is not simply a useful visual convention. The analyst intends it to mirror how the result has 'really' come about. The process is taken to be important to the result, perhaps even constitutive of it.

Causes may be seen to operate, but now it is possible to treat a given causal variable as operating in different ways (or indeed not at all) at different steps in the process. In an analysis of heroin addiction, race might be a crucial variable in explaining exposure to the possibility of using drugs, but once a person has started to use drugs, race might play no further part in affecting whether people so exposed in fact use drugs or, having used them, become addicted to their use (cf. Lindesmith, 1948).

What is to be explained is typically more complex than the relatively simple outcomes measured in the approaches described earlier. Instead of an outcome described as a value of a variable (so many steps up in a hierarchy, so much more or less income), the outcome is described as a different form of organizational or individual activity, a different way of putting together a number of common and interdependent activities. Thus, in his classic study of embezzlement, Cressey (1953) describes and explains the genesis of the commission of an act of violation of financial trust; Lindesmith (1948) describes and explains the complex of activity that characterizes the behaviour of opiate addicts.

Indeed, such analyses devote so much attention to how the result comes about that critics complain that the explanations are tautological (Turner, 1953) [see Chapter 9 – *Editors' Note*]. That is, drug addiction becomes nothing more than the total story of the road taken to it. The criminal violation of financial trust is the story of how the embezzler came to embezzle. When you've told how it happened, you've said all there is to say.

That observation can be made as a criticism, but it can also be embraced as an advantage. (In the language of the computer hacker, it's not a bug, it's a feature.) The analyst is performing an operation Paul Lazarsfeld described as the 'analysis of the dependent variable'. Instead of what is to be explained being taken as given – for example, variation in a person's class position or income, or the occurrence or non-occurrence of a revolution – at least one major object of the research becomes the discovery of what exactly the end result is. Cases that look alike are inspected carefully to see how they may differ. Analysts look to discover subvarieties of what seem on the surface to be one thing. They are interested in the interrelationships between the elements of the dependent variable, itself seen as multidimensional, so that its character cannot be expressed as one number on a ruler.

A model of such an exploration of the dependent variable is Cressey's explanation of the way his study of the causes of embezzling became a study whose dependent variable was defined as 'the criminal violation of financial trust'. [...] Later I will deal with the shift in Cressey's analysis further.

The research thus becomes, instead of the refinement of measures of association between independent and dependent variables, the story of how something inevitably got to be the way it is. Where the analysis of causes leads to a probabilistic statement of what might happen, and the conjunctural analysis leads to a description of all the things that must be present for a particular outcome to occur, the narrative analysis leads to what might well be called a tautology, the statement of a sequence in which is prefigured (to use Harrison White's evocative phrase) the end result. 'In my end is my beginning'.

Imagery

Behind all of these variations in analytic strategies, tactics and goals lies a phenomenon Herbert Blumer (1969) habitually, even obsessively, called attention to: the underlying imagery with which we approach the phenomenon we study. What do we think we are looking at? What is its character? Most importantly, given what we think it is, is the way we study it and report our findings congruent with that character?

Abbott's (1992) intriguing discovery – that authors who relentlessly speak of the action of variables when they report 'firm' results nevertheless start talking about real people when they have a result their analysis can't explain – reflects a problem in the congruence of their imagery with the world their work has revealed to them. These analysts envision a world in which variables do all the acting and interacting and produce a result they had foreseen. When it doesn't work out that way, they construct a more familiar kind of story based on our common knowledge of the world, 'common sense', in which people act the way people usually act.

Blumer thought, and so do I, that the basic operation in studying society is the production and refinement of an image of the thing we are studying. We learn a little something (maybe a lot, who knows?) about something we are interested in. On the basis of that little, we construct a pretty complete story of the phenomenon. Suppose we decide to study a city neighbourhood. We might begin by consulting a book of local statistics (the Chicago *Community Fact Book* or the relevant census publications) and seeing what kind of people live there. How many men? How many women? Of what ages? What is their median education? Their median income? With this basic information, I can work up, in my mind, a complete, if provisional, picture of the neighbourhood, deciding on the basis of the figures on income and education that it is a working-class neighbourhood, using the age distribution to guess at the nature of family life, seeing it as an area of people retiring or getting ready to retire or, conversely, as an area filled with young people just beginning their families. I add the variables of race and ethnicity and my picture becomes more complete.

My picture is more than a compilation of statistics. It includes details that are not in the books and tables I consulted, details I have invented on the basis of what those books told me. I 'know', for instance, what kinds of houses these people live in – I can practically see, as if in a photograph, the neat lawn with the plastic flamingos, the furniture 'suites' from the credit furniture store, and whatever else my stereotype of that kind of population produces. None of this is based on any real knowledge of the area I intend to study. It is imagery I have constructed imaginatively (or stereotypically) from a few facts. It includes, if I'm imaginative enough, the look of the streets and the smell of the kitchens ('Italians? Garlic!'), and, if I'm well read enough in social science, the kind of talk that goes on over the dinner table ('Working class? Restricted code – a lot of grunts and monosyllables, à la Basil Bernstein').

Imaginative, well-read social scientists can go a long way with a little fact. Since, however, we claim to be social scientists, we don't stop with imagination and extrapolation, as a novelist or filmmaker might. We do a little checking to see if we're right. Research. We gather data.

Now, however, we enter another, more abstract, realm of imagery. This imagery has to do with the kind of causality we think might be operating. Imagery about kinds of causes has a more professional source. Do we think the phenomenon we're studying is totally governed by chance, so that a model of random activity is appropriate? Do we think it is partly chance and partly something more deterministic? Do we think it is a story? In other words, in thinking about the phenomenon, we include in the picture we build up some notions about the kind of conclusion we will draw about it, the kind of paradigmatic thinking we will assimilate it to. These paradigms come to us out of our participation in a world of professional social scientists.

Narrative styles of analysis devote a lot of time and energy to developing this imagery, which is another way of talking about the analysis of the dependent variable. Developing imagery is a process in which we try to understand what we want to understand better. We do not search for causes so much as look for stories that explain what it is and how it got that way. When an analyst of causes has done the job well, the result is a large proportion of variance explained. When an analyst of narrative has done the job well, the result is a story that explains why it is inevitable that this process led to this result.

Narrative analysis produces something causal analysts are suspicious of, and properly so, given their presuppositions and working practices. Any probabilistic causal analysis that produced a perfect correlation would be dismissed as necessarily containing sizeable errors. Researchers know that there is too much noise in their data, too many measurement and other errors, for perfect correlations to occur. They expect imperfect correlations, even if their theory predicts a perfect one. But, while they know that there is error in their data (the errors that stand in the way of better correlations), they do not throw their imperfect data out, for they don't know which cases or measurements contain the errors. To be honest, they include all the cases and thus guarantee a probabilistic result. This upsets narrative analysts, who see the unexplained variance as a problem, not a natural feature of the landscape.

Narrative analysts, on the other hand, are not happy unless they have a completely deterministic result. Every negative case becomes an opportunity to refine the result, to rework the explanation so that it includes the seemingly anomalous case. A second way of dealing with anomalous cases, however, one which upsets probabilistic causal analysts, is to throw them out. Not exactly throw them out but, rather, decide by inspecting them carefully that they are not after all a case of the sort of thing we are explaining. Part of the process of constructing a narrative is a continuous redefinition of what the theory is explaining, of what the dependent variable actually is.

Cressey (1953, pp. 19–22) explains in detail why he redefined his dependent variable in the study of embezzling and what he threw out, as well as what he included that others might have left out, giving the category so constructed a new name, and in this way dealing with what might have been dismissed, from another point of view, as measurement error. He knew that

> the legal category [of embezzlement] did not describe a homogeneous class of criminal behavior. Persons whose behavior was not adequately described by the definition of embezzlement were found to have been imprisoned for that offense, and persons whose behavior was adequately described by the definition were confined for some other offense.

The category he defined as the object of his study was the 'criminal violation of financial trust', defined by the person first having 'accepted a position of [financial] trust in good faith', and then violating 'that trust by committing a crime'. This defined a category of criminals that was homogeneous and that included people convicted of forgery, confidence game and larceny by bailee who fitted his definition but would have been lost if he had stuck to the legal definition. More important for the point I want to make here, it allowed him to exclude cases – which would necessarily have been included if he had stuck to the original legal definition – in which the prosecutors found it convenient to indict for embezzlement but which did not fit his definition. In particular, it allowed him to exclude violators who had accepted positions of trust fully intending to steal money the first chance they got, the explanation of whose behaviour would be very different from the explanation of trust violation by people who had never intended to steal. Redefining the object of study, and eliminating cases, led to greater precision in the result.

Further Problems

A major problem in any form of social research is reasoning from the parts we know to something about the whole they and parts like them make up. This is not a sampling question in the conventional sense. We are not trying to find out, by learning the proportion of cases which have property X in our sample, what the similar proportion is in the universe from which our cases come, or anything formally similar to that. Rather, we want to create an image of the entire organization or process, based on the parts we have been able to uncover. The logic of such an analysis is different. We ask: What kind of an organization could accommodate a part like this? What would the rest of the organization have to be like for this part to be what it is? What would the whole story have to be for this step to occur as we have seen it occur? I don't know anywhere that the logic of such reasoning has been fully worked out, although a start was made in Paul Diesing's book on social science (1971) some years ago.

Another problem has to do with the social organization of social science and the way different styles of analysis are related to styles of work and the practicalities of contemporary modes of research. Sociologists of science, such as Kuhn (1962), Latour (1987), Star (1989) and Fujimura (1987, 1988) (also see the literature cited by Clarke and Gerson, 1990), have created some tools with which to approach these questions. We understand a technical problem by seeing its place in the entire work process of that kind of science. Logical problems become understandable, and solutions to them can be found, in the social organization in which they arise.

For instance, causal analyses in sociology typically, though not necessarily, involve large numbers of cases, and that means, in today's versions of social science, doing large-scale surveys or using the results of such surveys as they are given to us in censuses and similar documents. The economics of large-scale data gathering lead to a host of problems. Take a mundane, but not trivial, example: interviewer cheating. Some survey interviewers do not conduct the interviews they turn in, but just fake them, in order to increase their earnings. Survey organizations have, of course, devised techniques to get this under control, but it can hardly be said to be a problem that is solved. Roth (1966) analysed this as the 'hired-hand syndrome', applying a simple result from studies of the restriction of output in industry: workers who have no stake in the eventual product of a work process will maximize what is important to them – income – rather than what their employers are after – accurate data. If that's the kind of data you have, then an emphasis on probabilistic styles of causal analysis is almost logically entailed.

Similarly, large-scale data gathering inevitably means, given the restricted economic base of social science research, collecting relatively small amounts of data about the many cases studied. Studies of process, on the other hand, are typically done by a single researcher spending long periods of time with people and groups, in the classical anthropological style. The economics are quite different; the researcher need only find enough money to support the necessary time away from other paying occupations. The trade-off for this style of research is the opposite of that typical of analyses based on variables and causes construed in variable terms: you know much more about fewer cases. [...]

A final, and profoundly difficult, problem has to do with the ways we represent the knowledge our research produces (Kuhn, 1962; Becker, 1986; Latour, 1985). Professional social scientists typically use only a few of the very large number of possible ways of representing social science results, those few being parts of 'packages' of theories, methods, types of data and styles of analysis and representation which have been conventionalized in some working group. The contents of the package are interrelated, so that using one portion more or less entails using the whole package. Sociologists who do certain kinds of statistical analyses have, for instance, learned a simple method of representing causal relations between variables, in the form of arrows with statistical coefficients attached. They find this an effective shorthand, easily understood by other adepts.

Like the other agreed-on parts of a scientific package, such conventions of representation facilitate sociological work. But they also hamper it because, while they make communication of some results easy and efficient, they make communication of other kinds of results difficult or impossible. The arrows that convey the results of causal analyses so well are not very good at communicating the complex interdependencies embodied in stories or in the visual materials (still photographs, film and video) which social scientists are increasingly using (thereby finally catching up with the physical and biological sciences, where such materials have been routinely used almost since they were invented). But users of such methods have yet to develop the representational conventions which will make the communication of their results unproblematic.

These are problems for the future.

References

Abbott, A. (1992) 'What do cases do? Some notes on activity in sociological analysis', in C.C. Ragin and H.S. Becker (eds), *What is a Case? Exploring the Foundations of Social Inquiry*. Cambridge: Cambridge University Press.

Becker, H.S. (1986) 'Telling about society', in *Doing Things Together.* Evanston, IL: Northwestern University Press.

Blumer, H. (1969) *Symbolic Interactionism: Perspective and Method.* Englewood Cliffs, NJ: Prentice-Hall.

Clarke, A.E. and Gerson, E.M. (1990) 'Symbolic interactionism in social studies of science', in H.S. Becker and M.M. McCall (eds), *Symbolic Interaction and Cultural Studies.* Chicago: University of Chicago Press.

Cressey, D.R. (1953) *Other People's Money.* Glencoe, IL: Free Press.

Diesing, P. (1971) *Patterns of Discovery in the Social Sciences.* Chicago: Aldine.

Fujimura, J.H. (1987) 'Constructing doable problems in cancer research: articulating alignment', *Social Studies of Science,* 17: 257–93.

Fujimura, J.H. (1988) 'The molecular biological bandwagon in cancer research: where social worlds meet', *Social Problems,* 35: 261–83.

Kuhn, T. (1962) *The Structure of Scientific Revolutions.* Chicago: University of Chicago Press.

Latour, B. (1985) 'Visualization and cognition: thinking with eyes and hands', in H. Kuclick (ed.), *Knowledge and Society.* New York: JAI Press.

Latour, B. (1987) *Science in Action.* Cambridge, MA: Harvard University Press.

Lieberson, S. (1985) *Making It Count: The Improvement of Social Research and Theory.* Berkeley: University of California Press.

Lindesmith, A.R. (1948) *Opiate Addiction.* Bloomington, IN: Principia Press.

Ragin, C.C. (1987) *The Comparative Method: Moving beyond Qualitative and Quantitative Strategies.* Berkeley: University of California Press.

Ragin, C.C., Mayer, S.E. and Drass, K.A. (1984) 'Assessing discrimination: a Boolean approach', *American Sociological Review,* 49: 221–34.

Roth, J.A. (1966) 'Hired hand research', *The American Sociologist* 1: 190–6.

Star, S.L. (1989) *Regions of the Mind: Brain Research and the Quest for Scientific Certainty.* Stanford, CA: Stanford University Press.

CHAPTER 12

CASE STUDY AND THEORY

Martyn Hammersley, Roger Gomm and Peter Foster

A common charge against case study research is that its findings are not generalizable in the way that those of social surveys are. The question often raised is: How do we know that these findings are representative? Some advocates of case study respond to this by arguing that it is directed towards a *different kind* of general conclusion from that offered by survey research: they suggest that case study work is designed to produce theories. Thus, Yin (1994) argues that it aims at 'analytical' not 'empirical' generalization, while Mitchell (Chapter 8) claims that it involves 'logical' rather than 'statistical' inference.[1]

Various accounts have been produced of the role of case studies in producing theoretical conclusions. Abramson (1992) provides two versions which he acknowledges are contradictory: one framed in terms of a Baconian inductivist conception of science, the other in terms of Popperian falsificationism. Skocpol (1979, pp. 33–40; 1984) calls on the procedure of 'comparative historical analysis', which she sees as based on the methods of agreement and difference outlined by John Stuart Mill. Others appeal to interpretive or causal realism, arguing that case study gives access to the inner lives of people, to the emergent properties of social interaction, and/or to the underlying causal mechanisms which generate human behaviour (Burgess, 1927; Waller, 1934; Connolly, 1998). Finally, there is the notion of 'analytic induction', originally outlined by Znaniecki, which he contrasts with the 'enumerative induction' that underpins statistical method (Znaniecki, 1934; see also Lindesmith, 1937) – an account of how theory can be produced through case study which remains influential today (see Becker, 1998; see also Chapter 11).

These various rationales can be organized under two main headings: those which appeal to direct perception of causal relations; and those which emphasize the role of comparative method, in one form or another. We will discuss each type of rationale in turn.

Case study as revealing theoretical relations *in situ*

One way in which the theoretical value of case study is sometimes conceptualized is the argument that it can uncover the causal *processes* linking inputs and outputs within a system. These are the terms, for instance, in which Lacey (1970, 1976) justified studying a single school in order to throw light on the effects of academic differentiation on social class variations in educational performance. He pointed out that what went on within schools had previously been treated as a black box, and suggested that by opening this up the processes could be revealed through which differences in pupils' home backgrounds are translated into social class inequalities in educational outcomes. Moreover, some writers go beyond this to argue that through case study we can actually *see* causal relationships occurring in particular instances. Thus, Glaser and Strauss (1967) claim that 'in field work ... general relations are often discovered *in vivo*; that is, the field worker literally sees them occur' (p. 40).[2]

The idea that case study provides direct insight into causal relations can be filled out in different ways. The two most influential ones are both found in an early article by Willard Waller (1934). He begins from Gestalt psychology, arguing that the traditional Humean objection to the direct perception of causal relationships is based on a false associationist psychology. He argues that perception is always of patterns, rather than of isolated sense data; and that some of these patterns are temporal and capture causal relations. For Gestalt theory, he notes, cause is 'an elementary datum of experience'; and that 'if one perceives a single instance correctly, he can generalize from that instance' (p. 287). Thus, Waller rejects the view of some positivists that causality is a metaphysical assumption, and the idea that demonstrating causal relationships requires 'extra-mental manipulations' (p. 287). He argues that:

> In studying any set of phenomena directly, we pass them before our eyes in the attempt to discover recurrent patterns and, if possible, to make out the entire configuration of events. ... These recurrent patterns gradually crystallise into concepts. Concepts result from the capacity of the mind to perceive the similarity of configurations perceived in succession. Concepts may be defined as transposable perceptual patterns to which we have given names. Imagination is often called into play to fit together pieces of configurations, to perceive with insight configurations of events which have not actually been present to the senses. A high degree of insight into causal relations is implicit in the scientific concept. A concept must be transposable not only from one set of phenomena to another but also from one mind to another. The most effective way to communicate concepts is always to describe or to point to phenomena and to give to each configuration of events its name. (pp. 289–90)

On this basis, he suggests that science is 'akin to the artistic process; it is a process of selecting out those elements of experience which fit together and recombining them in the mind' (p. 290).

In the same article, Waller introduces a different (though by no means incompatible) argument that is specific to the understanding of other people and their actions. He refers to this variously as 'sympathetic understanding', 'sympathetic penetration' or 'sympathetic insight'. He argues that: 'The social sciences differ from the physical sciences in that our knowledge of human beings is internally as well as externally derived.' He quotes Cooley in support: '[Sympathetic penetration] is derived from contact with the minds of other men, through communication, which sets going a process of thought and sentiment similar to theirs and enables us to understand them by sharing their states of mind' (pp. 294–5).

This idea can be traced back to nineteenth-century German views about the role of *Verstehen* in historical scholarship (and beyond this to the writings of Vico in the eighteenth century). The argument is that since actions, institutions and societies are human products – or, in more recent language, are social constructions – they can be understood by human beings in a direct way that is not possible when it comes to physical objects.[3] In Waller's terms, understanding consists of 'imagining what it would be like to be somebody else' (p. 295). And he sees case study as the literary form 'which most usefully condenses and organises sympathetic insight' (p. 295).

In a much more recent article, Paul Connolly (1998) adopts a position which is similar in some key respects; though it appeals to a rather different epistemological view, what has come to be labelled 'critical realism' (see Harré, 1970, 1986; Bhaskar, 1975). Drawing on the work of Sayer (1992), he distinguishes between 'extensive' and 'intensive' research designs, arguing that the task of intensive research is 'identifying and analysing the particular social processes and practices that cause change'. Connolly (1998) suggests that detailed description can 'uncover the meaning' people 'attach' to their own and others' behaviour, and thereby 'begin to unravel the causes of an individual's or a group's behaviour' (p. 124). According to him, the primary goal of ethnographic studies is to discover the causal relationships operating in the case studied, rather than to test whether these relationships occur elsewhere; though he sees such analyses as drawing on accounts of causal mechanisms operating in other cases produced by earlier studies, and as being a resource for later work in other contexts.

Like Waller, Connolly treats quantitative and qualitative method as complementary, but with an emphasis on the value of the latter. He claims that quantitative work 'aims to produce generalisations but can tell us little about causal relations, while [qualitative work] can help to identify relations of causality, but is unable to generalise from these' (p. 124). While he does not see this difference as clear-cut, he believes that it points to the relative strengths of the two approaches. Thus, he concludes that while quantitative methods can try to isolate the effects of one variable on another, 'they can still never, in the last analysis, conclude with the degrees of certainty associated with qualitative methods that a particular correlation … is a causal one'. Indeed, he suggests that 'it remains the role of qualitative research to prove or disprove [causal claims] by exploring and analysing the meanings and justificatory frameworks that those involved attach to their actions' (p. 125). Here, then, as with Waller, we have the idea that causal relations can be found by direct study of particular cases – and, in particular, of the interpretations, intentions and motives of the people whose behaviour is to be explained.

Connolly is less explicit than Waller about the means by which causal relations can be uncovered through case study. What seems to be involved, though, is that once a correlation has been found by statistical means, case study researchers should investigate the causal mechanisms by which it was produced, through documenting the processes occurring in one or more cases relevant to that correlation. Thus, to use Connolly's own example, given the statistical documentation of inequalities in educational outcome between majority and minority ethnic groups in England, case studies are able to reveal the differential treatment of pupils from different ethnic backgrounds which generates those inequalities.

Neither version of the argument that case study can discover causal relations is unproblematic. Waller is surely right that our experience of the world is not simply an unrelated collection of sense data. We perceive patterns, some of these are temporal, and some of them embody causal relationships. However, Waller himself recognizes that perceptions can be mistaken, and this admission immediately raises the question of how causal attributions are to be checked. His answer to this is that we need to develop insight. He comments that 'the one and only remedy for false insight is true insight'; and that 'the really great men of sociology' had no 'method', in the sense of a fixed procedure. They searched for insight: 'they went "by guess and by God", but they found out things. They strove to perceive with insight' (Waller, 1934, p. 297). It hardly needs saying that this is a very unsatisfactory answer. It leaves us with the question: How are we to judge who has true insight and who merely claims it?

The notion of *Verstehen* also raises problems. While rejecting the idea that it amounts to introspection, Waller still treats it as a psychological matter, in which identical mental processes must be stimulated in interpreter and interpreted. Yet it is difficult to see how such identification could ever be validated in particular cases, or why it is assumed to be necessary. In response to such questions, there was a shift within German hermeneutics in the late nineteenth century from seeing understanding in psychological terms to treating it as a matter of cultural interpretation (see Palmer, 1969). However, this reformulation did not narrow the scope for error in *Verstehen*; in fact it raised the possibility of discrepant but equally valid interpretations of the same historical scene. These developments within hermeneutics foregrounded the question of the assumptions on which interpretations are based. After all, while it is true that – as human beings – both interpreter and inter-preted will share much in common, it is also true that they are often members of different cultures, and/or are located differently in society and history. Some writers have drawn sceptical or historicist conclu-sions from this argument; but, for those who do not, it highlights the need to check causal interpretations, and raises the question of how this is to be done.

Connolly's argument that case study can uncover causal mecha-nisms which generate correlations involves a couple of immediate problems. One is that the cases falling under the terms of any correla-tion will rarely be similar to one another in all relevant respects. And where these form part of a larger system, the correlation may arise from the distribution of these differences within the system, rather than from commonalities among cases. Thus, ethnic inequalities in educa-tional outcomes can be produced by differences *among* schools as well as by what goes on *within* them (see Gomm et al., Chapter 6; Gomm et al., 1998). The second problem is that any case is descriptively inex-haustible, and any description involves cultural interpretations that are always potentially open to question. It is not simply a matter of the researcher looking to see what processes are going on in a case. All manner of processes will be occurring there, and the identification of any one of them will involve cultural interpretations about which there may be reasonable disagreement.[4]

Connolly's appeal to critical realism highlights some further issues. One is the question of whether, or in what sense, meanings can be causes; and, therefore, of what we mean by 'cause'.[5] There is also the question of whether causal explanations rely on or imply theoretical ideas about universalistic relations among types of phenomena. Connolly seems to believe that ethnographic analysis of a single case can identify a causal relationship without the researcher being concerned with whether this relationship is found in other cases. And critical realism encourages this by treating causality in terms of powers possessed by particular agents and objects, rather than in terms of relations among categories of phenomena. While this can be a valuable perspective, it obscures the problem of how claims about such powers are to be validated.[6]

In our view, it is precisely the *general* nature of causal claims that allows us to check what caused what in a particular situation. Any explanation for events in one context necessarily treats them as an effect of a sort that is produced (under certain conditions) by some spe-cific *type* of cause; so that it can always be found in other contexts – at least in principle. In other words, explanations rely on assumptions about general causal relationships which cannot be validated solely through study of a single case.[7]

Our conclusion from this is that causal attribution necessarily depends on comparative analysis. While Hume's critique was based on an implausible associationist psychology, he was surely correct that we do not literally *see* the causal relationship when one billiard ball hits another: we only see a sequence of two events which we take to be causally related; an assumption which could always be mistaken.[8] Moreover, the causal relations operating in the social world are likely to be more complex than those in Hume's example: more factors are involved, and in diverse types of relationship (see Hage and Meeker, 1988). As a result, they are even less likely to be directly observable. The Humean argument is, of course, the basis for the frequently repeated insistence that correlation is not causation, and can never be entirely conclusive evidence for it. And, in our view, finding a correlation in a single case, or in a small number of cases, is usually an even less secure basis for identifying a causal relationship than finding a correlation in a larger sample of cases.

Case study and comparative method

Comparative method requires that data be available from more than one case, perhaps from a substantial number, such that the effects of various candidate causal factors can be controlled or assessed. The most powerful version of comparative method is experimentation, which involves creating the cases that are required for testing a causal claim. By contrast, the case study researcher has to search for naturally occurring cases that will provide the necessary comparative leverage. We will examine two influential interpretations of comparative method that have been appealed to by case study researchers: eliminative induction and analytic induction.

Eliminative induction

As we noted earlier, in her analysis of social revolutions Skocpol employs a form of comparative historical analysis which she claims is based on Mill's methods of agreement and difference. These methods were part of a codification of what Mill referred to, following Bacon, as eliminative induction. The first of these methods involves examining cases with a view to identifying factors which always occur when a particular outcome results: it searches for necessary conditions. By contrast, the method of difference involves searching for differences between those cases that display a particular type of outcome and those which do not. Here, the goal is to identify sufficient conditions. Mill recognized that the two methods could be used together, and

Skocpol applies both in seeking to explain successful social revolutions. The main cases she examines are the French, Russian and Chinese revolutions.[9] In looking at these, she identifies some factors shared in common; and she compares these cases with ones in which attempts at revolution were not successful, and with revolutions that were only political rather than social, with a view to identifying significant differences.

Skocpol argues that comparative historical method of this kind is analogous to multivariate statistical analysis – that it is the appropriate method in situations where only a very small number of cases are available for investigation; though she does not provide any sustained argument for this parallel (Skocpol, 1979, pp. 35–6). At the same time, she specifically denies that the form of analysis she employs is 'purely inductive' in character; and this signals some deviation from Mill. Indeed, her primary model seems to be the actual practice of such writers as Tocqueville, Marc Bloch and (especially) Barrington Moore; none of whom explicitly modelled his work on Mill's canons.[10] In effect, Skocpol appeals to the latter simply as a conveniently explicit formulation of the method for testing causal hypotheses which she believes comparative historians should use.

Skocpol's work has been subjected to methodological criticism, notably by Nichols (1986) [see also Chapter 10]. One criticism is that there is a lack of clarity about what she is seeking to explain. Is it only the success of the social revolutions she examines or their occurrence? And, if it is their success, how is 'success' being defined here? Another criticism is that she applies Mill's methods selectively, using them to eliminate some features of the cases studied (notably, ideological factors) but not applying them to the components of the compound causal factors which make up her theory. Nichols also points to problems raised for Skocpol's analysis by the fact that there are so few cases of successful social revolution.[11]

In order to explore the issues raised by this criticism, we need to look at Mill's conception of scientific method in more detail, so as to assess its viability as a basis for case study research. Before that, however, a little historical background is required. As already noted, to a large extent, we can find the origin of Mill's canons in the *New Organon* of Francis Bacon, published in 1620. And Bacon's position needs to be understood in the context of his rejection of the concept of science presented in Aristotle, which had dominated medieval thinking.

For Aristotle, science is knowledge of what is necessary, in the sense of what cannot be otherwise. Strictly speaking, there can be no knowledge of things that are contingent – we can only have opinions about these. Furthermore, scientific knowledge consists of a demonstrable understanding of the causes of properties (see Smith, 1995, pp. 47–9); and to demonstrate that something necessarily has a certain property requires a syllogistic argument from first principles that are self-evident. Aristotle believed that all sound reasoning or argument had this form; and that it paralleled the structure of reality, where consequences stem from the essential characteristics of things (see Hankinson, 1995, pp. 109–11).

For Aristotle, the process of inquiry was as follows. First, through observing particular facts we identify their common features. He seems to regard this as involving a direct apprehension of self-evident truths, rather than as a process of inference; though his account is open to different interpretations (see Smith, 1995, pp. 49–51). In the second stage of inquiry, the universals apprehended through observation are used as premises in deductive arguments, which are designed to provide causal explanations for the phenomena observed.

It is a feature of Aristotle's position, on our interpretation, then, that science operates on the basis of first principles which are non-inferential in character. At the highest level, these are general rules of reasoning, such as the law of non-contradiction, which apply to inquiry in all fields. Other principles are specific to each science, defining the genus or domain of things it studies and the differentiation of this into various species. These definitions identify essential forms or types of substance, from which can be derived other properties that members of a specific genus or species universally and permanently have. For example, though human beings have a sense of humour, having that feature is not part of the essence or definition of a human being. Such further properties flow from the essential form of each thing. Facts about these properties are what a 'science' is meant to give causal knowledge of. Thus, it consists of syllogisms in which the flow of conclusions from premises parallels the causal processes they represent (Woolhouse, 1988, pp. 51–3).[12]

Bacon rejected several key elements of this account. First, he criticized the Aristotelian idea that scientific thinking is deductive, in other words that it moves from universal premises to universal conclusions. He argued instead that it is inductive, that sound universal conclusions can only be reached by inference from the study of particulars; though he did also recognize the importance of deducing implications from inductively established principles – both to test these and to provide for practical applications. He claimed that, in achieving their first principles, Aristotelians relied on experience of a few cases from which they then leapt prematurely to universal conclusions. And he outlined various kinds of prejudice (the 'idols') which could distort induction. What is required for rigorous inquiry, he insisted, is careful and systematic investigation of cases, employing what he calls eliminative induction, a method which relies on 'the greater force of the negative instance' (Quinton, 1980).[13]

The starting point of inquiry for Bacon (1960) is the preparation of 'a natural and experimental history, sufficient and good' (p. 130). In other words, all known relevant cases must be laid out, and these must then be organized into a table of presence, a table of absence and a table of degrees. The table of presence includes all those cases where the effect which is to be explained is present. In the table of absence must be listed all those cases which share features in common with the cases included in the table of presence, but where the effect is not present. And in the table of degrees cases are presented which show a correlation between variation in the feature to be explained and variation in other characteristics. These tables allow identification of features of the cases that can be eliminated as causes because they are not always present when the effect occurs or because they *are* present when it *does not* occur. As this makes clear, the aim is to identify what is 'always present or absent with the given nature [that is, the thing to be explained], and always increases and decreases with it' (Bacon quoted in Woolhouse, 1988, p. 21). Moreover, it is worth emphasizing that, contrary to the way he is often interpreted, and to his own description of the process as 'mechanical', Bacon does not see eliminative induction as excluding the need for imaginative thinking about the path of causation. He does not believe that perusal of the tables always points clearly or reliably to the true cause. Indeed, he outlines various 'supports and rectifications of induction', some of which are similar in character to the ideas that case study researchers trade on (Woolhouse, 1988, pp. 21–3). For example, he argues that we should look for 'shining examples'; for 'solitary instances' – those which display the effect but seem to have little else in common with other cases displaying it; and for 'instances of the fingerpost' – in other words, crucial cases that help us decide between competing interpretations.

Mill's views were similar to those of Bacon in many respects. He was concerned to combat the idea that there is some other source of knowledge than experience: whether this be intuition, reliance on mathematical idealizations or reasoning from innate ideas. Mill believed that such methods were not only false but also encouraged conservatism in morals and politics. Undermining their stronghold in mathematics and science seems to have been one of his key motives in writing *A System of Logic* (1843; Ryan 1974, Chap. 3; see also Skorupski, 1993, Chap. 2).

Mill held that since all knowledge comes from the senses, the only form of inference that leads to genuinely new knowledge is induction. Thus, he argues that science is ultimately based on the spontaneous inductions that all people engage in during the course of life – which he labels enumerative induction. It involves noticing that several particular A's are B and concluding on this basis that all A's are B. Often, this is done in a largely unconscious way, but it can be made more self-conscious and explicit.[14] Even more important, though, according to Mill, is eliminative induction; and this is what his canons or methods are designed to formalize.[15] This builds on enumerative induction, but is specifically designed to eliminate false explanations, and thereby to leave the investigator with the true one.

Along with his championing of inductive inference, Mill also argued against the view that causal relations involve necessity, in the sense that they could not be otherwise. As we saw, for Aristotle the structure of reality paralleled that of the syllogistic proof, and true knowledge could only be of what *must* be, not simply of what contingently *is*. For Mill, by contrast, causal relations are simply regularities to be found in the world.[16] Mill's rejection of the idea that causal powers are involved, such that *A necessarily* produces *B*, is simply the other side of his rejection of deduction as a source of knowledge. From Mill's point of view, and that of many positivists, any notion of causal *necessity* is metaphysical, and must be abandoned as not open to empirical demonstration.[17]

Going back to Nichols' criticisms of Skocpol, these relate to some fundamental problems with Mill's canons as a basis for comparative case analysis. One concerns how we arrive at a proper formulation of the thing to be explained. For Mill this does not seem to be an issue of any significance. He apparently believes that we can produce a theory to account for *any* type of event.[18] And this leads to his acceptance that there can be multiple causes of the same phenomenon. By contrast, Skocpol gives considerable attention to the formulation of what it is she is setting out to explain, engaging in a critical discussion of previous work on revolutions and similar events to argue that 'successful social revolutions' is the appropriate focus. As we shall see, the character of what is to be explained is also a key concern for advocates of analytic induction. For them, phenomena have to be categorized in ways that are open to theoretical investigation; and this means the category employed must pick out phenomena produced by the same cause, and only by that cause. Moreover, for advocates of analytic induction, by contrast with Skocpol, the appropriate categorization of what is to be explained has to be found through empirical inquiry, rather than on the basis of prior theoretical reflection.

A second problem with Mill's position is that elimination of false explanations will only result in the identification of the true explanation if all relevant features of the cases have been included in the investigation. And this is made difficult by the fact that features of cases are not simply evident to the senses. Identifying them involves a process of conceptualization. This is especially clear in Skocpol's research: it is not difficult to see that such a large and complex set of events as the French Revolution is made up of a huge number of potentially relevant features, most of which are not (and were never) observable in any straightforward sense. Mill underplays the role of conceptualization in eliminative induction, then; presumably because he is keen to downgrade the significance of intuition and hypothesis in science.[19] This is another area where Skocpol specifically departs from Mill, emphasizing the role of theory in conceptualizing and selecting among potential explanatory factors (Skocpol, 1979, pp. 33–42).[20]

The third problem concerns the number of cases that needs to be investigated to reach a sound conclusion. For Mill, the task of inductive method is to produce knowledge that is demonstrably true, in the sense of knowledge whose validity is certain; analogous to the way the validity of a conclusion follows from true premises in a well-formed syllogism (see Scarre, 1998, pp. 112, 117–18). Yet, to infer the true cause of something with certainty by means of the methods of agreement and difference requires that *every* relevant case be studied. And the number of cases to which any causal claim relates is infinite; it includes all of those occurring in the past, the present and the future. Moreover, while Skocpol sees eliminative induction not as a logical procedure that guarantees sound conclusions, but rather as a means of checking the validity of theoretical interpretations, of discovering error rather than of establishing truth, the number of cases investigated is still a critical factor affecting the rigour of the test. And the need for a relatively large number of cases if false hypotheses are to be eliminated becomes even clearer once we take account of the potential causal role of absences of particular features and of combinations of features.[21]

In summary, there are problems intrinsic to eliminative induction, as formulated by Mill and to some extent as practised by Skocpol. These concern the conceptualization of what is to be explained and the selection and formulation of causal factors. In addition, contrary to what Skocpol claims, this method cannot provide convincing conclusions about causal relationships through comparison of only a handful of cases (see Lieberson, Chapter 10). While the checks she is able to exercise on the validity of her theory through comparative analysis may be better than nothing, they do not rule out all plausible alternatives. Moreover, the modifications she makes to Mill's methods weaken its capacity in this respect.

Analytic induction

Following the wane of Mill's influence in the late nineteenth and early twentieth centuries, there were some important changes in ideas about scientific method. Some writers continued to see it as inductive, but for them induction came to be interpreted as probabilistic, under the influence of developments in logic and the mathematics of probability (see Passmore, 1966, Chap. 6). Techniques were invented for inferring the characteristics of a finite population from data about a sample drawn from it, with specified levels of confidence; and there were also attempts to apply probability theory to scientific induction (most notably, that of Keynes, 1973). Others, however, rejected inductivist accounts of science, in favour of the hypothetico-deductive method. Most striking here is the work of Karl Popper, who denied that there could be a 'logic of discovery' – that induction plays any role in science. For him, where theoretical ideas come from is of no significance. The only requirement is that they produce hypotheses that are falsifiable, and that these are subjected to test. While the validity of no hypothesis– and thus of no theory – can be *proven*, a single failure in the course of testing establishes its falsity.[22]

In the same period, much attention came to be given to scientific method by American sociologists, in an attempt to put their work on a scientific footing. This gave rise to discussions about the relative importance of 'statistical' versus 'case study' method (see Bulmer, 1984; Hammersley, 1989). Some saw the former as providing the foundation for scientific investigation of social life, on the grounds that quantitative measurement is essential to all science.[23] By contrast, advocates of case study argued that quantitative measurement is not a necessary feature of scientific work. It is only a feature of *some* sciences: here the non-quantitative character of biology (at the time) was often contrasted with the quantitative character of physics. What *is* a defining feature of science, it was insisted, is that it produces universal laws, not mere statements of probability.[24] Moreover, the need for universal laws was seen as important in instrumental terms as well: on the grounds that the exception 'is the growing point of science' (see Mead, 1917, p. 221). The problem with a statistical approach, then, is not just that its conclusions are not of a scientific form, but that it introduces 'laxity' into the research process: cumulation becomes simply the addition of further explanatory factors, rather than leading to reformulation of the original elements of the theory.

One of the most influential versions of this argument appeared in Florian Znaniecki's book *The Method of Sociology* (1934). In it he contrasted what he referred to as enumerative and analytic induction. He characterized enumerative induction as involving examination of a set of cases identified as belonging to a particular common-sense category, and the description of features which predominate among them. This amounted to treating a factor which occurred frequently in cases where there was a particular outcome as a cause of that outcome. Znaniecki sees this approach as characteristic of practical rather than of scientific thinking.[25] He argued that the production of probabilistic 'explanations' arose when investigations started from, and stuck to, common-sense categorizations of the phenomena to be explained – rather than seeking scientific ones that are causally homogeneous.

So, Znaneicki draws a sharp distinction between practical common-sense understanding of the world, on the one hand, and scientific knowledge, on the other. And he treats conceptualization and hypothesis as playing a much more significant role in scientific inquiry than did Mill. He also sees causation as involving necessity. Indeed, in this respect he goes back to Aristotle; though he specifically rejects the idea that universal categories can be identified by direct apprehension, emphasizing the need for thorough empirical study of cases (see Znaniecki, 1934, pp. 222–8). Similarly, for him, causal analysis amounts to defining the essential features of the thing to be explained: those which make it what it is. These features are determined by closed, or semi-closed, systems of social action in which the relationship between cause and effect can be formulated in deductive terms. It is an especially important feature of Znaniecki's position that, for this to be achieved, what is being explained will often have to be redefined; this is what creates the gap between common-sense and scientific concepts. Thus, Znaniecki blends elements from the eliminative induction of Bacon and Mill with an Aristotelian understanding of the nature of causation.[26]

Alfred Lindesmith (1937) put forward a similar conception of scientific method as a basis for case study around the same time; though he does not use the term 'analytic induction' or refer to Znaniecki.[27] He, too, draws a sharp distinction between his own approach and 'the statistical or multivariate method' (Lindesmith, 1968, pp. 13–14). And, like Znaniecki, he sees the logic of analytic induction as that of the experiment, and argues that 'a valid theory … must account for the basic or essential aspects of [a phenomenon] by indicating that they form a system or pattern which is logically implied or predicted by the theory' (Lindesmith, 1968, p. 9).

Znaniecki did not provide a clear demonstration of the method of analytic induction in action. By contrast, Lindesmith applied this approach in a full-scale investigation of opiate addiction (see Lindesmith, 1937, 1938; see also Lindesmith, 1968). Starting with information about a few cases of addiction, he developed a hypothesis that fitted those cases. He then collected and analysed further cases, and this forced him to reformulate the hypothesis. He continued the investigation until additional cases no longer required him to revise the hypothesis; though he notes that new data may yet stimulate further revisions to the theory in the future (see Lindesmith, 1968, pp. 7–10). Lindesmith argues that the physical effects of opiates are not a sufficient explanation for addiction – social factors must also be taken into account. The necessity of this is made clear, he suggests, by the fact that there are cases of people who have taken these drugs but have not become addicted. His conclusion is that addiction occurs only where the person concerned recognizes that the distress he or she is suffering results from withdrawal of the drug, and decides to use it again to alleviate that distress. Thus, for Lindesmith, addiction involves a person using the drug in order to stay normal, rather than to pursue a drug-induced euphoria.[28]

Another major example of the application of analytic induction is the work of Cressey, whose initial focus was embezzlement. However, he found that he had to reformulate this as 'financial trust-violation', in order to eliminate cases where positions of financial trust had been taken with the intention of stealing money. In other words, the reformulation was required so as to produce a causally homogeneous category of cases to be explained. In this respect, Cressey's work is closer to what Znaniecki recommends than is Lindesmith's, with its shift from a common-sense category (embezzlement) to a scientific one (financial trust-violation) (see Cressey, 1950).[29]

Like eliminative induction, analytic induction has also attracted some criticism, most notably that of W.S. Robinson (Chapter 8; see also Goldenberg, 1993). Robinson argued that this procedure is structured so as only to discover necessary, not sufficient, conditions for the phenomenon being explained. In other words, for the most part, the cases studied are ones where the phenomenon to be explained is found. In Mill's terms, what is applied is the method of agreement, not the method of difference. Robinson insisted that a cause must specify both necessary and sufficient conditions. He also argued that during the twentieth century it had become clear that some scientific laws are probabilistic rather than deterministic, and that this means that a statistical approach to the study of causal relations in the social world is required: large, and representative, samples of cases need to be studied.

In fact, Lindesmith had recognized the importance of looking at cases where addiction has not occurred, to check whether the causal process his theory identified was present. Thus, he cites the case of someone who had been given morphine medically and not become addicted, but who later in life became 'a confirmed addict' (Lindesmith, 1938, pp. 600–3). Through this kind of comparison, he tries to show that where the features which his theory identifies are not all present addiction does not result, and that where they are all present it does. However, he comments that: 'obviously the number of instances in which a coincidence of this kind is likely to occur is very small, but those that have been found, unequivocally and without exception, indicate that if morphine is withdrawn carefully, without the patient recognizing or noticing the symptoms of abstinence, no craving for the drug develops' (Lindesmith, 1938, p. 602).[30] Thus, Lindesmith seems only to have investigated a small number of cases of difference, with the result that the sufficiency of his explanation has only been tested in a very limited way. Much the same is true of Cressey's work: he relies primarily on reports of the prior experience of those who had later committed trust-violation.

There is also a question about the character of the theories produced by analytic induction, and about their relationship to evidence. If it is true that the aim of analytic induction is to identify the essence of what is to be explained, in the sense of showing that effect follows necessarily from cause, is not the resulting theory deductive rather than inductive? In other words, is it not a tautology?[31] This seems to be the case with Lindesmith's theory. Turner comments: '[Lindesmith] has outlined the essential stages in becoming addicted by the time that he has arrived at his full definition of the phenomenon. The essential stages are implicit in the concept of addiction as he presents it' (Turner, Chapter 9, p. 201). As noted earlier, for Lindesmith, addiction occurs where withdrawal symptoms are experienced, are recognized for what they are, *and where a decision is made to use the drug to eliminate these symptoms*. The problem arises particularly with the last of these three elements, which seems to threaten the distinction between cause and effect. And, indeed, Lindesmith has argued that his focus is on the *process* of addiction, within which no clear distinction can be drawn between cause and effect. Appealing to the work of Dewey, he argues that this is true of causation generally (see Lindesmith, 1981). Yet, in other places, even within the same article, he seems to retain the idea that cause and effect are independent of one another; and it is difficult to see how this could be abandoned within the context of either eliminative or analytic induction.[32]

The prospects for comparative analysis in case study

We have outlined two interpretations of comparative method in case study research: that appealing to Mill's eliminative induction, and that formulated under the heading of analytic induction. We have also noted criticisms that have been made of both. It seems to us, however, that for the most part the criticisms simply point to areas in which reformulation may be required. Indeed, the two approaches have complementary strengths and weaknesses, as well as sharing much in common. Thus, in many ways analytic induction represents a useful modification of eliminative induction, as formulated by Mill, in giving a greater role to the process of conceptual thinking in formulating both what is to be explained and the factors explaining it. And, in relation to Skocpol's application of eliminative induction, the two applications of analytic induction we discussed point to the need for studying a relatively large number of cases.[33] On the other side, analytic induction requires modification, so as to provide for systematic testing of the hypothesis that has been developed: by seeking cases where the explanatory factor is known to be present so as to check whether it always has the effect predicted. In other words, analytic induction needs to employ the method of difference in a systematic way as well as the method of agreement, and on a more substantial scale than Lindesmith and Cressey do. Moreover, this could be taken further than it is in Mill's account of induction, along the lines suggested by both Bacon and Popper: seeking cases that would offer the stiffest test for a causal hypothesis. These modifications would enable comparative analysis to put forward relatively strong claims about necessary and sufficient conditions.

Nevertheless, serious problems remain with case study researchers' use of comparative method. Some of these are practical ones. It should be remembered that the paradigm of the comparative method is the experiment, and the essential feature of that technique is that the cases needed for comparison can be created through the manipulation of relevant variables. While case study work may have an advantage in minimizing procedural reactivity, its corresponding weakness is that all the cases are rarely available that would allow a full test of any hypotheses generated. Furthermore, as we have seen, quite a large number of cases may be required; and, given the intensive demands of case study work, it is unusual for more than a few cases to be studied in a single investigation. Much depends here, of course, on the size of the cases concerned. Where these are relatively small, as with the work of Lindesmith and Cressey, it may be practicable to investigate a relatively large number; but where cases are large – in temporal and/or spatial terms – the number that can be investigated at any one time is likely to be highly restricted, unless a large team of researchers is involved. While this problem does not necessarily rule out use of the comparative method, it does mean that case study researchers must build on one another's work. Follow-up studies need to investigate further cases selected specifically to develop and test the theory in new ways. Unfortunately, there are currently very few examples of cumulative case study work of this kind.[34] And, of course, there may be some types of event, 'successful social revolutions' could be one, that are so rare that effective comparative analysis is impossible.

Besides these practical problems with comparative method, there are also some more fundamental methodological ones. One is that use of comparative method relies on an assumption about the nature of the social world that is open to reasonable question. In fact, it is one that many qualitative researchers today explicitly reject. This is the idea that the social world is structured in terms of regularities that can be expressed as laws (see Lincoln and Guba, Chapter 2). Doubts about this have been based, in part, on the claim that social research has failed to produce convincing examples of such laws. But these doubts have also relied on philosophical arguments, for example that human beings exercise free will and that this is incompatible with social determinism.

It is unclear whether these doubts are well founded: much depends on what is meant by 'laws' and on how such notions as 'free will' are interpreted. Thus, a number of writers have suggested that what case studies produce are 'retrospective' or 'fuzzy' generalizations, which capture strong possibilities rather than deterministic or even probabilistic outcomes (Scriven, 1972; Stenhouse, 1978; Bassey, 1999). Of course, there are questions to be asked here about the kind of 'possibility' involved, and about whether this type of law differs in fundamental ways from those in the natural sciences. Either way, the dependence of comparative analysis on the existence of laws, of some kind, and the uncertainties surrounding this, need to be recognized and explored.[35]

Closely related to the issue of whether there are social laws is the fact that use of the comparative method involves abstracting from the details, from the uniqueness, of particular cases: the focus is on those respects in which cases are exemplars of some theoretical category. This is opposed by many case study researchers on the grounds that cases must be treated as wholes, or bounded systems, if they are to be properly understood (see, for example, Stake, Chapter 1; Simons, 1996). What is less clear, though, is how this position avoids reliance on causal assumptions in understanding individual cases. And there are other problems too. Thus, Simons sees case studies as investigating the unique with a view to producing universal knowledge. She describes this as a paradox, but believes it can be transcended. In this she appeals to the model of great art and literature. But she leaves obscure the nature of this process of transcendence.[36] Furthermore, if her argument is correct, it is unclear why we need case study research. Do not art and literature suffice?

We believe that it is important to draw a distinction between case study work that is designed to describe the features of a particular set of cases, or to explain what occurred in those cases, on the one hand, and research that is concerned with developing and testing theories, on the other. Case study *can* be used for the latter task, but it requires a different approach from work directed towards descriptive and explanatory goals. In theoretical research, interest in cases is indeed restricted to the ways in which they exemplify the relevant theoretical category. By contrast, where the aim is description and/or explanation, the task is to document what occurred in the particular case(s) being studied, and why. This will necessarily involve much more detailed attention to the distinctive features of those cases.

It is worth adding that the task of explanation (as contrasted with that of theory development) will frequently involve tracing part of the sequence of events which eventually resulted in what is to be explained. This is a point that Becker emphasizes in his discussion of narrative explanation (see Chapter 11 and Becker, 1998). He notes that often we can only understand an outcome by tracing the path by which it came about; and this may involve taking account of a wide range of factors operating at different stages. However, Becker goes on to argue that such explanation is identical with analytic induction; and this links back to Lindesmith's argument that his focus was on the addiction process – that his aim was to identify how 'the craving for drugs is generated in one identifiable, unitary type of experience'. Thus, he describes this experience as 'a complex interactional process involving many elements or variables in a series of happenings or events' (Lindesmith, 1968, p. 13).

However, it seems to us that this argument is misconceived: what analytic induction produces, as with experimental research, is a conditional theory – not a description of any particular process by which some type of event occurred in a particular case. It tells us what will happen *if* certain conditions are met. We can, of course, apply this theory to explain what happens in particular cases in which we have an interest. But no single theory of this kind will usually capture all the factors that are relevant to the task of explanation. In the case of addiction, for example, we may also want to know whether some people experience withdrawal symptoms more severely than others, or whether association with other addicts increases the likelihood that the symptoms will be recognized for what they are and that the decision will be made to use the drug to relieve these.[37] Moreover, what factors are relevant in an explanation is not determined by whether they form part of a single coherent theoretical system but rather by pragmatic considerations, for example whether they offer some assistance in solving a practical problem or provide a basis for assigning blame.

Another problem is that both the versions of comparative method we have discussed assume *deterministic* laws: in other words, laws which state that if A occurs then B will *always* follow, wherever certain conditions are met. This is why both eliminative and analytic induction can treat a single negative instance as disconfirming a hypothesis. Yet if laws in the social world were to be probabilistic rather than deterministic in character, as they may well be, the task facing case study researchers seeking to draw theoretical conclusions would be much more difficult. If laws are probabilistic, a negative result in one case cannot be treated as conclusive disproof; even aside from the possibility of methodological error. Instead, a relatively large sample of cases would need to be investigated in order to detect trends that reflect such laws.[38]

Conclusion

In this chapter we have examined the arguments supporting the idea that case study research can produce causal explanations or theories.

We looked first at those versions of this argument which appeal to the capacity of case study to uncover causal relations *in situ*. We argued that there are serious problems with the main forms of this argument. Adequate knowledge of such relations is not simply given in perception, and so causal hypotheses have to be checked. And this requires comparison across cases. In the second section, we looked at two forms of comparative analysis to which case study researchers often appeal. We discussed Mill's concept of eliminative induction, and compared it with the more recent notion of analytic induction. We argued that the latter corrected some problems in Mill's approach – notably neglect of the role of theory and hypothesis – but underplayed his method of difference. We argued that a version of comparative analysis drawing on both could be viable; but we also pointed to a number of remaining problems. Some of these are practical in character, for example the fact that effective use of comparative analysis probably requires the investigation of a relatively large number of cases. Others are more fundamental, for example to do with whether we can reasonably assume deterministic laws of human behaviour. This issue links back to a point that we mentioned in the earlier section: whether meanings can be causes, and if they can, what sort of causes they are.

In summary, then, there are important and difficult problems still to be resolved concerning the role of case studies in producing valid theories. It is perhaps worth saying, though, that we do not see resolution of these problems as depending solely on abstract analysis of the kind we have engaged in here. To a large extent, case study research directed towards producing theory can only make progress through practical investigation of what is and is not achievable. At the same time, case study researchers need to be aware of the problems that face them in this task, and must address these.

Notes

1 Of course, some survey research is explicitly concerned with producing theories. Whether case study is directed towards a different *kind* of theory, for example one underpinned by systematic rather than genetic causation, or whether it is simply a different route to the same kind of theory, is not something about which there is agreement among case study researchers. For the distinction between genetic and systematic causation, see Cressey (1953, Introduction).

2 Both Lacey and Glaser and Strauss also use the comparative method in their attempts to identify causal relationships. Thus, Lacey justifies his selection of Hightown Grammar for study on the grounds that it controls a key variable (see Hammersley, 1985). Glaser and Strauss's concept of theoretical sampling is specifically concerned with maximizing and minimizing differences among cases in order to develop well-grounded theories.

3 The concept of *Verstehen* also draws on a more general notion that was applied by some of the Romantics to experience of the natural world: the idea that 'visible appearances

of nature excite in us by an inherent law ideas of the invisible things on which they are dependent' (see Anschutz, 1968, p. 148). On the influence of the romantics on Cooley, see Hammersley (1989, pp. 61–3).

4 We have pointed out elsewhere how questionable are some of the interpretations made in the research on racism in education with which Connolly is concerned (see Foster et al., 1996; Hammersley, 1998).

5 The book by Sayer which Connolly cites in support of his position includes only a brief discussion of this issue, referring the reader to Bhaskar (1989, Chap. 3) (Sayer, 1992, pp. 110–11). This is a difficult and complex issue. For different philosophical views about reasons and causes, see Anscombe (1963), Ayer (1963), Goldman (1970) and Davidson (1980). On causation in general, see Brand (1976) and Sosa and Tooley (1993).

6 This is illustrated, it seems to us, by Sayer's (1992, Chap. 7) discussion of 'verification and falsification'.

7 It is worth noting that the reason why Waller believes that generalization can be made from a single correctly perceived case is precisely that the case is taken to be an instance of a generally occurring causal relationship.

8 Hume writes that observation gives us no impression of 'any power or necessary connection; any quality, which binds the effect to the cause, and renders the one an infallible consequence of the other' (quoted in Woolhouse, 1998, p. 148).

9 In a later article she also investigates the Iranian Revolution (see Skocpol, 1982).

10 On Tocqueville's use of comparison, see Smelser (1971). For a useful discussion of Bloch's advocacy of comparative method, see Sewell (1967). Sewell points out that for Bloch this method is primarily concerned with testing hypotheses not generating them (p. 217). See also Hill and Hill (1980) who suggest that Bloch drew his comparativism from historical linguistics; though he did not follow this model consistently. On Barrington Moore, see Skocpol (1994, Chap. 1) and Skocpol and Somers (1994, pp. 79–80).

11 While Skocpol noted this problem in her initial analysis, she did not regard it as a barrier (Skocpol, 1979, pp. 33–42). And she does not change her mind about this in response to criticism (see Skocpol, 1986). For a critique of Skocpol's treatment of ideology see Sewell (1985); Skocpol (1985) is her reply.

12 It is worth noting that the surviving documents from Aristotle's scientific work do not correspond closely to the approach outlined here, which is the one presented in the *Posterior Analytics* (see Hankinson, 1995). For one thing, his scientific work includes knowledge of 'that which is for the most part' as well as of 'that which is always'; in other words, probabilistic as well as deterministic laws.

13 As Quinton points out, some twentieth-century criticism of Bacon, including that of Popper, has tended to overlook this emphasis on the negative instance (see also Urbach, 1982, 1987). Note also, though, that what Bacon was proposing here can be interpreted as a more systematic form of what Aristotle saw as the first stage of inquiry. Indeed, the methods of agreement and difference had been anticipated by philosophers working within an Aristotelian framework in medieval times (see Losee, 1972, pp. 32–4; see also Weinberg, 1965). On the whole issue of what Bacon retained from the older point of view, and where he broke with it, see Malherbe (1996).

14 Careful scrutiny of instances and methodical recording of results was also emphasized by Bacon as essential to science (see Quinton, 1980, p. 55).

15 Besides the methods of agreement and difference, Mill also identifies the method of residues, and that of concomitant variation. We will not give these any attention here: they are generally regarded as of secondary importance to the methods of agreement and difference.

16 This idea was anticipated in the work of the medieval philosophers Duns Scotus and William of Ockham, who argued that God can do anything that does not involve a logical contradiction. From this it follows that everything which happens in the world is contingent on His will (see Losee, 1972, pp. 33–4).

17 In the late nineteenth and early twentieth centuries many positivists even rejected the concept of cause itself as metaphysical (as had Comte). Waller's article, discussed earlier, is in part a polemic against one version of this view, found in the writings of Karl Pearson (see Pearson, 1892).

18 This is not entirely true: he does recognize that there are 'capricious' phenomena, and others where regularities break down (see Skorupski, 1989, p. 174). Nevertheless, Mill gives little attention to the task of formulating what is to be explained; largely because he tends to treat this as a matter of observation.

19 Completion of *A System of Logic* seems to have been stimulated by the appearance of Whewell's *Philosophy of the Inductive Sciences*, which assigned an important role to hypothesis. On the debate between Mill and Whewell, see Strong (1955) and Scarre (1998).

20 In fact, Mill himself argued that eliminative induction could not be applied in sociology. Here he recommends instead what he calls the 'physical method'. Skocpol recognises this, though she does not discuss Mill's argument (see Skocpol and Somers, 1994, p. 88). Mill's 'physical method' involves 'concrete deduction', which he sees as characteristic of astronomy. What seems to be implied here is that sociology must be founded on *psychological* laws which will themselves have been produced through eliminative induction. The sociological task is then to use these laws to deduce explanations and predictions that take account of the compositional effects produced by the operation of multiple causes.

21 For discussions of these complexities, see Mackie (1967) and Skorupski (1989, Chap. 6).

22 See Popper (1959, 1963). We noted earlier that Abramson (1992) appeals to Popper's work to justify case study work. This appeal is rare, even though case study's role in investigating crucial cases is emphasized by some writers.

23 The inscription on the wall of the Social Sciences Research Building at the University of Chicago, often seen as a bastion of case study method, reads: 'When you cannot measure, your knowledge is meagre and unsatisfactory – Lord Kelvin' (see Bulmer, 1984, p. 151).

24 Note that this argument was used before the widespread acceptance of quantum theory.

25 It is important to note that Znaniecki's definition of 'enumerative induction' is different from that of Mill. In particular, it implies that this form of inference is explicitly probabilistic.

26 Also in line with Aristotle, Znaniecki sees a first task in sociological work as identifying the various types or species of social action. His book *Social Actions* (1936) is devoted to this task. For a useful discussion of Znaniecki, see Bierstedt (1969).

27 Lindesmith refers to Znaniecki in later work, quoting him with approval but suggesting that the distinction between enumerative and analytic induction is an old one that is also discussed by writers on logic like Keynes (1973).

28 Lindesmith emphasizes that the literature was not studied at the beginning of the research, for fear of introducing bias, but that it was explored extensively later in pursuit of negative cases (Lindesmith, 1938, p. 2; 1968, p. 7). For criticism of his theory, see McAuliffe and Gordon (1974) and Weinberg (1997).

29 It should be noted that Lindesmith did restrict his focus to drugs which produce withdrawal distress, thereby excluding cocaine and marijuana, for example – on the grounds that a theory of addiction could not cover both categories (see Turner, Chapter 9, p. 201). Both Lindesmith (1952, p. 492) and Cressey (1953, p. 14) trace analytic induction back to Mill's methods. And, indeed, some of Mill's formulations show similarities, for example:

> The process of tracing regularity in any complicated, and at first sight confused set of appearances, is necessarily tentative [...] the simplest supposition which accords with the more obvious facts, is the best to begin with; because its consequences are the most easily traced. This rude hypothesis is then rudely corrected, and the operation repeated;

and the comparison of the consequences deducible from the corrected hypothesis, with the observed facts, suggests still further correction, until the deductive results are at last made to tally with the phenomena. (Mill, 1974; Book III, pp. 496–7)

What is missing from this account, though, is precisely the idea that categorizations of the thing to be explained may need to be revised.

30 The kind of comparison Lindesmith uses here has the advantage of controlling some other factors: those that are permanent features of the person concerned. However, the two cases being compared – the initial administration of the drug, and the later use of the drug which resulted in addiction – are not independent: the second may have been influenced by the person's earlier experience with the drug. It is worth noting that Skocpol uses the same strategy – she compares events in Russia in 1905, as a failed revolution, with those in 1917; though she uses the method of difference in other ways as well.

31 Robinson (1952) mentions this, but does not discuss it. This is a complicated issue: much depends on what is meant by 'deductive'. See Skorupski's distinction between the narrow and the broad definitions of analyticity (Skorupski, 1989, pp. 85–6).

32 The problem could be avoided in the case of Lindesmith's research by defining 'addiction' as sustained use of opiates over a long period, as distinct from the initial decision to use them in order to alleviate withdrawal symptoms.

33 Lindesmith studied over fifty cases, and Cressey over a hundred.

34 The best example we are aware of is the work of Hargreaves (1967), Lacey (1970), Ball (1981), and Abraham (1995) on the effects of differentiation of pupils in school (see Hammersley, 1985).

35 The issue of what type of law, if any, applies to human social life has been studied most effectively in the philosophy of history (see Scriven 1959; Dray 1964; Martin, 1977; see also Hammersley, 1992, Chap. 2). Social anthropology has been the discipline where the debate about comparative method has been most intense. For evidence of the strong reaction against this method on the British scene in recent years, see Holy (1987) and Ingold (1992).

36 The parallel between historical investigation and art was considered in considerable depth in the nineteenth century, for example by Dilthey (see Hodges, 1949; see also Znaniecki, 1934, pp. 195–6).

37 Of course, these other factors may form part of other theories. However, the idea that we could put all relevant theories together to produce a complete explanation is an illusion: the number of explanatory factors that could be appealed to is potentially infinite.

38 For discussion of the implications of the probabilistic character of laws, see Lieberson (1985, 1992).

References

Abraham, J. (1995) *Divide and School: Gender and Class Dynamics in Comprehensive Education.* London: Falmer.

Abramson, P.R. (1992) *A Case for Case Studies: An Immigrant's Journal.* Newbury Park, CA: Sage.

Anschutz, R.P. (1968) 'The logic of J.S. Mill', in J.B. Schneewind (ed.), *Mill: A Collection of Critical Essays.* London: Macmillan (First published in Mind, 58, 19, 1949).

Anscombe, E. (1963) *Intention.* Oxford: Blackwell.

Ayer, A. (1963) *The Concept of a Person.* New York: St Martin's Press.

Bacon, F. (1960) *The New Organon and Related Writings.* Indianapolis: Bobbs-Merrill. (First published in 1620.)

Ball, S.J. (1981) *Beachside Comprehensive.* Cambridge: Cambridge University Press.

Bassey, M. (1999) Case Study Research in Educational Settings. Buckingham: Open University Press.

Becker, H.S. (1998) Tricks of the Trade: How to Think about your Research while you're Doing It. Chicago: University of Chicago Press.

Bhaskar, R. (1975) A Realist Theory of Science. Leeds: Leeds Books.

Bhaskar, R. (1989) The Possibility of Naturalism (2nd edn). Hassocks: Harvester.

Bierstedt, R. (1969) 'Introduction', in F. Znaniecki, Of Humanistic Sociology Chicago: University of Chicago Press.

Brand, M. (ed.) (1976) The Nature of Causation. Urbana, IL: University of Illinois Press.

Bulmer, M. (1984) The Chicago School of Sociology. Chicago: University of Chicago Press.

Burgess, E.W. (1927) 'Statistics and case studies as methods of sociological research', Sociology and Social Research, 12: 103–20.

Connolly, P. (1998) '"Dancing to the wrong tune": ethnography, generalization, and research on racism in schools', in P. Connolly and B. Troyna (eds), Researching Racism in Education. Buckingham: Open University Press.

Cressey, D. (1950) 'Criminal violation of financial trust', American Sociological Review, 15: 738–43.

Cressey, D. (1953) Other People's Money. Glencoe, IL: Free Press.

Davidson, D. (1980) Essays on Actions and Events. Oxford: Oxford University Press.

Dray, W. (1964) Philosophy of History. Englewood Cliffs, NJ: Prentice-Hall.

Foster, P., Gomm, R. and Hammersley, M. (1996) Constructing Educational Inequality. London: Falmer.

Glaser, B.G. and Strauss, A.L. (1967) The Discovery of Grounded Theory: Strategies for Qualitative Research. Chicago: Aldine.

Goldenberg, S. (1993) 'Analytic induction revisited', Canadian Journal of Sociology, 18 (2): 161–76.

Goldman, A. (1970) A Theory of Human Action. Princeton, NJ: Princeton University Press.

Gomm, R., Foster, P. and Hammersley, M. (1998) 'From one to many, but how? Theory and generalization in case study research', paper given at a conference on Case Study Research in Education, Centre for Development and Appraisal in Education, University of Warwick.

Hage, J. and Meeker, B.F. (1988) Social Causality. London: Unwin Hyman.

Hammersley, M. (1985) 'From ethnography to theory: a programme and paradigm for case study research in the sociology of education', Sociology, 19 (2): 244–59.

Hammersley, M. (1989) The Dilemma of Qualitative Method: Herbert Blumer and the Chicago tradition. London: Routledge.

Hammersley, M. (1992) What's Wrong with Ethnography? London: Routledge.

Hammersley, M. (1998) 'Partisanship and credibility: the case of antiracist research', in P. Connolly and B. Troyna (eds), Researching Racism in Education: Politics, theory and practice. Buckingham: Open University Press.

Hankinson, R.J. (1995) 'Philosophy of Science', in J. Barnes (ed.) The Cambridge Companion to Aristotle. Cambridge: Cambridge University Press.

Hargreaves, D.H. (1967) Social Relations in a Secondary School. London: Routledge.

Harré, R. (1970) The Principles of Scientific Thinking. London: Macmillan.

Harré, R. (1986) Varieties of Realism. Oxford: Blackwell.

Hill, A.O. and Hill, B.H. (1980) 'Marc Bloch and comparative history', American Historical Review, 85: 828–57.

Hodges, H.A. (1949) Wilhelm Dilthey: An Introduction (2nd edn). London: Routledge & Kegan Paul.

Holy, L. (ed.) (1987) Comparative Anthropology. Oxford: Blackwell.

Ingold, T. (ed.) (1992) Key Debates in Social Anthropology. London: Routledge.

Keynes, J.M. (1973) *A Treatise on Probability. The Collected Writings of John Maynard Keynes* (Vol. VIII). London: Macmillan for the Royal Economic Society. (First published in 1921.)

Lacey, C. (1970) *Hightown Grammar*. Manchester: Manchester University Press.

Lacey, C. (1976) 'Problems of sociological fieldwork: a review of the methodology of Hightown Grammar', in M. Shipman (ed.), *The Organization and Impact of Social Research*. London: Routledge & Kegan Paul.

Lieberson, S. (1985) *Making it Count: The Improvement of Social Research and Theory*. Berkeley: University of California Press.

Lieberson, S. (1992) 'Einstein, Renoir and Greeley: evidence in sociology', *American Sociological Review*, 57: 1–15.

Lindesmith, A. (1937) *The Nature of Opiate Addiction*. Chicago: University of Chicago Libraries.

Lindesmith, A. (1938) 'A sociological theory of drug addiction', *American Journal of Sociology*, 43: 593–609.

Lindesmith, A. (1968) *Addiction and Opiates*. Chicago: Aldine.

Lindesmith, A. (1952) 'Comment on W.S. Robinson's "The logical structure of analytic induction"', *American Sociological Review*, 17: 492–3.

Lindesmith, A. (1981) 'Symbolic interactionism and causality', *Symbolic Interaction*, 4 (1): 87–96.

Losee, J. (1972) *A Historical Introduction to the Philosophy of Science*. London: Oxford University Press.

McAuliffe, W.E. and Gordon, R.A. (1974) 'A test of Lindesmith's theory of addiction: the frequency of euphoria among long-term addicts', *American Journal of Sociology*, 79 (4): 795–840.

Mackie, J.L. (1967) 'Mill's methods of induction', in P. Edwards (ed.), *The Encyclopedia of Philosophy*. New York: Macmillan.

Malherbe, M. (1996) 'Bacon's method in science', in M. Pettonen (ed.), *The Cambridge Companion to Bacon*. Cambridge: Cambridge University Press.

Martin, R. (1977) *Historical Explanation: Re-enactment and Practical Inference*. Ithaca, NY: Cornell University Press.

Mead, G.H. (1917) 'Scientific method and the individual thinker', in J. Dewey, A. Moore, H. Brown, G.H. Mead, B. Bode, H. Stuart, J.H. Tufts and H.M. Kallen, *Creative Intelligence: Essays in the Pragmatic Attitude*. New York: Holt.

Mill, J.S. (1843) *A System of Logic*. London: Longman.

Mill, J.S. (1974) *A System of Logic, Ratiocinative and Inductive: Being a Connected View of the Principles of Evidence and the Methods of Scientific Investigation*. Toronto: University of Toronto Press. (First Published in 1843.)

Nichols, E. (1986) 'Skocpol on revolution: comparative analysis vs. historical conjuncture', *Comparative Social Research*, 9: 163–86.

Palmer, R.E. (1969) *Hermeneutics*. Evanston, IL: Northwestern University Press.

Passmore, J. (1966) *A Hundred Years of Philosophy* (2nd edn). Harmondsworth: Penguin.

Pearson, K. (1892) *The Grammar of Science*. London: Adam & Charles Black.

Popper, K.R. (1959) *The Logic of Scientific Discovery*. London: Hutchinson.

Popper, K.R. (1963) *Conjectures and Refutations*. London: Routledge & Kegan Paul.

Quinton, A. (1980) *Bacon*. Oxford: Oxford University Press.

Robinson, W.S. (1952) 'Rejoinder to comments on "The logical structure of analytic induction"', *American Sociological Review*, 17: 494.

Ryan, A. (1974) *J.S. Mill*. London: Routledge.

Sayer, A. (1992) *Method in Social Science* (2nd edn). London: Routledge.

Scarre, G. (1998) 'Mill on induction and scientific method', in J. Skorupski (ed.), *The Cambridge Companion to Mill*. Cambridge: Cambridge University Press.

Scriven, M. (1959) 'Truisms as the grounds for historical explanations', in P. Gardiner (ed.), *Theories of History*. New York: Free Press.

Scriven, M. (1972) 'Objectivity and subjectivity in educational research', in L.G. Thomas (ed.), *Philosophical Redirection of Educational Research*. Chicago: National Society for the Study of Education.

Sewell, W. (1967) 'Marc Bloch and the logic of comparative history', *History and Theory*, 6 (2): 208–18.

Sewell, W. (1985) 'Ideologies and social revolutions: reflections on the French case', *Journal of Modern History*, 57 (1): 57–85.

Simons, H. (1996) 'The paradox of case study', *Cambridge Journal of Education*, 26 (2): 225–40.

Skocpol, T. (1979) *States and Social Revolutions: A Comparative Analysis of France, Russia, and China*. Cambridge: Cambridge University Press.

Skocpol, T. (1982) 'Rentier state and Shi'a Islam in the Iranian Revolution', *Theory and Society*, 11: 265–300.

Skocpol, T. (1984) 'Emerging agendas and recurrent strategies in historical sociology', in T. Skocpol (ed.), *Vision and Method in Historical Sociology*. Cambridge: Cambridge University Press.

Skocpol, T. (1985) 'Cultural idioms and political ideologies in the revolutionary reconstruction of state power: a rejoinder to Sewell', *Journal of Modern History*, 57 (1): 86–96.

Skocpol, T. (1986) 'Analyzing causal configurations in history: a rejoinder to Nichols', *Comparative Social Research*, 9: 187–94.

Skocpol, T. (1994) *Social Revolutions in the Modern World*. Cambridge: Cambridge University Press.

Skocpol, T. and Somers, M. (1994) 'The uses of comparative history in macrosocial inquiry', in T. Skocpol (ed.), *Social Revolutions in the Modern World*. Cambridge: Cambridge University Press.

Skorupski, J. (1989) *John Stuart Mill*. London: Routledge.

Skorupski, J. (1993) *English Language Philosophy 1750–1945*. Oxford: Oxford University Press.

Smelser, N.J. (1971) 'Toqueville as comparative analyst', in I. Vallier (ed.), *Comparative Methods in Sociology: Essays on Trends and Applications*. Berkeley: University of California Press.

Smith, R. (1995) 'Logic', in J. Barnes (ed.), *The Cambridge Companion to Aristotle*. Cambridge: Cambridge University Press.

Sosa, E. and Tooley, M. (eds) (1993) *Causation*. Oxford: Oxford University Press.

Stenhouse, L. (1978) 'Case study and case records: towards a contemporary history of education', *British Educational Research Journal*, 4 (2): 21–39.

Strong, E.W. (1955) 'William Whewell and John Stuart Mill: their controversy about scientific knowledge', *Journal of the History of Ideas*, 16: 209–31.

Urbach, P. (1982) 'Francis Bacon as a precursor to Popper', *British Journal for the Philosophy of Science*, XXXIII: 113–32.

Urbach, P. (1987) *Francis Bacon's Philosophy of Science*. La Salle, IL: Open Court.

Waller, W. (1934) 'Insight and scientific method', *American Journal of Sociology*, XL (3): 285–97.

Weinberg, J.R. (1965) *Abstraction, Relation and Induction: Three Essays in the History of Thought*. Madison and Milwaukee: University of Wisconsin Press.

Weinberg, D. (1997) 'Lindesmith on addiction: a contextual interpretation', *Sociological Theory*, 15 (2): 150–61.

Woolhouse, R.S. (1988) *The Empiricists*. Oxford: Oxford University Press.

Yin, R.K. (1994) *Case Study Research: Design and Methods* (2nd edn). Thousand Oaks, CA: Sage.

Znaniecki, F. (1934) *The Method of Sociology*. New York: Farrar & Rinehart.

Znaniecki, F. (1936) *Social Actions*. New York: Farrar & Rinehart.

AN ANNOTATED BIBLIOGRAPHY

Other key works on case study methodology are listed below. For the most part, we have restricted the list to contributions that are explicitly concerned with case study, ignoring the literature on ethnography, participant observation, life history interviews, and so on.

Abramson, P.R. (1992) *A Case for Case Studies: An Immigrant's Journal.* Newbury Park, CA: Sage.

As the combination of the title and subtitle indicate, this book is a peculiar mixture. Most of it is taken up with the presentation of a journal written by the grandfather of the author. However, the third section consists of a discussion of case study methodology in the context of psychology. The author examines two rationales for case study research, in terms of induction and the hypothetico-deductive method. In particular, this form of research is examined in the context of Popper's philosophy of science. There is also a comparison with single-case experimental designs.

Bassey, M. (1999) *Case Study Research in Educational Settings.* Buckingham: Open University Press.

This is an account of case study research which relates quite specifically to the field of education, and to a very particular interpretation of the approach. Bassey contrasts educational research with social scientific inquiry into educational topics, the distinctive feature of the former being its commitment to 'inform educational judgements and decisions in order to improve educational action' (p. 39). In many ways his starting point is the work of Stenhouse, and the classroom action research which this stimulated. The most important feature of the book is a discussion of what case studies produce. Bassey reports that he has changed his mind about this. Where before he did not believe that case studies could produce generalizations, he now argues that they are able to do this; but that what they produce is a different kind of generalization from the 'scientific generalizations' characteristic of natural science, and from the 'statistical generalizations' typical of social science research. He calls this distinctive product of case study research in education 'fuzzy generalizations', drawing a parallel with fuzzy logic. These generalizations tell us 'that something *may* happen, but without any measure of its probability'. They are 'qualified generalizations', 'carrying the idea of possibility but no certainty' (p. 46). Bassey argues that by formulating fuzzy generalizations from their work, educational researchers can make a very important contribution to the professional discourse of educators; not least because these generalizations have the accessibility of 'sound bites'. Bassey discusses some of the practical issues involved in case study research in education of the kind he advocates, and includes three substantial examples of such work.

Becker, H.S. (1968) 'Social observation and social case studies', in D.L. Sills (ed.), *International Encyclopedia of the Social Sciences* (Vol. 14). New York: Crowell, Collier and Macmillan. Reprinted in H.S. Becker (1971) *Sociological Work.* Chicago: Aldine.

As its source suggests, this is a review of case study method, tracing its origins to the medical case study, and discussing its aims and methods and some of the problems surrounding them. Becker treats case study as primarily qualitative in character, though he does discuss the use of quasi-statistics. He emphasizes its dual character: concerned both with documenting a particular case and developing 'more general theoretical statements about regularities in social structure and process' (p. 233). He notes that 'the case study cannot be designed single-mindedly to test general propositions'. Rather, it 'must be prepared to deal with a great variety of descriptive and theoretical problems. The various phenomena uncovered by the investigator's observations must all be incorporated into [the] account of the group and then be given theoretical relevance' (p. 233). And Becker comments that, so stated, the aim of case study is utopian: one cannot see, describe and find the theoretical relevance of everything. Hence, case studies tend to focus on 'a few problems that seem to be of major importance in the group studied' (p. 233). However he argues that the utopian goal is of value since it prepares the researcher to deal with unexpected findings, forces him or her to consider the multiple interrelations of the particular phenomena observed, and saves the investigator from making assumptions that may turn out to be incorrect about matters that are relevant to the aims of the study. The bulk of the article provides a practical outline of participant observation research.

Becker, H.S. (1990) 'Generalizing from case studies', in E. Eisner and A. Peshkin (eds), *Qualitative Inquiry in Education.* New York: Teachers College Press.

Becker argues for thinking about generalizability in terms of generic activities. Once these have been identified, they provide the basis for generalization to whole areas of social life. He cites as examples of this approach Goffman's work on total institutions and on stigma. On this basis, particular cases can be examined in terms of how they represent different values on some generic variables or processes. He suggests that this produces a 'classier' sort of generalization; involving what others have referred to as theoretical inference or theoretical generalization.

Bromley, D.B. (1986) *The Case Study Method in Psychology and Related Disciplines*. Chichester: Wiley.

This book locates case study in the context of psychology. Bromley's emphasis is on the scientific character of this method, and on the way in which it complements experimental and psychometric approaches. The line taken is a clinical one, so that the aim of case study research is treated as both providing advice and help to the people who are the cases and developing and testing theoretical ideas about particular types of case. Theory is seen in quasi-judicial terms as 'case-law' framed in terms of prototypical instances.

Burgess, E.W. (1927) 'Statistics and case studies as methods of sociological research', *Sociology and Social Research*, 12: 103–20.

A classic article arising out of the debate about case study and statistics in American sociology in the first half of the twentieth century. (For discussions of this, see M. Bulmer, *The Chicago School of Sociology*, Chicago: University of Chicago Press, 1984; M. Hammersley, *The Dilemma of Qualitative Method*. London: Routledge, 1989, Chaps 3 and 4; J. Platt '"Case study" in American methodological thought', *Current Sociology*, 40: 17–48.) Burgess questions the identification of scientific with statistical method, while yet recognizing the value of statistics in providing the basis for comparison, indicating significant social processes, identifying correlations and making predictions. In particular, he argues that the way in which statistical method tends to be used presupposes an atomistic rather than an organic conception of society. He charts what he refers to as 'the emancipation of the case-study from the domination of statistics' (p. 115), in the work of Spencer, Sumner and especially Thomas and Znaniecki. At the same time, he criticizes the tendency to treat each case as individual and independent rather than as a specimen or type, the latter being essential for science. He concludes that case study is a distinct method from statistics with its own criteria of excellence; but that the two are mutually complementary.

Feagin, J.R., Orum, A.M. and Sjoberg, G. (eds) (1991) *A Case for the Case Study*. Chapel Hill: University of North Carolina Press.

The introduction to this book makes a case for case study research in terms of its focus on natural settings, holistic orientation, concern with time and history, and facilitation of theory generation. The question of the reliability and validity of case studies is also addressed. This argument is extended in the first chapter, which presents a critique of the dominance in American sociology of quantitative method based on the model of natural science. Emphasis is placed on the value of case study research in challenging bureaucratic secrecy to provide an understanding of the role of power in the global order, and giving a voice to vulnerable and disadvantaged people. The remaining chapters include accounts of particular examples of case study research by the researchers concerned (including the second restudy of Middletown and an influential investigation of homelessness), as well as discussions of case study research in particular fields (criminology, gender and family research). Several of these chapters are effectively discussions of particular research projects, and say relatively little about case study in general, but they have illustrative value.

Geertz, C. (1973) 'On thick description', in C. Geertz, *The Interpretation of Culture*. New York: Basic Books.

While not primarily addressed to case study, what Geertz says here is very relevant to it, and the article has become a key source in the literature. He argues for a 'semiotic' conception of culture, and spells out the implications of this for social inquiry. In the course of this argument, he introduces the concept of 'thick description' – borrowed from the philosopher Gilbert Ryle (*Collected Papers* (Vol. 2), London, Hutchinson, 1971, Chaps 36 and 37) – and proposes that producing thick descriptions should be the aim of anthropological research. He contrasts such descriptions with those which are concerned solely with the external aspects of behaviour. Moreover, he stresses that understanding what people are doing, and why, requires us to take account of the context in which they are acting. He argues that this does not make anthropology any less a science than physics or chemistry, but that it does make it a different kind of science. At the same time, he compares the task of the anthropologist with that of the literary critic. In these terms, he suggests, ethnography is analogous to trying to construct a reading of a manuscript, one that is 'foreign, faded, and full of ellipses, incoherencies, suspicious emendations and tendentious commentaries' (p. 10). And, as a result, the task of validating interpretations is more difficult than it is in other sciences. The notion of an interpretive science also has implications for the issue of generalizability. Geertz argues that the production of general conclusions takes place not through studies building on one another, in the sense of starting from where previous ones left off, but rather by their using the theoretical resources that previous work has produced in order to try to deepen our understanding of universal human themes. He criticizes two ways in which social scientists have often sought to generalize from single cases: the 'Jonesville-is-the-USA' model, where the case studied is treated as a microcosm of the whole society; and the 'Easter Island as a test case' approach, where a case is selected in order to test some theoretical idea. Instead, Geertz argues for a distinction between the locus and the focus of study. Anthropologists study *in* villages, he argues, rather than simply studying villages. And what they study in villages are social processes that will be found elsewhere; or, at least, their work provides knowledge about particulars that can be used to think more deeply about general social processes.

Hamilton, D. (1980) 'Some contrasting assumptions about case study research and survey analysis', in H. Simons (ed.), *Towards a Science of the Singular: Essays about Case Study in Educational Research and Evaluation* (CARE Occasional Publications no. 10). Norwich: Centre for Applied Research in Education, University of East Anglia.

Writing in the context of educational research, Hamilton argues that case study research operates with a 'diametrically opposed, yet equally sophisticated, set of domain assumptions' from survey analysis, even though they share 'similar goals at the practical level' (p. 78). He suggests that case study is distinct in studying single settings or events, and in not assuming that these can be pooled to form a homogeneous aggregate. He also specifies a number of other contrasts in terms of which case study inquiry differs from survey analysis. First, survey research is modelled on natural science method, whereas case study adopts procedures according to whether they facilitate an understanding of educational phenomena. Second, it treats those phenomena as more social and artefactual than natural and invariant. Third, survey research tries to map surface complexity by means of multivariate analysis, whereas case study seeks to eliminate complexity through in-depth analysis. Fourth, survey analysis reduces concepts to measures, whereas case study explores the relationships between concepts and instances. Fifth, survey research is concerned with generalization, assuming the invariance of the world, whereas case study engages in 'interpretation in context'. Finally, survey research studies large samples, seeking to identify factors common to multiple cases, whereas case study interprets 'idiosyncracies' in order to learn from them.

Hammersley, M. (1992) 'So, what are case studies?', in *What's Wrong with Ethnography?* London: Routledge.

Here 'case study' is defined quite narrowly as a case selection strategy, being contrasted with narrow definitions of 'survey' and 'experiment', in terms of number of cases studied and whether the cases investigated are created or found. So, case study is the investigation of, or the use of information from, a relatively small number of naturally occurring cases. These contrasts are also used to highlight both the advantages and the disadvantages of case study. The advantage is the capacity to generate detailed information about each case, and as part of this to carry out more thorough checking of the descriptions produced. The disadvantage in comparison with survey research is the problem of generalization to a larger population; and by comparison with experimental research it is the weak basis provided for identifying causal relationships. However, the author argues that case studies are capable of producing both types of general conclusion, and strategies are identified that case study researchers use to do this.

Kennedy, M.M. (1979) 'Generalizing from single case studies', *Evaluation Quarterly*, 3 (4): 661–78.

This article considers the problem of generalization from case studies very much in the context of evaluation research. It argues that there are ways in which such generalizations can be made both in replicated/multi-case studies and in studies of a single case. She outlines some of these, for example specifying considerations that need to be borne in mind when comparing the characteristics of the case studied with those of the target population. She also provides a discussion of generalizing single case study findings in terms of what has come to be called transferability, explicating the analogies with legal precedent and clinical judgement.

Merriam, S.B. (1988) *Case Study Research in Education: A Qualitative Approach*. San Francisco: Jossey-Bass.

This is an introduction to doing case study research. It focuses specifically on the field of education, but much of the advice is applicable more generally. There is an initial outline of case study research, 'within the naturalistic or qualitative paradigm' (p. 3), and a discussion of the types and uses of case study. The rest of the book covers defining a research problem; literature review; effective interviewing; observation; analysing documents; processing and analysing data; dealing with validity, reliability and ethics; and writing the case study report. In short, it covers much the same ground as other introductions to qualitative research.

Platt, J. (1988) 'What can case studies do?', *Studies in Qualitative Methodology*, 1: 1–23.

Platt reviews some definitions of case study and then examines the literature on the rhetorical and logical functions of this method. She discusses the diversity of purposes case study can serve, but also argues that it is not the best method for all purposes. She emphasizes the importance of the selection of cases for study, while recognizing that some studies are successful as a result of 'happy accident'. A particular strength of case study work, Platt suggests, is its capacity to make surprising discoveries.

Ragin, C.C. and Becker, H.S. (eds) (1992) *What is a Case? Exploring the Foundations of Social Inquiry.* Cambridge: Cambridge University Press.

This book is a collection of papers focused on case analysis that come from a workshop addressing the question in the title. The papers are quite diverse in terms of the areas of research they discuss (for example, research on railroad tramps, the work of a rural mechanic, and a dairy-farm community, all in the chapter by Harper; and work on commercial fraud, on NASA and the space shuttle *Challenger* disaster, and on intimate relationships, all in the chapter by Vaughan). There is also variety in the approach to case analysis they adopt. Some represent a quantitative or mathematical approach, others are more qualitative in character. As far as providing an answer to the question in the title, the book must be judged a failure. However, it is an interesting failure, full of ideas that may be of use to case study researchers. One striking feature is the extent to which there is agreement, on the part of those at the opposite ends of the spectrum in approach, about the failings of much quantitative analysis of social phenomena, and the scope for approaches that are more concerned with examining the social processes involved in a small number of cases. An example is the parallel between Abbott's analysis of narrative and Becker's discussion of the narrative analysis characteristic of analytic induction in qualitative work. There are discussions of case analysis as practised in different fields, some with a single substantive focus, others more comparative in character. There are also interesting discussions about what are taken to be cases, and how the concept of case is to be interpreted, notably by Ragin and Platt.

Runyan, W. McKinlay (1982) 'The case study method', in *Life Histories and Psychobiography: Explorations in Theory and Method.* New York: Oxford University Press.

Runyan writes in the context of psychology, where case study is closely related to clinical approaches. He outlines the debate between the advocates and critics of case study, identifying a number of key issues: the reliance of some case studies, notably life histories, on retrospective reports; the qualitative and 'subjective' character of the data employed; and the role of case studies in the generation and testing of causal theories. He considers the arguments on each side, seeking to identify the role that case studies can play in serving particular purposes and in complementing other approaches. His primary focus is on case studies which systemically present information about a person for clinical purposes. Within this field, he identifies different types of case study, and distinguishes them from 'psychological reports' and 'life histories'. In an attempt to clarify and improve case study methodology of this kind, he examines three examples in detail; considers the relationship of case studies to single-case experimental designs; examines the criteria to be used in evaluating case studies, in light of the criticisms often made of them; and considers the prospects for future work, recommending the 'quasi-judicial' approach developed by Bromley.

Shaw, C.R. (1931) 'Case study method', *Publications of the American Sociological Society*, 21: 149–57.

A classic discussion of case study in the context of Chicago studies of delinquency, and especially of life history material. Shaw argues that this method 'reveals the process or sequence of events, in which individual factors and the particular social environment to which the child has been responsive have united in conditioning the habits, attitudes, personality, and behavior trends' (p. 150). Shaw treats case study as complementing statistical method.

Simons, H. (ed.) (1980) *Towards a Science of the Singular: Essays about Case Study in Educational Research and Evaluation* (CARE Occasional Publications no. 10). Norwich: Centre for Applied Research in Education University of East Anglia.

This set of papers comes from a conference on 'case study methods in educational research and evaluation', and the context is very much that of educational evaluation of an illuminative or democratic kind. It includes Hamilton's comparison of the assumptions built into case study and survey research. The distinctive approach to case study research characteristic of the SAFARI project is presented (see also Walker, below), plus the critique of it by Jenkins.

Simons, H. (1996) 'The paradox of case study', *Cambridge Journal of Education*, 26 (2): 225–40.

In this article, Simons argues that the original conception of case study has been distorted through pressure from conventional notions of science and from the increasingly instrumental demands of policy makers. She insists that case study is a form of research in its own right, with its own principles. At the heart of it, she suggests, is the paradox that 'by focusing in depth and from a holistic perspective, a case study can generate both unique and universal understandings' (p. 225). She argues that the tension between the unique and the universal generates new forms of understanding. Moreover, these are attuned to the 'vocabulary of action' of practical actors. Simons argues that case study's ability to produce universal knowledge through study of the unique can be understood in terms of a parallel with great art and literature. Indeed, she suggests that case study fuses science with art. Thus, the task is as much to stimulate people to think in different ways as to express conclusions, to maximize diversity in ways of thinking rather than to produce certainty, and to identify new problems more than to offer solutions to already recognized ones. In line with this, she emphasizes the creative role of the researcher: that there are always alternative ways of representing a situation; that every account involves some misrepresentation; and that all accounts have ethical and political implications – for which the case study researcher must take responsibility.

Stake, R.E. (1994) 'Case studies', in N.K. Denzin and Y.S. Lincoln (eds), *Handbook of Qualitative Research*. Thousand Oaks, CA: Sage.

Stake, R.E. (1995) *The Art of Case Study Research*. London: Sage.

(See also R.E. Stake (1988) 'Case study methods in educational research: seeking sweet water', in R.M. Jaeger (ed.), *Complementary Methods for Research in Education*. Washington, DC: American Educational Research Association. This is a 'hypothetical dialogue' between Stake, some students and some fellow advocates of case study research.)

In 'Case studies' and *The Art of Case Study*, Stake develops themes from his article 'The case study method of inquiry'. He starts from the idea that 'case study is not a methodological choice, but a choice of object to be studied. We choose to study the case' (Stake, 1994, p. 236). And he defines a case as a 'functioning specificity' or 'bounded system'. The starting point for him, then, is a particular phenomenon that has intrinsic interest. Indeed, he notes that often the case for study is not specifically chosen for theoretical or other reasons but is 'of prominent interest before formal study begins' (Stake, 1994, p. 243). And he stresses 'potential for learning' as a criterion for selection over notions of typicality. So, while Stake recognizes that case study researchers often have what he calls an instrumental interest in cases (in other words, that they are concerned with what can be inferred about other cases), his emphasis is on what he calls intrinsic case study. Here, the aim is to allow the case 'to reveal its own story' (Stake, 1994, p. 237), to capture the particular, indeed the unique, in all its complexity. And he draws a contrast between 'seeking to identify cause and effect' and 'seeking understanding of human experience' (Stake, 1995, p. 38), which is more a matter of chronology than causality (Stake, 1995, p. 39). Furthermore, he argues that 'often, the researcher's aim is not veridical representation so much as stimulation of further reflection, optimizing readers' opportunity to learn (Stake, 1995, p. 41). Case study provides the basis for what Stake calls naturalistic generalizations: 'conclusions arrived at through personal engagement in life's affairs', but which can also be based on vicarious experience, including that provided by case study researchers. He contrasts such naturalistic generalizations with propositional generalizations, which is what quantitative research aims at. So, for Stake, case study is investigation of a single case to understand it in its particularity, this understanding necessarily being reliant on the personal characteristics of the researcher, and designed to provide vicarious experience for readers, so as to facilitate the process of naturalistic generalization.

Stenhouse, L. (1978) 'Case study and case records: towards a contemporary history of education', *British Educational Research Journal*, 4 (2): 21–39.

Stenhouse, L. (1980) 'The study of samples and the study of cases', *British Educational Research Journal*, 6 (1): 1–6.

Stenhouse, L. (1988) 'Case study methods', in J.P. Keeves (ed.), *Educational Research, Methodology and Measurement: An International Handbook*. Oxford: Pergamon Press.

The focus in these articles is very much on the role of case study research in the field of education. Furthermore, Stenhouse develops his argument in the context of a distinctive view of classroom research as central to the activity of the schoolteacher (see L. Stenhouse, *An Introduction to Curriculum Research and Development*, London: Heinemann, 1975). Much of his argument is concerned with highlighting the differences between case study and the quantitative approaches which had previously dominated educational research in Britain. He formulates this contrast as the study of cases versus the study of samples. He draws a parallel between case study inquiry and the work of historians, as a basis for clarifying what is required for case studies to meet the requirements of verification and cumulation; this involving quite different principles from those characteristic of the experimental model. He argues that in history, verification takes place through communal criticism of evidence 'which is available on the same terms to all scholars' (Stenhouse, 1978, p. 22). He therefore argues that there is a need in educational research for the development of archives of case records, the data on the basis of which case studies rely. Similarly, he argues that in history, cumulation depends on retrospective rather than predictive generalizations, retrospective generalizations being an attempt to 'map the range of experience rather than to perceive within that range the operation of laws in a scientific sense'. The kind of historical work he has in mind here is comparative, rather than linear or narrative. Furthermore, he emphasizes the practical value of historical research, in equipping us 'to understand the unpredicted by being able to fit it very rapidly into a systematically ordered and interpreted grasp of experience so far'. He comments: 'Where predictive generalisations claim to supersede the need for individual judgement, retrospective generalisations seek to strengthen individual judgement where it cannot be superseded' (Stenhouse, 1978, p. 22). What he is arguing for here is analogous to what Stake refers to as naturalistic generalization. His argument rests on the assumption that the social world is not open to understanding in terms of universal laws, at least in the sense of predictive generalizations which could provide methodical rules for teachers or other professional practitioners to follow. He notes that practitioners must deal with cases in their uniqueness, not simply as instances of some general category. Another way of formulating this contrast is in terms of the judgement of wholes, as opposed to the analysis of factors that may parsimoniously predict outcomes. Much of Stenhouse's argument, then, involves outlining a conception of practical action that is at odds with that which is built into what he calls the 'psycho-statistical model'. The paper entitled 'Case study methods' is a broader discussion prepared for a handbook. It outlines different styles of case study, discusses some practical considerations in the conduct of this kind of work, and briefly considers the role of theory and ethical issues.

Tripp, D.H. (1985) 'Case study generalization: an agenda for action', *British Educational Research Journal*, 11 (1): 33–43.

Tripp notes that case study researchers have often sought to generalize their findings in terms of notions of naturalistic generalization or transferability. He argues that there is a problem here for the researcher in identifying what are features that must be documented if the findings are to be transferable to other cases, and for the user of case study research in identifying useful studies from which to transfer findings. As a solution to this he advocates the development of comprehensive theory on the basis of case study work that would provide guidance to both researchers and users.

Walker, R. (1978) 'The conduct of educational case studies: ethics, theory, and procedures', in W. Dockrell and D. Hamilton (eds), *Rethinking Educational Research*. London: Hodder & Stoughton.

(See also B. McDonald and R. Walker (1977) 'Case study and the social philosophy of educational research', in D. Hamilton, D. Jenkins, C. King, B. MacDonald and M. Parlett (eds), *Beyond the Numbers Game: A Reader in Educational Evaluation*. London: Macmillan.)

Here Walker outlines the approach used at the time he was writing by some curriculum researchers associated with the Centre for Applied Research in Education at the University of East Anglia; notably in the SAFARI project. He starts from the claim that there is much cultural fragmentation, and thus much misunderstanding, among different groups and individuals within the educational world. And he sees case study as contributing to overcoming this. He describes it as involving collecting the 'definitions of the situation', or perspectives, of groups and individuals within an educational setting, publishing these within that setting, and later more widely. What is required for this is what he calls 'condensed fieldwork', by comparison with the much more lengthy forms characteristic of ethnography, whose results cannot be made available to participants until long after the event. He discusses two possible problems with what he proposes: that the short period of data collection threatens the validity of the results; and that it raises the problem of how a relationship of trust can be established between researcher and participants. He argues that the first problem is not as serious as it might seem, given that the aim is simply the documenta-tion of perspectives, rather than establishing 'what really goes on' in a setting. The solution he suggests for the second problem is a set of pro-cedures agreed with participants that gives them control over subse-quent publication of the data. Indeed, he puts forward a more general argument to the effect that people own the data about their own lives, particularly where these are their own perceptions and perspectives.

R.K. Yin (1994) *Case Study Research: Design and Methods* (2nd edn). Thousand Oaks, CA: Sage.

Yin approaches case study very much in the context of applied social research, and his book is geared to providing practical guidance about doing this kind of work. There is a companion volume (*Applications of Case Study Research*, Thousand Oaks, CA: Sage, 1993) which supplies more extended concrete examples. Yin's approach is to treat case study as an alternative to quantitative research, in the sense of a method that is to be used when appropriate and that offers findings that are as reli-able (in the common-sense sense of that term) as those from experi-mental and survey research. He argues that the kind of product towards which case study is directed is different from that characteris-tic of much quantitative research. Whereas the latter is often concerned with statistical generalization, case study research is aimed at analytic generalization. For Yin, case study investigates a contemporary phe-nomenon in its real-life context, takes account of many variables through the triangulation of multiple sources of evidence, and benefits from the prior development of theoretical propositions to guide data collection and analysis. This definition rules out historical case studies, as well as the kind of inductive approach which is quite common among many who see themselves as engaged in case study inquiry. Yin distinguishes between exploratory, descriptive and explanatory case studies. However, he believes that criteria common to all research methods are applicable to case study research: for example, construct validity, internal validity, external validity and reliability.

INDEX